The

Lost Art

of the

Great Speech

Also by Richard Dowis (with Richard Lederer)

Sleeping Dogs Don't Lay
St. Martin's Press

The Write Way
Pocket Books

The

Lost Art

of the

Great Speech

How to Write It ⋆ How to Deliver It

Richard Dowis

AMACOM

American Management Association

New York • Atlanta • Boston • Chicago • Kansas City • San Francisco • Washington, D.C.
Brussels • Mexico City • Tokyo • Toronto

Special discounts on bulk quantities of AMACOM books are available to corporations, professional associations, and other organizations. For details, contact Special Sales Department, AMACOM, an imprint of AMA Publications, a division of American Management Association, 1601 Broadway, New York, NY 10019. Tel.: 212-903-8316   Fax: 212-903-8083

This publication is designed to provide accurate and authoritative information in regard to the subject matter covered. It is sold with the understanding that the publisher is not engaged in rendering legal, accounting, or other professional service. If legal advice or other expert assistance is required, the services of a competent professional person should be sought.

Library of Congress Cataloging-in-Publication Data

Dowis, Richard, 1930–
        The lost art of the great speech : how to write it, how to deliver it / Richard Dowis.
        p.   cm.
    Includes bibliographical references and index.
    ISBN 0-8144-7054-8
    1. Public speaking.   2. Oratory.   I. Title.
PN4121.D78   1999
    808.5'1—dc21   *99-35742*
                                                            CIP

Printing number

10   9   8   7   6   5   4   3   2   1

Speeches have their origins in antiquity. . . . As man's progress developed, the need for speech-making increased. The more gifted speakers became the lawmakers and leaders. By the time civilization flowered in Athens, oratory became the fine art of government and culture. And so it has continued to our own stormy times.

Lewis Copeland
From the Introduction to *The World's Great Speeches*

This book is dedicated to
George Goodwin
my friend and mentor for three decades

Some men look out into the night and see only the dark;
others see moonlight and stars and fireflies,
and they hail the promise of the dawn.

Contents

Foreword

Many years ago, when I was laboring in obscurity as employee-newsletter editor for a small textile company, my boss asked me to prepare brief remarks for the president of the company to deliver at a gathering of longtime employees. I accepted the challenge with considerable trepidation. The situation was not ideal even for an experienced speech writer, certainly not for me, whose experience was absolute zero. The deadline was tight and I would not be given the opportunity to talk with the president to find out what he wanted to say. Guidance from my boss was minimal. It was left to me to decide *what* the president would say as well as *how* he would say it. Nevertheless, I somehow muddled through.

To my amazement, the president delivered the speech exactly as I had written it. Even more to my amazement, he sounded good. As I listened to him speak, I was conscious of every pause, every emphasis, every nuance that I had tried so hard to put into the remarks. I had made no effort to "sound" like the man. In truth, I couldn't have done so if I had tried, for I had met him only briefly and had never heard him make a speech. What I wrote for him was what I thought he ought to say and how I thought he ought to say it. That, I learned much, much later, is the speech writer's first duty.

The whole exercise was enormously satisfying. In later years, I was to experience the same satisfaction, the feeling that I had at least some influence on the direction of the company for which I was writing. I enjoyed hearing my words delivered by a good speaker.

After a brief stint as publications manager for The Coca-Cola Company, I joined the international public relations agency of Manning, Selvage & Lee, and over a quarter of a century with that firm I honed my skill as a speech writer. This book is a compilation of what I learned about writing speeches and, in the process, about delivering them, because writing and delivery are inseparable. So the book is intended both for people who write speeches for others and for people who write and deliver their own. It is also a defense of the written speech. I am not of the school that believes all good speeches are extemporaneous.

Because the book is to a large extent a memoir, I have written in the first person throughout. In addition to using examples from actual speeches to illustrate points, I have included at the end of each chapter at least one full speech or substantial excerpt from a speech by a well-known person. These speeches are selected both for their historical significance and to illustrate points made in the book. I believe reading and listening to speeches is one of the keys to learning how to write and deliver them.

Richard Dowis
Waleska, Georgia

The

Lost Art

of the

Great Speech

—— Chapter One ——

Opportunity Knocks

Winston Churchill was arguably the most eloquent and dynamic speaker of the twentieth century. During the bleakest days of World War II, the great man used his eloquence and the medium of radio to inspire his countrymen and bolster their resolve to fight on to defeat the seemingly unstoppable Nazi war machine. His words brought hope and courage to millions of Britons who, in those terrible times, had little else to cling to, knowing that the survival of their empire and their way of life was at stake.

Who can forget those ringing Churchillian phrases—"the iron curtain," "their finest hour," and his most famous one, "I have nothing to offer but blood, toil, tears, and sweat"? That simple but powerful phrase is from a speech Churchill made to Parliament on May 13, 1940, shortly after he became Prime Minister. With that speech, the people of Great Britain and the rest of the world were first made aware of the bulldog determination that was to become Churchill's trademark. Listen:

> *You ask, what is our policy? I say it is to wage war by land, sea, and air. War with all our might and with all the strength God has given us, and to wage war against a monstrous tyranny never surpassed in the dark and lamentable catalogue of human crime. That is our policy.*
>
> *You ask, what is our aim? It is victory at all costs—victory in spite of all terrors—victory however long and hard the road may be, for without victory there is no survival.*

And later, after the Nazis threatened to invade England:

> *We shall fight on the beaches. We shall fight on the landing grounds. We shall fight in the fields and streets. We shall fight in the hills. We shall never surrender.*

Powerful, powerful words. Words that literally might have changed the course of history.

Many years after the war, President John F. Kennedy, no mean phrasemaker himself, said of Churchill, "He mobilized the English language and sent it into battle." High praise, indeed, from the man who inspired his own people with "Ask not what your country can do for you. Ask what you can do for your country."

You may not aspire to the eloquence of a Churchill or a Kennedy. And it's extremely unlikely that you will ever have the opportunity to "mobilize the English language and send it into battle." It is quite likely, however, that you will have the opportunity to make a speech or perhaps to write a speech for someone else to deliver. And you just might be able to use such an opportunity to mobilize the language in the service of your company, church, civic club, political party, or other organization—or perhaps some special cause to which you are committed.

A holistic approach

If you're like most people, you've probably taken a course in public speaking at one time or another. Most courses I'm familiar with concentrate on the techniques of speaking. They're strong on such topics as posture, voice control, and overcoming fear. These are important topics, and as we continue there'll be plenty of suggestions for improving your speaking techniques.

This book, however, takes what might be called a holistic approach. By that I mean we consider the whole area of public speaking—from researching and writing your speech and preparing your manuscript to delivering the speech and handling questions from the audience. In addition, we'll be discussing some things you're not likely to find in any speech course.

You cannot separate the speech from the speaker or the delivery from the message. No matter how skillful you are at speaking, you will not be a good speaker if you have nothing important to say or if the words and phrases you choose are inappropriate for the occasion. Nor can you be an effective speaker if you do not master the fundamentals of good delivery. Even the unforgettable words of Churchill would have fallen flat if they had come from an orator of less skill.

A logical sequence

In writing this book, I tried to provide instruction in all the various aspects of public speaking. I began the way most speeches begin—with someone being given an opportunity to make a speech.

I know that many people reading this book are especially concerned about the mechanics of delivery, so from time to time, I have included a brief discussion of a way in which you can improve your technique and be more poised and confident when you mount the podium. I call these practical suggestions "Podium Presence" tips.

Make a speech? Me?

Most speeches begin with someone being given the opportunity to make a speech. I like to use the word *opportunity* when I talk about speaking. An invitation to speak is an opportunity—not something to be avoided like a root canal or an IRS audit. Let's assume for a moment that you're the one who has been given the opportunity. I can almost hear you saying, "Yes, but I don't have anything worthwhile to talk about."

Nonsense. If somebody didn't think you had something worthwhile to offer, you would never have been invited to speak. Besides, a subject doesn't have to be a world-shaker to be interesting. If the subject is appropriate for the audience, and if the speech is well crafted and well delivered, it will be worthwhile.

"Yes, but there are others, experienced speakers, who could do a better job of representing my organization."

Don't bet on it. Most of your colleagues probably have the same misgivings that you have about making a speech. In any case, experience isn't always the best teacher. I know experienced speakers who ought to spend some time looking for ways to improve their speaking techniques. Such people may be asked to speak often because of the positions they hold, not because they're especially good speakers. One of the most boring speakers I ever heard was the president of a large company. Yet, despite his ineptitude, his name appeared often on programs. An experienced speaker can bore an audience just as easily as a novice can.

"Yes, but I'm scared out of my skull when I have to stand up before a group. I even get nervous when I'm asked to lead my Sunday School class in silent prayer."

Good line. That kind of humor will help you win your audience over. We'll talk about the use of humor in public speaking later, and we'll also give you some practical tips for overcoming fear and nervousness.

You're not alone

If you shake in your proverbial boots when you have to speak before a group, you're not alone. Even such great speakers as Lincoln,

Churchill, Adlai Stevenson, and the esteemed editor Henry W. Grady suffered from stage fright. Fear of speaking in public shows up in *The Book of Lists* as one of the fourteen things Americans fear most, along with the fear of high places, the fear of sickness and death, and the fear of insects. Can you guess how the fear of public speaking ranks on that list? Number *one.*

Sickness and death? That's way down in sixth place. So, when someone says, I'd rather *die* than make a speech, he just might be speaking the literal truth.

Although increasing your ability to serve your organization or your special cause is reason enough to improve your ability to write and deliver a speech, there are other substantial benefits.

You gotta believe

Self-confidence is essential. Never doubt for a moment that you have it within yourself to make a great speech. You *can* move your audience. You can sell them on your point of view. You can even make them laugh, if that's your goal. Lack of confidence is a common problem with beginning speakers. Even Moses lacked confidence in his speaking ability. The Old Testament relates that when God ordered Moses to lead the Children of Israel out of bondage in Egypt, Moses tried to beg off, saying, "Oh, my Lord, I am not eloquent, either heretofore or since thou hast last spoken to thy servant; but I am slow of speech and of tongue. . . . Oh, my Lord, send, I pray, some other person."

And so the Lord sent Charlton Heston.

Carpe diem

Let's say you're a junior executive in a large company. One day your boss comes to you and tells you she has to make a twenty-minute talk to a group of customers and wants you to write it for her. Or maybe she has a conflict that day and wants you to pinch-hit and deliver the speech. What do you do? Well, you can arrange to break your arm so you can't write. Or tell her that your grandmother is planning to die soon and the funeral will be on the date of the speech. But broken arms are painful, and grandmothers can die only so many times.

Or, you can accept the opportunity gratefully to pinch-hit for the boss as a writer or speaker or both. If you do a good job, you'll not only earn the gratitude of the boss, you'll enhance your prestige in the company. And if you continue to accept and seek out speaking opportunities, your poise, your self-assurance, even your standing in the company and in the eyes of your colleagues will increase. So will your mastery of other skills that are important in business and professional life.

Write better

Learning to write a good speech will help you write better letters, memos, and other communications. Although speech writing is different from other kinds of writing in the sense that ear appeal is essential, a well-crafted speech has many characteristics that ought to be present in other kinds of writing. A speech must be organized logically so it is easily understandable on the first pass. A letter, memo, or report should be organized the same way. A reader shouldn't have to reread. A listener can't go back and relisten. A good speech makes use of active verbs and vivid nouns, which I call "gut" words. A lot of writing would benefit from more of that kind of language.

A good speech often relies on anecdotes and human-interest examples to carry its message—another characteristic that's appropriate for many kinds of writing.

Although speeches are written primarily to be *heard*, they are often seen in print as well. Many companies publish their executives' most important speeches in pamphlet form for distribution to shareholders, customers, and employees. Key speeches are sometimes published in magazines and newspapers, either in whole or in part. In these ways, a speech can have a life far beyond the twenty or thirty minutes the speaker spends in delivering it.

Other benefits

Writing and delivering speeches will make you more aware of your appearance, your posture, and your voice. You'll learn to enunciate more clearly and pronounce words correctly. You'll learn to pay more attention to grammar and word usage. Your "people skills" will improve. You'll become a better listener and more conscious of how words affect you and others.

And here's something even more important: If you become an accomplished speaker, you will be a more interesting person. As your self-confidence as a speaker grows, so will your self-confidence in other aspects of your business and personal life.

As your ability and confidence grow, you might find that making a speech can actually be fun. Or, if not fun, certainly gratifying. I once asked a frequent speaker if he enjoyed speaking. He answered, "No, but I enjoy *having spoken*." In other words, he liked the prestige, the satisfaction, the sense of accomplishment that come from delivering an effective speech. If speaking is a challenge to you, consider the words of the late General George S. Patton: "Accept the challenges so that you may feel the exhilaration of victory."

Speakers, speech writers in short supply

Despite the many advantages of learning the craft of speech making, good speakers are in short supply. Exaggerated fear of facing an audience, lack of confidence, concern about selecting a subject—these and other problems, both real and imagined, conspire to keep many capable people in the audience rather than at the lectern.

In the business world today, good speech writers are much in demand. Busy executives often turn to speech writers for help, either because they themselves are not good writers or because they just don't have time to devote to writing their own speeches. Many large corporations employ full-time speech writers, who are well-paid, respected, and have the ear of management. Other companies retain public relations firms or freelance writers to provide speech-writing help for their top executives. It isn't at all unusual for a speech writer to command a fee of three, four, or five thousand dollars or more for crafting a twenty- to thirty-minute speech. And you must believe me when I say that a really good speech is cheap at those prices, considering what a good speech can do for a company. Or, to be negative about it, what a bad speech can do *to* a company.

Clearly, you are a person who wants to become a more proficient speaker or speech writer, or both. Otherwise, you would not have invested your money in this book. If you are willing to invest further in time and effort by learning and applying the principles discussed here, you can and will reach your goal.

But it ain't easy, folks

None of this is meant to imply that preparing a speech and delivering it in public are easy. You must work hard and practice diligently to apply these fundamentals to your own opportunities and needs. How hard? How diligently? Some accomplished speakers say they spend as much as two or three hours of preparation time for each minute of speaking time. The great cleric Harry Emerson Fosdick reportedly spent ten hours of prep time for each minute of pulpit time.

A friend of mine who is a professional speech writer claims facetiously that Abraham Lincoln has been responsible for many a badly written speech. My friend doesn't say that the Emancipator himself wrote bad speeches. But because Lincoln is reputed to have scribbled his best-known speech on the back of an envelope while riding the train from Washington to Gettysburg, some speech makers think they don't have to spend a lot of time in preparation. Chances are, though, that Lincoln had been working on his incomparable Gettysburg Address for a long time and had it all in his head, if not on paper, before he took that famous train ride.

Read and listen

Throughout the book, I'll be sharing with you some of my experiences and observations, not only as a speech writer but also as one who has read and listened to many, many speeches—some of them good, some of them bad, and a few of them truly great. I believe that listening to and reading good speeches is an excellent way to learn to write and deliver a speech. It has been my pleasure, through the miracle of recording, to hear the voices of some of the great speakers of the twentieth century. For this I have used a set of tapes titled "Great Speeches of the 20th Century." The boxed set is available from Rhino Records, Inc. I highly recommend it.

When I cannot listen to a speech, I enjoy reading one. Collections of speeches are available in books and on CD-ROM. A recent collection, compiled by William Safire, *New York Times* columnist and self-described language maven, is *Lend Me Your Ears: Great Speeches in History*. This is especially interesting and useful because Safire introduces each selection with insightful commentary.

Throughout the book I have used speech excerpts to illustrate points, and at the end of each chapter, I have included one or two speeches or excerpts from speeches that I especially like. Many of these speeches are historically significant; all are instructive and technically interesting. As you read the speeches and excerpts, try to envision the speaker. Listen to the speeches with your mind's ear. Consider where dramatic pauses would come, how the speaker's thoughts and ideas are emphasized, and why particular words were chosen to express them. Doing this will help you begin to think as a speaker and speech writer, and it will help you in writing and delivering your own speech.

"Their Finest Hour"

I want to share with you an excerpt from a speech delivered by Prime Minister Winston Churchill on June 18, 1940. In the speech the prime minister discussed the Allies' military setbacks in France and proclaimed the end of the Battle of France and the beginning of the Battle of Britain. It was at the end of this speech that he uttered his immortal line, "Their finest hour":

We may now ask ourselves in what way has our position worsened since the beginning of the war. It is worsened by the fact that the Germans have conquered a large part of the coast of the Allies in Western Europe, and many small countries have been overrun by them. . . . We must not forget that from the moment we declared war on September 3, it was always possible for Germany to turn all her air force on this country. There would be other devices of invasion, and France could do little or nothing to prevent her. We have therefore lived under this danger during all these months. . . . If we are now called upon to endure what [the French] have suffered, we will emulate their courage, and if final victory rewards our toils they shall share the gain—aye, freedom shall be restored to all. We abate nothing in our just demands.

What General Weygand called the Battle of France is over. The Battle of Britain is about to begin. On this battle depends the survival of Christian civilization. Upon it depends our own British life and the long continuity of our institutions and our empire. The whole fury and might of the enemy must very soon be turned upon us. Hitler knows he will have to break us in this island or lose the war.

If we can stand up to him all Europe may be freed and the life of the world may move forward into broad sunlit uplands; but if we fail, the whole world, including the United States and all that we have known and cared for, will sink into the abyss of a new dark age made more sinister and perhaps more prolonged by the lights of a perverted science.

Let us therefore brace ourselves to our duty and so bear ourselves that if the British Commonwealth and Empire last for a thousand years, men will still say This was their finest hour.

"A Date Which Will Live in Infamy"

Another great wartime leader, President Franklin Delano Roosevelt, was Churchill's near equal as an orator. Here is the full text of his speech to Congress on December 8, 1941, in which he formally asked for a declaration of war against Japan:

Yesterday, December 7, 1941, a date which will live in infamy, the United States of America was suddenly and deliberately attacked by naval and air forces of the Empire of Japan. The United States was at peace with that nation and, at the solicitation of Japan, was still in conversation with its government and its Emperor looking toward the maintenance of peace in the Pacific. Indeed, one hour after Japanese air squadrons had commenced bombing in Oahu, the Japanese Ambassador to the United States and his colleague delivered to the Secretary of State a formal reply to a recent American message. While this reply stated that it seemed useless to continue the existing diplomatic negotiations, it contained no threat or hint of war or armed attack.

It will be recorded that the distance of Hawaii from Japan makes it obvious that the attack was deliberately planned many days or even weeks ago. During the intervening time the Japanese government had deliberately sought to deceive the United States by false statements and expressions of hope for continued peace.

The attack yesterday on the Hawaiian Islands has caused severe damage to American naval and military forces. Very many American lives have been lost. In addition American ships have been reported torpedoed on the high seas between San Francisco and Honolulu.

Yesterday the Japanese government also launched an attack against Malaya.

Last night Japanese forces attacked Hong Kong.

Last night Japanese forces attacked Guam.

Last night Japanese forces attacked the Philippine Islands.

Last night the Japanese attacked Wake Island.

This morning the Japanese attacked Midway Island.

Japan has, therefore, undertaken a surprise offensive extending throughout the Pacific area. The facts of yesterday speak for themselves. The people of the United States have already formed their opinions and well understand the implications to the very life and safety of our nation.

As Commander in Chief of the Army and Navy I have directed that all measures be taken for our defense.

Always will we remember the character of the onslaught against us. No matter how long it may take us to overcome this premeditated invasion, the American people in their righteous might will win through to absolute victory.

I believe I interpret the will of the Congress and of the people when I assert that we will not only defend ourselves to the utmost but will make very certain that this form of treachery shall never endanger us again.

Hostilities exist. There is no blinking at the fact that our people, our territory, and our interests are in grave danger.

With confidence in our armed forces, with the unbounded determination of our people, we will gain the inevitable triumph—so help us God. I ask that the Congress declare that since the unprovoked and dastardly attack by Japan on Sunday, December 7, a state of war has existed between the United States and the Japanese Empire.

— Chapter Two —

Before You Speak

This chapter will cover some factors to be considered before you accept an invitation and some of the things you should do in preparation for writing your speech. First, let me quickly review some of the key points discussed so far.

- An invitation to make a speech should be looked upon as an opportunity to serve your company, organization, or special cause.
- Never doubt that you have within yourself the ability to make a good speech, but, you must develop that ability.
- If the thought of speaking in public strikes fear in your heart, you are not alone. Even experienced speakers suffer from stage fright and lack of confidence.
- Learning to write and deliver a speech will increase other skills needed in your business or professional career.
- Learning to speak in public will make you a more confident, more interesting person.

Some red flags

Now that I have persuaded you to look upon an invitation to speak as an opportunity and to accept it enthusiastically, I want to hedge a bit and say that there may be some speaking invitations you should refuse. Well, perhaps "refuse" is too strong. Let's just say that certain situations ought to raise red flags.

Who's on first?

Suppose you're a sales manager of Wonder Widget, Inc., and you're invited to appear with three other speakers to discuss "Widget Marketing in the Twenty-First Century." Now, that's a broad enough subject to support four speakers, but unless you're scheduled to be the first speaker, or, you know well in advance what your fellow participants are going to say, you run the risk of having a previous speaker say what you had planned to say. And what could be more embarrassing, disconcerting, or boring to your audience than to find yourself having to plow somebody else's field?

If you happen to be last on the program, your speech will have to be especially interesting to hold the attention of an audience that undoubtedly will be growing weary. After hearing three speeches, the audience might be so tired by the time you rise to speak that they wouldn't listen if you told them a foolproof way to pick the winning lottery number.

Several years ago, an executive for whom I often wrote speeches accepted such an invitation. He learned after accepting that he would be number three of three speakers on the program. He was apprehensive because he was almost certain the other speakers would have already said much of what he wanted to say. He knew he probably would have to tailor his remarks to what the others had said or risk boring the audience by going over the same material. Although this executive was an experienced speaker, he liked to work from a prepared text. "Winging it" was not something he was good at, and he was unhappy at the prospect of having to change his prepared remarks on the spot to accommodate the previous speakers.

The situation posed a real challenge for my client. It required him to come up with some ideas and information that his fellow speakers would not have or would not think to use, so that on-the-spot tinkering with his prepared remarks would be minimal. He asked me to work with him on the project. My first suggestion was that he contact the other speakers and ask what particular aspects of the subject they planned to cover. This would have been an ideal solution to the problem, except that the other speakers were competitors, and my client was reluctant to ask for their help.

After considerable effort, we developed what we thought was a good speech that stood a reasonable chance of being significantly different from what either of the other two speakers would say. We couldn't be certain, of course; and there was still the problem of audience fatigue. Moreover, it was a morning program, and the speech was the last item before lunch. So the fatigue problem could be compounded by hunger.

In writing the final draft, I inserted a bit of humor near the beginning to remind the audience of what the speaker faced as the last one on the program and to gain their appreciation of his effort. Here is what I wrote for insertion into the speech shortly after the obligatory opening niceties:

> *Being the last speaker of the day, I feel somewhat like Liz Taylor's latest husband on their wedding night—I know what I'm supposed to do, but I'm not sure I know how to make it interesting. Of course, there is one advantage to being last. By the time you get up to speak, the audience thinks they've heard everything worthwhile, so their expectations are low, and no one blames you if you don't say anything new. Nevertheless, I believe I can offer you some additional insight into our subject.*
>
> *And you'll want to pay close attention to what I have to say, because I'm going to say some nice things about you.*

I wasn't at the meeting, but I was told that the speech went over well and the Liz Taylor joke got a good laugh. We were lucky. I admit it wasn't original, but it served.

A definite maybe

The question is: Should you accept an invitation to be one of several speakers on a program? My answer to that is a definite maybe. You have to decide for yourself after considering the particular circumstances.

If you're certain that you have something to say on the subject that other speakers cannot, or probably will not, say, or if you can bring a new perspective to the subject, then you can change that definite maybe to a definite probably. Even then, I would not relish the idea of being last on a program.

If you happen to know that you'll be first or even second on the program, there should be no problem. Beyond second, though, you might have cause for concern. Of course, you might not be told at the time you're invited what position you'll have. You could ask, but if you make being first a condition of acceptance, your attitude could be interpreted as rude or egotistical. The program planner might not be sympathetic. His job is to put together a group of experts, each of whom will give a unique perspective on the subject, holding the audience in rapt attention. Fine in theory, but it doesn't necessarily turn out that way in practice.

Programs with multiple speakers often take the form of a panel discussion, which includes participation by the audience and the moderator. Panel discussions pose less of a problem because much of a speaker's time is spent responding to questions. Even so, the panel format might call for opening and closing remarks by each panelist. These remarks should be carefully prepared, and the danger of duplication still exists.

Know the format before you accept the invitation. If it seems reasonable, by all means accept.

Control the topic

Another important consideration in deciding whether to accept an invitation is the subject you are asked to discuss. You should not agree to speak on a subject you are uncomfortable with or that you feel you don't know enough about. I have been a professional writer most of my life, but I have had very little experience in writing advertising copy. I would welcome the chance to speak to a group of marketing executives on, say, why advertising and public relations should use coordinated messages, but I would not speak to the same group on the essentials of good advertising copy. It's simply not my field. I have some opinions on the subject, but I have no credentials that make my opinions worthy of consideration.

Before you accept an invitation, be certain that the person issuing it has a realistic understanding of your credentials. Otherwise, you might be oversold to the audience and thus be unable to meet their expectations. Not long ago, I was asked to speak to a "literary" exchange club. Now, I don't think of myself as a "literary" person. My writing has been mostly of the commercial variety—that is, speeches, financial reports, brochures, etc. Although I enjoy good literature, I read for pleasure and rarely think about symbolism and deeper meanings. I told the program chairman this and she assured me that the club members would appreciate some practical tips on writing. Only after receiving that assurance did I accept the invitation. Because the group's expectations were realistic, the meeting was a success.

Topic criteria

In many instances, you will be asked to speak on a subject of your choice, but if you're assigned a topic that you're uncomfortable with, feel free to suggest an alternative. In either case, there are several criteria you should consider.

First, of course, your topic should be appropriate for the occasion, the event, and the audience. A young minister was invited to speak to a group of elderly men and women. The subject he chose was "The Sin of Lust." After the speech, a sweet little old lady came forward to shake the minister's hand. "That was a nice message, Sonny," she said, "but with this group, it would be more appropriate to talk about rust."

If you do suggest a topic that's different from the one the organization asked for, try to stay as close as possible to the original. It probably is safe to assume that the person who issued the invitation thought the assigned subject would be of interest to the audience. For example, if you're sales manager of Wonder Widget and you're invited to speak on "Widget Technology: Where Is It Leading?" you might say, "Well, I'm a marketing person; I'm concerned with the here and now. I wouldn't be credible talking about the future of widget technology. That's a subject for our research director." That would allow the program chairman to withdraw the invitation gracefully.

A reasonable alternative might be something like "Widget Technology: What Today's Consumer Wants." With that alternative, you would be in the technology ballpark but you would be putting the emphasis on satisfying consumers, which you, as a marketing person, ought to know and care about.

In addition to suitability and credibility, your subject should be one that is important to you as well as the audience. If it's not important to the audience, it will bore them; if it's not important to you, it will sound phony. This doesn't mean that every topic has to be a grand passion. After all, you're not freeing the slaves, calling the nation to arms, or launching a presidency.

If you have trouble deciding on a suitable subject, make a list of topics you would feel comfortable with. Then consider each one separately in light of what you know about the organization, the occasion, and the audience. By this process, you can narrow down the list to perhaps three possible topics; then ask the program chair to rate them according to how they might appeal to the audience.

Decide on the purpose

Perhaps the most important consideration in the selection of a topic and in writing your speech is the purpose. What do you want the audience to do or think or feel as a result of what you say? This is a question you should ask not only yourself but also your sponsors. They had a reason for inviting you to speak and they ought to know what they want the speech to accomplish.

It is a good idea to write down a brief statement of purpose and keep it at hand as you write your speech.

From my experience in reading and writing speeches, I have concluded that there are six basic purposes of a speech:

1. To entertain
2. To inform
3. To inspire
4. To motivate
5. To advocate
6. To convince or persuade

These can overlap, and of course a speech can have more than one purpose. Churchill's speeches were meant to both inspire and motivate his countrymen. A president's state-of-the-union address usually is intended to inform members of Congress of the progress his administration has made, to convince them that his policies are good for the country, and to motivate them to work hard to pass his favorite programs. The best state-of-the-union speeches may also be inspirational, persuasive, and even entertaining. But usually one or two of the six basic purposes predominate.

Although many fine speeches contain humor, to entertain is rarely the purpose of a speech. Instead, the humor helps to carry a point or to win over an audience—that is, to make the audience more receptive to the important things a speaker has to say. There will be more on humor in later chapters.

Is the time right?

Finally, be certain that your topic—whether chosen or assigned—can be managed within the time allotted. If you're asked to speak for fifteen or twenty minutes on a subject that cries out for thirty minutes, you should decline the invitation, ask for more time, or suggest an alternate topic.

Once in a while, the opposite situation might arise. You may be allotted more time than you can reasonably fill with the assigned topic, and this situation should also raise a red flag. Trying to expand thirty minutes worth of material to fill forty-five minutes is like trying to write a thousand-word article on a subject that could easily be covered with five hundred or six hundred words. The product, whether it's an article or a speech, will be flat, tedious, and boring.

I conduct one-day business-writing seminars for groups of nine or ten people. I'm sometimes invited to conduct a mini-seminar, usually an hour or an hour and a half for a larger group. Although I have plenty of prepared material to fill that much time, I would not want to lecture for an hour and a half because I know that holding the attention of an audience for more than about forty-five minutes is difficult, if not impossible. To solve the problem, I pass out writing and editing exercises for the audience to complete and discuss. This breaks up the time into smaller segments and allows members of the audience to be participants in the program. Audience participation is not always practical, but when it is, it can be a powerful tool for a speaker.

I once accepted an invitation to talk on "Essential Elements of a Community Relations Program." I had no problem with the subject. I know it well, and I thought I could cover it nicely in twenty minutes and allow ten minutes for a question-and-answer session. It never occurred to me that I would have more than thirty minutes, but when I saw the printed program, which the chairman mailed to me just a few days before the event, I was astounded to learn that I was expected to hold forth for one full hour. Because the program was already set and in print, there was no graceful way to correct the problem.

The chairman used bad judgment in not asking me how much time I needed, but I used worse judgment in not asking how much time I would have.

Don't assume anything

Even the most well-meaning program chairperson cannot always be counted on to arrange conditions that are favorable to the speaker or to provide all the information the speaker should have. The chairperson might feel that her responsibility is over once you have made a commitment to speak. It is up to you, the speaker, to inquire about details of the event. It is perfectly appropriate to do so.

Let's consider some of the details you will want to know after you have accepted and before you start to prepare your remarks. To use a phrase popularized during the national debate on healthcare legislation in 1992, the devil is in the details.

Obviously, you will get all the necessary information, such as date, time, and place. I suggest you ask for this kind of information to be confirmed in writing to eliminate any possibility of a mix-up. Don't forget to ask for the name, address, and telephone number of the president, program chair, or someone else in the organization whom you can call or write for additional information. Be certain you know how to pronounce any names you might use in your speech.

Know the organization

Find out everything you can about the organization and its membership: How many members does the organization have? What kind of people compose the membership? Men or women only, or both? Young? Middle-aged? All ages?

What kind of organization is it? Business or professional? Service club? Church group? What is its purpose? Its philosophy?

Is it a national or international organization, or is it strictly local?

What are its main activities or projects?

Some of this information might be useful for your speech. Certainly, the speech should reflect some knowledge of the sponsoring organization. There's nothing more flattering to an audience than for a speaker to refer to some worthwhile activity of their organization. For example, if you're speaking to a Lions Club, a reference to the organization's extensive work on behalf of the blind would be well-received.

I recall hearing a speech delivered to a Jaycee club (formerly the Junior Chamber of Commerce) of which I was a member. The speaker used a very clever opening that showed he had at least some knowledge of the organization. In those days, the Jaycees' organizational structure provided for two vice presidents. One was called internal vice president; the other, external vice president. Perhaps that organizational structure still prevails, but since Jaycees "graduate" at age 36 and many years have passed since my own graduation, my knowledge of the organization is dated.

In any case, the speaker made a few preliminary remarks and then launched into a story about efforts to organize a Jaycee chapter at the state penitentiary. "The inmates responded enthusiastically to the idea of having a Jaycee chapter in the prison," the speaker said, "but when it came time to elect officers for the new chapter, no one wanted to run for president." He paused for what must have been three or four seconds before delivering his zinger:

"However, there were 37 candidates for *external* vice president."

The speaker was not a Jaycee. He had simply taken time to learn some things about the organization, including the fact that Jaycees were forming chapters in penitentiaries. As he continued his speech, he further demonstrated his knowledge by mentioning some other worthwhile activities of the organization.

President Ronald Reagan delighted employees of the Ivorydale Soap Manufacturing plant in St. Bernard, Ohio, on October 3, 1985, with the following:

> *There's a rising Tide of good Cheer in the land. We see new Zest in the economy every day. And all we need now is a Bold Dash to Safeguard the Gain we've already made.*

Tide, Cheer, Zest, Bold, Dash, Safeguard, and Gain are all brand names of soaps.

More devilish details

Find out about the make-up of the audience: How many are likely to be there? Will there be guests? If so, will they be guests of the club or guests of individual members? Will there be any public officials or distinguished guests? What different professions will be represented? Often, all of the audience will be members of the same profession. In that case, you need to learn something about the profession so that you can make suitable remarks.

Inquire about the occasion and agenda: Does the program have a theme? Is this to be a regular meeting or some special occasion? Is it a luncheon or dinner meeting? Will there be other speakers? If so, find out who they are and try to learn something about them. Will you be the main, or featured, speaker? Exactly when do you speak? What's on the program immediately before and after you speak? How long will you be expected to speak? Should you allow time for questions? Who will introduce you? Will you need to send the introducer a prepared introduction?

Find out about the physical facilities: How large is the room? Will the audience be seated theater style or at tables? Will there be a head table? Will there be a lectern? How about the sound system? If you plan to use visuals, is the facility suitable? Can charts be placed so as to be visible to all the audience? Can the room be darkened for slides? Are there electrical outlets for a projector or other equipment you might need?

Not every one of the above items will be relevant to every speaking assignment, but when they are relevant, they will help you in deciding on a topic, working with the program chair, writing your speech, and preparing for the event.

Podium Presence Tip

In the next chapter, we will begin together the actual writing of your speech, and I'll give you some good reasons for having a written speech even if you don't want to follow it to the letter. But now, here's the first of the Podium Presence Tips:

Sincerity is perhaps the most essential ingredient in a speech. You must believe, really believe, in what you are saying. If so, you will be more relaxed, less nervous, more confident. If you are insincere, your audience will know it and will respond, or *not* respond, accordingly. Martin Luther King, Jr., was passionate for his cause; his audiences felt his passion when he spoke, and his words moved a nation. William Jennings Bryan put it this way: "The speech of one who knows what he is talking about and means what he says—it is thought on fire."

So before you accept an invitation, certainly before you select a topic and begin to prepare your remarks, ask yourself, "Do I have any reservations about making this speech to this audience?" If your answer is "yes," you need to back off and look carefully at the situation.

"The Awesome Power of Disobedience"

During a long and successful career as an actor, Charlton Heston developed a reputation for social activism and became an articulate spokesman for causes in which he believed. One of those causes was the 2nd Amendment to the United States Constitution—the right to keep and bear arms. In the following speech to the Harvard Law School in February 1999, Mr. Heston uses several of the professional techniques that will be discussed in later chapters. The series of sentences beginning with "If you," near the end of the speech, is an excellent example of an especially effective technique called anaphora:

I remember my son when he was five, explaining to his kindergarten class what his father did for a living. "My Daddy," he said, "pretends to be people."

There have been quite a few of them. Prophets from the Old and New Testaments, a couple of Christian saints, generals of various nationalities and different centuries, several kings, three American presidents, a French cardinal and two geniuses, including Michelangelo.

If you want the ceiling re-painted I'll do my best.

It's just that there always seems to be a lot of different fellows up here. I'm never sure which one of them gets to talk. Right now, I guess I'm the guy.

As I pondered our visit tonight it struck me: If my Creator gave me the gift to connect you with the hearts and minds of those great men, then I want to use that same gift now to re-connect you with your own sense of liberty—your own freedom of thought—your own compass for what is right.

Dedicating the memorial at Gettysburg, Abraham Lincoln said of America, "We are now engaged in a great Civil War, testing whether this nation or any nation so conceived and so dedicated can long endure." Those words are true again—believe that we are again engaged in a great civil war, a cultural war that's about to hijack your birthright to think and say what lives in your heart.

I fear you no longer trust the pulsing lifeblood of liberty inside you—the stuff that made this country rise from wilderness into the miracle that it is.

Let me back up a little. About a year ago I became president of the National Rifle Association, which protects the right to keep and bear arms. I ran for office, I was elected, and now I serve—I serve as a moving target for the media who've called me everything from "ridiculous" and "duped" to a "brain-injured, senile, crazy old man." I know, I'm pretty old—but I sure, Lord, ain't senile.

As I have stood in the cross hairs of those who target Second Amendment freedoms, I've realized that firearms are not the only issue.

No, it's much, much bigger than that. I've come to understand that a cultural war is raging across our land, in which, with Orwellian fervor, certain acceptable thoughts and speech are mandated. For example, I marched for civil rights with Dr. King in 1963—long before Hollywood found it fashionable. But when I told an audience last year that white pride is just as valid as black pride or red pride or anyone else's pride, they called me a racist.

I've worked with brilliantly talented homosexuals all my life. But when I told an audience that gay rights should extend no further than your rights or my rights, I was called a homophobe.

I served in World War II against the Axis powers. But during a speech, when I drew an analogy between singling out innocent Jews and singling out innocent gun owners, I was called an anti-Semite.

Everyone I know knows I would never raise a closed fist against my country.

But when I asked an audience to oppose this cultural persecution, I was compared to Timothy McVeigh.

From *Time* magazine to friends and colleagues, they're essentially saying, "Chuck, how dare you speak your mind like that! You are using language not authorized for public consumption!"

But I am not afraid. If Americans believed in political correctness, we'd still be King George's boys, subjects bound to the British crown.

In his book, *The End of Sanity*, Martin Gross writes that "blatantly irrational behavior is rapidly being established as the norm in almost every area of human endeavor. There seem to be new customs, new rules, new anti-intellectual theories regularly foisted on us from every direction.

Underneath, the nation is roiling. Americans know something without a name is undermining the country, turning the mind mushy when it comes to separating truth from falsehood and right from wrong. And they don't like it."

Let me read a few examples.

At Antioch college in Ohio, young men seeking intimacy with a coed must get verbal permission at each step of the process from kissing to petting to final copulation—all clearly spelled out in a printed college directive.

In New Jersey, despite the death of several patients nationwide who had been infected by dentists who had concealed their AIDS the state commissioner announced that health providers who are HIV-positive need not—need not—tell their patients that they are infected.

At William and Mary, students tried to change the name of the school team "The Tribe" because it was supposedly insulting to local Indians, only to learn that authentic Virginia chiefs truly like the name.

In San Francisco, city fathers passed an ordinance protecting the rights of transvestites to cross-dress on the job, and for transsexuals to have separate toilet facilities while undergoing sex change surgery.

In New York City, kids who don't speak a word of Spanish have been placed in bilingual classes to learn their three R's in Spanish solely because their last names sound Hispanic.

At the University of Pennsylvania, in a state where thousands died at

Gettysburg opposing slavery, the president of that college officially set up segregated dormitory space for black students.

Yeah, I know—that's out of bounds now. Dr. King said "Negroes."

Jimmy Baldwin and most of us on the March said "black." But it's a no-no now.

For me, hyphenated identities are awkward—particularly "Native-American." I'm a Native American, for God's sake. I also happen to be a blood-initiated brother of the Miniconjou Sioux.

On my wife's side, my grandson is a thirteenth generation native American—with the capital letter on "American."

Finally, just last month—David Howard, head of the Washington, D.C., Office of Public Advocate, used the word "niggardly" while talking to colleagues about budgetary matters. Of course, "niggardly" means stingy or scanty. But within days Howard was forced to publicly apologize and resign.

As columnist Tony Snow wrote: "David Howard got fired because some people in public employ were morons who (a) didn't know the meaning of niggardly, (b) didn't know how to use a dictionary to discover the meaning, and (c) actually demanded that he apologize for their ignorance."

What does all this mean? It means that telling us what to think has evolved into telling us what to say, so telling us what to do can't be far behind.

Before you claim to be a champion of free thought, tell me: Why did political correctness originate on America's campuses? And why do you continue to tolerate it? Why do you, who're supposed to debate ideas, surrender to their suppression?

Let's be honest. Who here thinks your professors can say what they really believe? That scares me to death. It should scare you too, that the superstition of political correctness rules the halls of reason.

You are the best and the brightest. You, here in the fertile cradle of American academia, here in the castle of learning on the Charles River, you are the cream. But I submit that you, and your counterparts across the land, are the most socially conformed and politically silenced generation since Concord Bridge. And as long as you validate that—and abide it—you are by your grandfathers' standards cowards.

Here's another example. Right now at more than one major university, Second Amendment scholars and researchers are being told to shut up about their findings or they'll lose their jobs. Why? Because their research findings would undermine big-city mayors' pending lawsuits that seek to extort hundreds of millions of dollars from firearm manufacturers.

I don't care what you think about guns. But if you are not shocked at that, I am shocked at you. Who will guard the raw material of unfettered ideas, if not you? Democracy is dialogue!

Who will defend the core value of academia, if you supposed soldiers of free thought and expression lay down your arms and plead, "Don't shoot me."

If you talk about race, it does not make you a racist.

If you see distinctions between the genders, it does not make you sexist.

If you think critically about a denomination, it does not make you anti-religion.

If you accept but don't celebrate homosexuality, it does not make you a homophobe.

Don't let America's universities continue to serve as incubators for this rampant epidemic of new McCarthyism. But what can you do? How can anyone prevail against such pervasive social subjugation? The answer's been here all along. I learned it thirty-six years ago on the steps of the Lincoln Memorial in Washington D.C., standing with Dr. Martin Luther King and two hundred thousand people.

You simply—disobey.

Peaceably, yes. Respectfully, of course. Nonviolently, absolutely.

But when told how to think or what to say or how to behave, we don't. We disobey social protocol that stifles and stigmatizes personal freedom.

I learned the awesome power of disobedience from Dr. King . . . who learned it from Gandhi, and Thoreau, and Jesus, and every other great man who led those in the right against those with the might.

Disobedience is in our DNA. We feel innate kinship with that disobedient spirit that tossed tea into Boston Harbor, that sent Thoreau to jail, that refused to sit in the back of the bus, that protested a war in Viet Nam. In that same spirit, I am asking you to disavow cultural correctness with massive disobedience of rogue authority, social directives and onerous laws that weaken personal freedom.

But be careful—it hurts. Disobedience demands that you put yourself at risk. Dr. King stood on lots of balconies.

You must be willing to be humiliated—to endure the modern-day equivalent of the police dogs at Montgomery and the water cannons at Selma. You must be willing to experience discomfort. I'm not complaining, but my own decades of social activism have left their mark on me.

Let me tell you a story. A few years back I heard about a rapper named Ice-T who was selling a CD called "Cop Killer" celebrating ambushing and murdering police officers. It was being marketed by none other than Time/Warner, the biggest entertainment conglomerate in the world. Police across the country were outraged. Rightfully so. At least one had been murdered. But Time/Warner was stonewalling because the CD was a cash cow for them, and the media were tiptoeing around it because the rapper was black.

I heard Time/Warner had a stockholders meeting scheduled in Beverly Hills. I owned some shares at the time, so I decided to attend. What I did there was against the advice of my family and colleagues. I asked for the floor. To a hushed room of a thousand average American stockholders, I simply read the full lyrics of "Cop Killer," every vicious, vulgar, instructional word.

"I got my 12 gauge sawed off I got my headlights turned off I'm about to bust some shots off I'm about to dust some cops off. . . ."

It got worse, a lot worse. I won't read the rest of it to you. But trust me, the room was a sea of shocked, frozen, blanched faces. The Time/Warner executives squirmed in their chairs and stared at their shoes. They hated me for that.

Then I delivered another volley of sick lyric brimming with racist filth, where Ice-T fantasizes about sodomizing two 12-year old nieces of Al and Tipper Gore.

"She pushed her butt against my. . . ."

Well, I won't do to you here what I did to them. Let's just say I left the room in echoing silence. When I read the lyrics to the waiting press corps, one of them said "We can't print that." "I know," I replied, "but Time/Warner's selling it."

Two months later, Time/Warner terminated Ice-T's contract. I'll never be offered another film by Warner, or get a good review from *Time* magazine. But disobedience means you must be willing to act, not just talk. When a mugger sues his elderly victim for defending herself—jam the switchboard of the district attorney's office.

When your university is pressured to lower standards until 80% of the students graduate with honors—choke the halls of the board of regents.

When an eight-year-old boy pecks a girl's cheek on the playground and gets hauled into court for sexual harassment—march on that school and block its doorways. When someone you elected is seduced by political power and betrays you—petition them, oust them, banish them. When *Time* magazine's cover portrays millennium nuts as deranged, crazy Christians holding a cross as it did last month—boycott their magazine and the products it advertises.

So that this nation may long endure, I urge you to follow in the hallowed footsteps of the great disobediences of history that freed exiles, founded religions, defeated tyrants, and yes, in the hands of an aroused rabble in arms and a few great men, by God's grace, built this country.

If Dr. King were here, I think he would agree.

"Today, I Am an Inquisitor"

At the opposite end of the political spectrum from Charlton Heston, the late Representative Barbara Jordan, of Texas, was just as articulate in espousing and defending her beliefs. The first black woman to be elected to Congress, Ms. Jordan was a member of the House Judiciary Committee that held hearings on the possible impeachment of President Richard Nixon. In the following speech, delivered during the hearings in 1974, she used irony, anaphora, quotations, and antithesis to make her points. After you have read about these techniques in later chapters, you might want to return to this speech and try to identify examples of them.

Mr. Chairman, I join my colleague Mr. Rangel in thanking you for giving the junior members of this committee the glorious opportunity of sharing the pain of this inquiry. Mr. Chairman, you are a strong man, and it has not been easy but we have tried as best we can to give you as much assistance as possible.

Earlier today we heard the beginning of the Preamble to the Constitution of the United States, "We, the people." It is a very eloquent beginning. But when that document was completed, on the seventeenth of September in 1787, I was not included in that "We, the people." I felt somehow for many years that George Washington and Andrew Hamilton just left me out by mistake. But through the process of amendment interpretation, and court decision, I have finally been included in "We, the people."

Today I am an inquisitor. I believe hyperbole would not be fictional and would not overstate the solemness that I feel right now. My faith in the Constitution is whole, it is complete, it is total. I am not going to sit here and be an idle spectator to the diminution, the subversion, the destruction of the Constitution.

"Who can so properly be the inquisitors for the nation as the representatives of the nation themselves?" [*Hamilton*, Federalist, no. 65.] The subject of its jurisdiction are those offenses which proceed from the misconduct of public men. That is what we are talking about. In other words, the jurisdiction comes from the abuse or violation of some public trust. It is wrong, I suggest, it is a misreading of the Constitution for any member here to assert that for a member to vote for an article of impeachment means that that member must be convinced that the president should be removed from office. The Constitution doesn't say that. The powers relating to impeachment are an essential check in the hands of this body, the legislature, against and upon the encroachment of the executive. In establishing the division between the two branches of the legislature, the House and the Senate, assigning to the one the right to accuse and to the other the right to judge, the framers of this Constitution were very astute. They did not make the accusers and the judges the same person.

We know the nature of impeachment. We have been talking about it awhile now. "It is chiefly designed for the president and his high ministers" to some-how be called into account. It is designed to "bridle" the executive if he engages in excesses. "It is designed as a method of national inquest into the conduct of public men." [*Hamilton,* Federalist, no. 65.] The framers confined in the Con-gress the power if need be, to remove the president in order to strike a delicate balance between a president swollen with power and grown tyrannical, and pres-ervation of the independence of the executive. The nature of impeachment is a narrowly channeled exception to the separation-of-powers maxim; the federal convention of 1787 said that. It limited impeachment to high crimes and mis-demeanors and discounted and opposed the term "maladministration." "It is to be used only for great misdemeanors," so it was said in the North Carolina ratification convention. And in the Virginia ratification convention: "We do not trust our liberty to a particular branch. We need one branch to check the others."

The North Carolina ratification convention: "No one need be afraid that officers who commit oppression will pass with immunity."

"Prosecutions of impeachments will seldom fail to agitate the passions of the whole community," said Hamilton in the *Federalist Papers, no. 65.* "And to divide it into parties more or less friendly or inimical to the accused." I do not mean political parties in that sense.

The drawing of political lines goes to the motivation behind impeachment; but impeachment must proceed within the confines of the constitutional term "high crimes and misdemeanors."

Of the impeachment process, it was Woodrow Wilson who said that "nothing short of the grossest offenses against the plain law of the land will suffice to give them speed and effectiveness. Indignation so great as to overgrow party interest may secure a conviction; but nothing else can."

Common sense would be revolted if we engaged upon this process for petty reasons. Congress has a lot to do. Appropriations, tax reform, health insurance, campaign finance reform, housing, environmental protection, energy suffi-ciency, mass transportation. Pettiness cannot be allowed to stand in the face of such overwhelming problems. So today we are not being petty. We are trying to be big because the task we have before us is a big one.

This morning, in a discussion of the evidence, we were told that the evi-dence which purports to support the allegations of misuse of the CIA by the president is thin. We are told that that evidence is insufficient. What that re-cital of the evidence this morning did not include is what the president did know on June 23, 1972. The president did know that it was Republican money, that it was money from the Committee for the Re-Election of the President, which was found in the possession of one of the burglars arrested on June 17.

What the president did know on June 23 was the prior activities of E. Howard Hunt, which included his participation in the break-in of Daniel Ells-berg's psychiatrist, which included Howard Hunt's participation in the Dita

Beard ITT affair, which included Howard Hunt's fabrication of cables designed to discredit the Kennedy administration.

We were further cautioned today that perhaps these proceedings ought to be delayed because certainly there would be new evidence forthcoming from the president of the United States. There has not even been an obfuscated indication that this committee would receive any additional materials from the president. The committee subpoena is outstanding, and if the president wants to supply that material, the committee sits here.

The fact is that yesterday, the American people waited with great anxiety for eight hours, not knowing whether their president would obey an order of the Supreme Court of the United States.

At this point I would like to juxtapose a few of the impeachment criteria with some of the president's actions. Impeachment criteria: James Madison, from the Virginia ratification convention. "If the president be connected in any suspicious manner with any person and there be grounds to believe that he will shelter him, he may be impeached."

We have heard time and time again that the evidence reflects payment to the defendants of money. The president had knowledge that these funds were being paid and that these were funds collected for the 1972 presidential campaign.

We know that the president met with Mr. Henry Petersen twenty-seven times to discuss matters related to Watergate and immediately thereafter met with the very persons who were implicated in the information Mr. Petersen was receiving and transmitting to the president. The words are "if the president be connected in any suspicious manner with any person and there be grounds to believe that he will shelter that person, he may be impeached."

Justice Story: "Impeachment is intended for occasional and extraordinary cases where a superior power acting for the whole people is put into operation to protect their rights and rescue their liberties from violations."

We know about the Huston plan. We know about the break-in of the psychiatrist's office. We know that there was absolute complete direction in August 1971 when the president instructed Ehrlichman to "do whatever is necessary." This instruction led to a surreptitious entry into Dr. Fielding's office.

"Protect their rights." "Rescue their liberties from violation."

The South Carolina ratification convention impeachment criteria: Those are impeachable "who behave amiss or betray their public trust."

Beginning shortly after the Watergate break-in and continuing to the present time, the president has engaged in a series of public statements and actions designed to thwart the lawful investigation by government prosecutors. Moreover, the president has made public announcements and assertions bearing on the Watergate case which the evidence will show he knew to be false.

These assertions, false assertions, impeachable, those who misbehave. Those who "behave amiss or betray their public trust."

James Madison again at the Constitutional Convention: "A president is impeachable if he attempts to subvert the Constitution."

The Constitution charges the president with the task of taking care that the laws be faithfully executed, and yet the president has counseled his aides to commit perjury, willfully disregarded the secrecy of grand jury proceedings, concealed surreptitious entry, attempted to compromise a federal judge while publicly displaying his cooperation with the processes of criminal justice.

"A president is impeachable if he attempts to subvert the Constitution." If the impeachment provision in the Constitution of the United States will not reach the offenses charged here, then perhaps that eighteenth-century Constitution should be abandoned to a twentieth-century paper shredder. Has the president committed offenses and planned and directed and acquiesced in a course of conduct which the Constitution will not tolerate? That is the question. We know that. We know the question. We should now forthwith proceed to answer the question. It is reason, and not passion, which must guide our deliberations, guide our debate, and guide our decision.

—— CHAPTER THREE ——

Preparing to Write

I hope you enjoyed reading President Roosevelt's memorable declaration of war at the end of Chapter One. For those of us who recall World War II, reading that speech is like stepping onto the page of a history book. Another great presidential speaker was John F. Kennedy. He made many memorable speeches and spoke many memorable lines. He was perhaps at his best in his inaugural address on January 20, 1961, when he challenged Americans to "ask what you can do for your country."

Did Kennedy himself write that speech? Probably not. No doubt he put a lot of himself into the writing, but he almost certainly worked with at least one speech writer. Kennedy's main speech writer was Ted Sorensen. In his 1965 book about Kennedy, Sorensen tells us that the president never pretended he had time to write the first draft of a speech. Knowing how much work is involved in writing a good speech, I can easily understand that. One would certainly hope that the president of the United States has more important ways to spend his time.

But Sorensen also points out that Kennedy edited the work of his speech writers with a heavy hand. He often added or deleted words, sentences, or whole paragraphs. Sometimes he would even edit the speech writer's outline. Crafting a speech was a cooperative effort between Kennedy and Sorensen. That's the way it ought to be with speech writers and their principals.

One of the first speeches I ever wrote was ripped to shreds by the corporate executive for whom I wrote it. I was disappointed. The disappointment must have shown on my face during the editing conference, because afterward, the executive made it a point to thank me for my help. And then he said, "Don't worry about all my editing, Dick. I always do that. Your draft was just what I needed. Without it, I wouldn't have had anything to edit. It gave me something to disagree with."

Was that damning with faint praise? Maybe; but I continued to write for that executive. He continued to edit my work heavily, but as we came to know each other better, he edited less. In time, I learned to respect his preferences and to anticipate his disagreements. We became a pretty good team.

Should speeches be written?

In this chapter, you will learn the preliminary steps to follow before you begin to write the speech. First, let's deal with a question that almost always arises in discussions of speech making: Should a speaker even use a written speech?

Some experts argue against it. They say a written speech is nothing more than a crutch. When a speaker uses a written speech, so goes the argument, he or she tends to read it word for word and it comes out stiff and stilted. It's true, of course, that nothing can be duller than a speech delivered in an expressionless, droning voice by a speaker whose eyes are glued to a written script. But such a performance is the fault of the speaker, not the manuscript. Some people can speak well without a manuscript; most cannot. If you're among the latter group, don't be concerned or self-conscious about relying on a script. You must, of course, learn how to use the script effectively. The key to using a written speech well is to know it well.

I recall writing an important speech for a prominent banker. I had never written for him before, nor had I heard him speak. His reputation, however, preceded him: He was generally considered to be a terrible speaker. He liked the speech I wrote, and I was in the auditorium the evening he delivered it before a large crowd. After listening for about five minutes, I could tell he was following the script exactly. And he was doing a surprisingly good job. I knew he was reading it, because I knew what was in the text, but I doubt that the audience could tell it. The speech sounded so good that I almost dislocated my shoulder patting myself on the back. At the same time, I wondered why people said my client was such a bad speaker. Well, he was no Ronald Reagan, but what the heck. . . .

Then I found out. About halfway through the speech, he suddenly departed from the text to ad lib a point that, presumably, he had just thought of. After that, it was all downhill. He couldn't get back on track. The speech that we both thought was so strong on continuity had become disjointed. The connectives and transitions I had inserted so carefully seemed now to have an effect that was just the opposite of what was intended. If the written speech was a crutch, he hobbled noticeably after tossing it aside.

And so this man's reputation as a bad speaker survived intact. If he had stuck with the speech, well . . . who knows?

President Ronald Reagan, the great communicator, always seemed natural and relaxed when he spoke, yet he almost always read his major addresses from a TelePrompTer™. Watching one of his speeches on television, I could actually glimpse the TelePrompTer now and then. Of course, he was a trained actor; however, many speakers who are not trained actors can read a speech, whether from a typescript or TelePrompTer, and sound natural.

I once wrote a videotape script for an executive who had almost no speaking experience. The tape was to be distributed to branch offices to announce a major change in company policy. The subject was so important to the company that the executive wanted to deliver it word for word. I wrote the script, and together we went over it carefully. Knowing that he was going to read it, I wanted to be certain that I had used words and phrases he was comfortable with. We underlined the words that needed to be emphasized and marked the places where he needed to pause. Then we had the text transferred to a TelePrompTer. For the taping, I suggested that he read from the TelePrompTer while sitting on the edge of his desk. For some speakers, this might seem contrived. For him, it was natural because he often sat on the edge of his desk when he spoke informally with visitors. Everyone who saw the tape thought the speaker seemed natural and relaxed. Yet, he had read the script word for word. The success of this important communication was a result of careful preparation and practice.

I'm not saying that you or any speaker should always read a speech word for word. I am saying that you can read a speech without sounding stilted. Whether a speech is delivered directly from the text depends on the occasion, the type of speech, and, most of all, the skill, experience, and inclination of the speaker. In any case, I believe strongly that almost every speech should begin with a written text, even if the speaker prefers not to use it.

Defense of written speeches

A well-written speech is a disciplined speech. It doesn't ramble. It gets to the point. It fits the time allotted. It contains no superfluous detail, but it doesn't leave out anything important. If you're speaking from cue cards, as some speakers like to do, the chances of leaving something out are high.

Writing—writing anything—is just about the best discipline I know of. Simply stated, writing makes you think. In writing this book, I had to think more about speeches, speech making, and speech writing than ever before. It's one thing to do something; it's quite another to tell someone else how to do it. Try telling someone how to ride a bicycle, swing a golf club, or play a guitar. It's not so easy.

The kind of thinking you have to do when you write is more than just letting the subject turn over and over in your mind, although that, too, can be useful. Writing forces you to think in specifics. It forces you to think in a directed way. Just putting your thoughts on paper in a sort of stream of consciousness might be a useful way to get started, but it's not writing. Writing is the application of discipline to creativity.

It seems to me that writing a speech is a lot like making a movie. In filmmaking, much of the footage that's shot ends up on the cutting-room floor. The result is a fast-paced, entertaining picture that holds the attention of the audience from beginning to end. That's what you want a speech to do.

Having a written, polished script in hand well before the date of the speech will give you confidence. If you've gone through the process of writing it all down and editing it thoroughly, you'll know the subject better. Even if you prefer to speak from notes, your notes will be more useful if they're made from a written text.

Business benefits

For business men and women, there's another important point to be made in favor of written speeches. If your speech is newsworthy, it's a good idea to have copies to pass out to any news media people who attend the event and to mail to any who request it. Your company's public relations department might also need a copy for use in preparing a news release about the speech. Some companies reprint their executives' speeches in booklet form and give them wide distribution.

In the 1970s, when the ecology movement was in its infancy, the late Paul Austin, who was then president of The Coca-Cola Company, delivered a masterful, deeply felt speech on ecology. One purpose of the speech was to outline the company's policy on matters of ecology at a time when a lot of ecology-minded people were screaming for a ban or tax on nonreturnable packaging for soft drinks as a means of controlling litter and solid waste.

Mr. Austin's thoughtful and acclaimed speech went a long way toward dispelling some misconceptions about soft drink cans and bottles while making some important points about ecology. The company had the speech printed and widely distributed. It was a PR coup. No doubt it helped make things go better with Coke—and probably with Pepsi, too.

Research: the first step

Writing a speech begins with research. The type and amount of research you need to do depends on the occasion, the nature of the speech, the subject, and how much you and the audience already know about it. Basically, research means reading up on the subject, especially recent books and articles, to be certain your information is up-to-date. It might also entail interviewing experts in the field to get varying points of view. Before you begin to write, you must have a working knowledge of your subject, whether it comes from your experience, from interviews, or from reading. Most often, the knowledge will come from a combination of these sources.

Depending on the subject, you might need to spend some time in the library or to call forth some articles from one of the on-line research services. Virtually unlimited information on many subjects is available on the Internet.

There's at least one organization I know of that will furnish you, at a very modest cost, copies of actual speeches on a wide variety of subjects. It's called the Executive Speaker. You'll find the address in Appendix B of this book. The subject file of Executive Speaker is extensive.

Your research should also include efforts to come up with quotations, anecdotes, analogies, statistics, and humor to help carry your points. Anecdotes from your own experience are always best, but most speech writers make use of the many sourcebooks available.

Writing for someone else

If you're writing a speech for someone else, you'll still need to do some research, no matter how knowledgeable the speaker might be. The more you know the better you can serve your client. Familiarity with the subject will enable you to ask questions designed to draw out your speaker's views and help him shape his thoughts. That's part of your job.

It's a good idea to ask your speaker, well in advance of the first session, to provide you with any pertinent materials he or she has available. Some executives will have all the necessary research material on file and will be happy to lend it to you to read before the two of you meet. Some will have thought the subject through before the first meeting with the writer. Others will be poorly prepared, or not prepared at all, at the first meeting. In any case, you should be prepared. Otherwise, your meeting will be unproductive, and you are likely to get off on the wrong foot with the client. It is not up to you to anticipate how well prepared your client might be.

Go to the first conference armed with a list of questions designed to draw the speaker out, to get him to think about the subject. Play the devil's advocate. Probe. Disagree. Argue. Challenge the speaker with questions and statements such as the following:

- "I don't quite understand."
- "Can you explain that in simpler terms?"
- "Does that have any practical application?"
- "Can you give me an example?"
- "Can you clarify that point?"
- "Let's examine that a little more closely."
- "Why is this important to the people who'll be in the audience?"
- "Are you certain that's the correct position?"
- "What else can you tell me about that?"

By the time of your first meeting, you should already know about the makeup of the audience. And you should have a good idea as to what extent the audience is familiar with the subject. Sometimes an expert on a subject will assume the people in the audience know more or less than they do and will tend to talk either down to them or over their heads. Don't let your client make that mistake.

In summary, when you write for another person, you're part of a team. If you're content to simply take down what the speaker tells you and feed it back in different words, you'll never be all you could be as a speech writer.

Brainstorming: a useful technique

Another good way to prepare for writing a speech is a technique commonly called "brainstorming." In a brainstorming session, several people get together in a comfortable, relaxed setting and just talk informally about the subject. The group should not be large—five may be the ideal number—but it should be composed of people of varied skills and backgrounds. The composition can be important for a number of reasons. For example, if you have five participants and one happens to be the boss, some of the others might be reluctant to express their thoughts freely. Or they might be all too eager to provide "input" just to impress the boss.

For brainstorming to work well, participants must check their inhibitions at the door. During the session, no idea, thought, or comment should be rejected or ridiculed. Even the most far-fetched idea can spark a better thought in someone else. This ground rule must be made clear from the beginning and gently enforced by the moderator, with such comments as "That's an interesting idea, Bob. What do you think about it, Kathi?" or "I had never thought of it exactly that way; let's get some other ideas."

I recall sitting in on a brainstorming session in which the boss of one man, let's call him Phil, was present. Phil made one suggestion early in the meeting. It wasn't a bad idea, but Phil's boss said, more thoughtlessly than maliciously, "I considered that a long time ago, Phil, and I can tell you straight out, it won't fly." Well, predictably, Phil clammed up. And who could blame him? A good moderator would have salvaged the idea and tried to encourage Phil's continued participation.

Putting together a brainstorming session might not be practical or possible for you. But when it can be done, it can be very effective. There are computer programs available that substitute for the real thing. The one I'm most familiar with is called "Idea Fisher." The name derives from the name of its originator, Marshall Fisher, who got the idea for Idea Fisher while he was taking a course in humor writing at UCLA. The concept is based on word and idea association. The software includes two linked databases: Q-Bank and Idea-Bank. Q-Bank contains nearly 6,000 questions to clarify problems, modify ideas, and evaluate solutions. Idea-Bank contains more than 65,000 idea words and 775,000 associated links. Both Q-Bank and Idea-Bank are intended to stimulate thinking about any subject you choose. Bear in mind, though, that no computer program can think for you. At best, it gives you some tools to help you think for yourself.

Several add-ons to Idea Fisher are available, including one especially for speeches and presentations.

Why am I doing this?

The next step in preparing to write is to set forth the purpose of the speech. Don't even think about writing until you have a clear notion of what the speech is supposed to accomplish.

Remember from the previous discussion that the six basic purposes of speeches are to entertain, inform, inspire, advocate, motivate, and convince or persuade. These are expressed here as one-word generalities, but the statement of purpose that you write for your speech should be more specific and more detailed. Include in the statement exactly what you want members of the audience to do, feel, or think, and how you want them to react. As examples, I composed statements of purpose for four speeches from my files. I wrote the statement from the speeches, but I tried to make them as realistic as possible. They are much as they would be if they had been prepared by the speech writer (or the speaker) before the writing began.

The first was delivered to a group of engineers and other technical people at a conference on federal regulations concerning the handling of toxic materials. The PR executive was a recognized expert on disclosure requirements of the Clean Air Act and other laws. Here is how the purpose might have been expressed:

> *The purpose of this speech is to inform the audience of the importance of including a detailed, professional program of communications, public disclosure, and community relations when they make plans for siting or expanding a facility that handles toxic materials. The speech should also convince them that developing such a communications program should be done expertly. By implication, the speech should also persuade the audience to call on the speaker's company for assistance when the need arises.*

Note that the statement includes two of the six purposes.

The next example is from a speech by a corporate CEO to shareholders in a year when the company's sales and earnings were disappointing:

> *The primary purpose of this speech is to inform the shareholders of the year's financial results, but it is important to convince them that the relatively poor performance of the company was the result of unfavorable economic conditions and not of any operations problems. Further, the speech should inform the shareholders of the company's prospects for growth by discussing several promising new products. After the speech, the shareholders should leave the meeting feeling good about their company. They should have renewed confidence in the management and should feel their investment is in good hands.*

Obviously, the CEO of a company must provide facts and figures about the company's operations, but in this instance it was important to persuade the shareholders to continue their support of the company and to convince them that management was doing its job.

The third example is based on a keynote speech delivered by a business executive at an awards luncheon honoring outstanding high school students. The audience included not only students but also teachers, principals, other education officials, and community leaders:

> *This speech should be largely inspirational. It should stress the importance of education in our society. It will provide some startling facts [inform] about the declining level of excellence in American education. The speech will call for a change of attitude toward education [advocate] and urge a return to basic American values [motivate].*

As head of a major corporation, the speaker mentioned several business-related examples, but he was careful not to mention the name of his company or even to name the industry of which it was a part. Presumably, he wanted to avoid seeming to be self-serving.

The last example is from a speech made by a company president to the company's national sales force. It is highly inspirational and motivational, essentially a pep talk:

> *What this speech should do is really "fire up" the sales force. It should make the salespeople feel they are truly part of a team. It should compliment them on the fine job they have done in the past year. In addition, it will describe some of the things the company is doing to make the salespeople more productive, which will pay dividends in the form of higher commissions. Since one purpose of the annual sales meeting is to promote camaraderie and esprit de corps within the company, the speech should be entertaining as well as informative and motivational.*

Each of these four statements has more than one purpose, and you will find that to be true of almost every speech you hear or read. When you write a statement of purpose, do not try to make it conform to one or even two or more of the six categories. The important thing is to get something on paper to guide you through the writing of the speech.

If you're writing a speech for a client, make the development of this statement of purpose a joint exercise. It will help both you and your client. Put it in writing so that both of you can have a copy as you continue to work on the speech. The time you spend on this exercise will be well spent.

The speech writer's road map

Once you have formulated a clear, specific statement of purpose for the speech, it's time to begin work on an outline. Making an outline is like planning a trip: You don't leave until you've mapped out your route. You know where you want to go, and maybe you have a general idea of how to get there. But until you plot your course on a map, you can't be certain of every road you'll have to take and every town you'll pass through along the way. The outline is the speech writer's road map.

There's no set way to develop an outline, and it's probably a mistake to become too involved in the procedure itself. Use the method or format that works best for you. One way to begin is to make a list of the points you want to make in the speech. For a twenty- to thirty-minute speech, there could be as many as eighteen or twenty. The number really doesn't matter.

Once you have these potential points on paper, go through the list again and evaluate each one carefully. You'll find that some are more important than others. Try to pare the list to three or four—I'd say a maximum of five—that are really important. One thing you do not want is to overload your speech. Most audiences just won't absorb too many ideas or too much information at once. Look at it this way: The more ideas you pack into your speech, the less attention any single idea will get. Be certain that the focus remains on the most important points.

In the process of paring down your list, you'll probably find that many of the discarded points will remain in the speech but will be relegated to supporting, explanatory, or reinforcing roles.

From this paring-down exercise, a thesis for the speech should evolve. A thesis is a single, strong, unifying idea that seems to put the entire speech in perspective. This idea, or core statement as it might be called, may or may not be expressed somewhere in the speech. Whether it is or not, it is what the speech is all about.

Identify the thesis

In preparing to write this discussion of the speech thesis, I pulled several speeches from my bulging files. In each one, I was able to pick out a single statement that I would call the thesis statement. For example, I looked at a speech I wrote some years ago for a client to deliver to a management conference in Canada. The title of the speech is "Management Challenges of the Future." I found the thesis on page 7:

> *So the question is not whether today's management has the ability to meet the challenges of the future, but whether it has the will. The free enterprise economic system that we enjoy in North America is the most dynamic, the most vibrant, the most resilient system ever devised to direct the economic affairs of man. It can overcome honest errors and even a certain amount of deliberate tampering. But it cannot tolerate neglect. It cannot survive a lack of will on the part of those who profess to believe in it.*
>
> *If we have the will to make this system work as it has worked in the past, the future of business in North America is bright; if not, we can look for steady erosion of our economic base and our standard of living.*

The speech was just over sixteen pages long. Everything that appeared before page seven of the speech led to that statement. Everything after page seven of the speech supported it.

Some speech writers advocate writing a thesis statement at the beginning, but it seems to me that the thesis grows out of the list of main points. Either way, every good speech has a thesis, and in many cases it is stated somewhere in the speech, often in more than one place and in different words. Sometimes it comes near the beginning; sometimes it constitutes a wrap-up.

At this point in the preparation process, you have:

- A written statement of purpose,
- A list of what you want the speech to accomplish,
- A list of your main points and supporting points, and
- A thesis, or core statement, for the speech.

These four items are needed to structure a good, workable outline. To complete the outline—the road map that tells you how you expect to get where you want to be—arrange your main points in the order you want them to appear, along with the appropriate supporting points, keeping in mind the purpose, the thesis, and what you want the speech to accomplish.

"GLORY AND HOPE"

To many black South Africans, Nelson Mandela must seem to be George Washington, Abraham Lincoln, and Martin Luther King Jr. rolled into one. Imprisoned in 1962 and released 28 years later at the age of 72, Mandela became the first black to be elected president of South Africa. The speech below, delivered on the day of his election in May 1992, is a moving tribute to the indomitability of the human spirit. It is especially noteworthy for its eloquent language and rich imagery, and it also uses triads, anaphora, and other techniques, to be discussed later:

Your majesties, your royal highnesses, distinguished guests, comrades and friends: Today, all of us do, by our presence here, and by our celebrations in other parts of our country and the world, confer glory and hope to newborn liberty. Out of the experience of an extraordinary human disaster that lasted too long must be born a society of which all humanity will be proud. Our daily deeds as ordinary South Africans must produce an actual South African reality that will reinforce humanity's belief in justice, strengthen its confidence in the nobility of the human soul and sustain all our hopes for a glorious life for all.

All this we owe both to ourselves and to the peoples of the world who are so well represented here today.

To my compatriots, I have no hesitation in saying that each one of us is as intimately attached to the soil of this beautiful country as are the famous jacaranda trees of Pretoria and the mimosa trees of the bushveld. Each time one of us touches the soil of this land, we feel a sense of personal renewal. The national mood changes as the seasons change. We are moved by a sense of joy and exhilaration when the grass turns green and the flowers bloom.

That spiritual and physical oneness we all share with this common homeland explains the depth of the pain we all carried in our hearts as we saw our country tear itself apart in terrible conflict, and as we saw it spurned, outlawed and isolated by the peoples of the world, precisely because it has become the universal base of the pernicious ideology and practice of racism and racial oppression.

We, the people of South Africa, feel fulfilled that humanity has taken us back into its bosom, that we, who were outlaws not so long ago, have today been given the rare privilege to be host to the nations of the world on our own soil. We thank all our distinguished international guests for having come to take possession with the people of our country of what is, after all, a common victory for justice, for peace, for human dignity. We trust that you will continue to stand by us as we tackle the challenges of building peace, prosperity, nonsexism, nonracialism and democracy.

We deeply appreciate the role that the masses of our people and their democratic, religious, women, youth, business, traditional and other leaders have played to bring about this conclusion. Not least among them is my Second Deputy President, the Honorable F.W. de Klerk.

We would also like to pay tribute to our security forces, in all their ranks, for the distinguished role they have played in securing our first democratic elections and the transition to democracy, from bloodthirsty forces which still refuse to see the light.

The time for the healing of the wounds has come.

The moment to bridge the chasms that divide us has come.

The time to build is upon us.

We have, at last, achieved our political emancipation. We pledge ourselves to liberate all our people from the continuing bondage of poverty, deprivation, suffering, gender and other discrimination.

We succeeded to take our last steps to freedom in conditions of relative peace. We commit ourselves to the construction of a complete, just and lasting peace.

We have triumphed in the effort to implant hope in the breasts of the millions of our people.

We enter into a covenant that we shall build the society in which all South Africans, both black and white, will be able to walk tall without any fear in their hearts, assured of their inalienable right to human dignity—a rainbow nation at peace with itself and the world.

As a token of its commitment to the renewal of our country, the new Interim Government of National Unity will, as a matter of urgency, address the issue of amnesty for various categories of our people who are currently serving terms of imprisonment.

We dedicate this day to all the heroes and heroines in this country and the rest of the world who sacrificed in many ways and surrendered their lives so that we could be free.

Their dreams have become reality. Freedom is their reward.

We are both humbled and elevated by the honor and privilege that you, the people of South Africa, have bestowed on us, as the first President of a united, democratic, nonracial and nonsexist South Africa, to lead our country out of the valley of darkness.

We understand it still that there is no easy road to freedom.

We know it well that none of us acting alone can achieve success.

We must therefore act together as a united people, for national reconciliation, for nation building, for the birth of a new world.

Let there be justice for all.

Let there be peace for all.

Let there be work, bread, water and salt for all.

Let each know that for each the body, the mind and the soul have been freed to fulfill themselves.

Never, never and never again shall it be that this beautiful land will again experience the oppression of one by another and suffer the indignity of being the skunk of the world.

The sun shall never set on so glorious a human achievement!

Let freedom reign. God bless Africa!

"The Woman I Love"

Fifty-six years and a continent away from Nelson Mandela's historic ascension to the presidency of South Africa, another historic event occurred: England's King Edward VIII took the unprecedented action of abdicating his throne for "the woman I love," an American divorcée named Wallis Warfield Simpson. Opinions to this day remain divided as to whether his action was selfish or courageous, but the story still holds a fascination for many people.

In the next chapter, I'll take you step-by-step through the process of outlining a speech. Right now, let's drift back in time and read Edward's short statement to Parliament. The date was December 11, 1936.

At long last I am able to say a few words of my own. I have never wanted to withhold anything, but until now it has not been constitutionally possible for me to speak. A few hours ago I discharged my last duty as King and Emperor, and now that I have been succeeded by my brother, the Duke of York, my first words must be to declare my allegiance to him. This I do with all my heart.

You all know the reasons which have impelled me to renounce the throne. But I want you to understand that in making up my mind I did not forget the country or the empire, which, as Prince of Wales and lately as King, I have for twenty-five years tried to serve.

But you must believe me when I tell you that I have found it impossible to carry the heavy burden of responsibility and to discharge my duties as King as I would wish to do without the help and support of the woman I love.

And I want you to know that the decision I have made has been mine and mine alone. This was a thing I had to judge entirely for myself. The other person most nearly concerned has tried up to the last to persuade me to take a different course.

I have made this, the most serious decision of my life, only upon the single thought of what would, in the end, be best for all.

This decision has been made less difficult to me by the sure knowledge that my brother, with his long training in the public affairs of this country and with his fine qualities, will be able to take my place forthwith without interruption or injury to the life and progress of the empire. And he has one matchless blessing, enjoyed by so many of you, and not bestowed on me—a happy home with his wife and children.

During these hard days I have been comforted by her Majesty my mother and by my family. The ministers of the crown, and in particular Mr. Baldwin, the Prime Minister, have always treated me with full consideration. There has never been any constitutional difference between me and them, and between me and Parliament. Bred in the constitutional tradition by my father, I should never have allowed any such issue to arise.

Ever since I was Prince of Wales, and later on when I occupied the throne, I have been treated with the greatest kindness by all classes of the people wherever I have lived or journeyed throughout the empire. For that I am very grateful.

I now quit altogether public affairs and I lay down my burden. It may be some time before I return to my native land, but I shall always follow the fortunes of the British race and empire with profound interest, and if at any time in the future I can be found of service to his Majesty in a private station, I shall not fail.

And now, we all have a new King. I wish him and you, his people, happiness and prosperity with all my heart. God bless you all! God save the King!

— Chapter Four —

Outlining and Organizing

In Chapter Three, I offered several suggestions for preparing to make an outline of your speech. Let me summarize those suggestions:

- Do a thorough job of researching the subject.
- Prepare a written statement of the specific purpose of the speech.
- Write down exactly what you want the audience to think or feel or do as a result of the speech.
- Based on your research, list all the points you might want to make.
- Pare the list down to three, four, or possibly five truly important points, discarding the remaining ones or converting them into supporting points.
- Identify the thesis, or unifying theme, that emerges from the paring-down process.
- Arrange the points and supporting points in the proper order.

What you then will have is your outline. Writing the speech is a matter of converting the outline into a full text, which you will edit, refine, and polish. You or your client will use the text, or notes made from it, to deliver a speech. It will be a good speech. The audience will be moved. You will be a hero. Or, if you're both writer and speaker, you'll enjoy one of the most satisfying experiences of your life.

But you still have a way to go before you can savor the applause.

Developing the outline

Near the end of Chapter Three, I promised to take you through the preparation of an outline. To do that, I want you to consider a mostly imaginary situation based on a real speech and a real situation.

Let's say that you're a top executive of a large business. You have been invited to speak to the Rotary Club of Washington, D.C., a prestigious organization whose membership includes many government officials. You feel very strongly that government regulation of business has gone much too far, that regulations increase the cost of doing business and thus inhibit the creation of jobs. You believe the time has come to curb government growth. You do not believe, however, that all government regulation of business is bad, but you believe a workable balance in the relationship of government and business should be the objective.

You do not want to spend a lot of time talking about your own company, except perhaps to use some of your business experiences to illustrate your points.

Your research into the subject has consisted mainly of finding quotations, anecdotes, statistics, and other materials to support your contentions. You have done the research and thought about the topic at length. You've titled the speech "Government and Business: A Balancing Act."

You remember that I recommend beginning with a formal, written statement of purpose for a speech. Keep in mind the six basic purposes of a speech: to entertain, inform, inspire, motivate, advocate, and convince or persuade. A statement of purpose for "Government and Business: A Balancing Act" would encompass three of the six purposes—to inform, to advocate, and to convince.

The statement of purpose should include what you want members of the audience to do, think, or feel as a result of the speech. Here is how your statement of purpose might be expressed:

> *The purpose of this speech is to present my views on the subject of why too much government regulation of business is inappropriate in a free-enterprise economy and to advocate a return to balance in the government-business relationship. I want members of the audience to be more aware of the effect of government regulation on business and more receptive to efforts to curb the growth of government in order that the proper balance might be restored. In addition, I want the audience to gain a favorable impression of me and, by extension, of my company.*

It is important to note that the statement of purpose does *not* say anything about motivating the audience to write their congressmen or to try in any way to influence any particular impending legislation. You have decided that it would be inappropriate to make such suggestions to this audience.

The next step in developing an outline is to list the points the speaker might want to make. For this speech, let's say that your research has led you to list fourteen such points:

1. Federal government regulations pervade almost every facet of our business and personal lives.
2. The presidential election is coming soon, and people in Washington are concerned about how the election will affect their lives.
3. Both candidates have agreed that something must be done to curb awesome federal power.
4. Cite the quotation from an article published in a major news magazine entitled "Can Congress or the President really bring the government to heel?"
5. People of all political persuasions are convinced that it is time to curb government growth. Cite an opinion poll.
6. Opposing forces are at work in our complex society. A Harvard sociologist claims that our society is "an uneasy amalgam of contradictory principles."
7. Vast majority of Americans are between the two extremes of political thought.
8. Cite the quotation from Conference Board Information Bulletin: "Business people must make active political efforts to ensure the survival of the socio-economic and political system that makes possible the function of the free-enterprise system."
9. The political system and economic systems are tied together. They are mutually dependent, and it is imperative to maintain a workable balance between the two.
10. The economy will need to create millions of new jobs over the next several years to provide for the men and women coming into the workforce.
11. Only business can create jobs. It is the responsibility of business to create jobs.
12. Anything that adds to the cost of business contributes to unemployment by increasing product cost and decreasing demand. Higher costs reduce the amount of capital available for businesses to invest in job-creating expansion.
13. Government's role should be to facilitate; the role of business should be to innovate.
14. The time has come to get rid of the adversary relationship that exists between government and business.

These are all good points, but the list needs to be more manageable. You must examine each point and consider to what extent it supports the stated purpose of the speech, how the audience might react to it, and its relative importance in the overall context.

The next step is to identify among the list the three or four most important points. Ask yourself, "What are the key points that will do the most to fulfill the stated purpose of the speech and induce the audience to do, think, or feel the way I want them to?" Another way to look at it is this: "If I could tell this audience only three or four things, what would I want them to be?"

In this careful scrutiny of the fourteen possible discussion points, you will combine some, perhaps eliminate some, and relegate others to supporting roles. You will end up with three, four, or five really important points. These are the foundation on which to build the speech.

For your speech, let's say you decide the four key points are:

1. Government is much too deeply involved in almost every aspect of our personal and business lives.
2. Government regulations add to the cost of doing business and make it difficult for business to meet its responsibility of creating jobs for Americans.
3. The role of business is to create jobs. This is something the government cannot do. The role of government should be to facilitate the creation of jobs.
4. Not all government involvement in business is bad. What is needed is a workable balance in the government-business relationship.

Paring down the list of possible points and distilling the list into a few key points leaves you with a manageable amount of material. The thinking required in the paring-down process probably will generate a thesis statement. At this point, you might consider writing the thesis statement very much as it would appear in the speech. Remember that we have defined the thesis as a single, unifying idea or theme of the speech. Here is a possible thesis for the speech:

> *The free-enterprise system and the American political system that has made possible the highest degree of individual liberty the world has ever known are not mutually exclusive concepts. They are, in fact, dependent upon each other. Simply stated, you cannot have political freedom without economic freedom, and you cannot have economic freedom without political freedom. The imperative we face today is to attain and maintain a workable balance in the relationship between government and business. And I stress the*

word "attain" because I do not think we have such a bal-
ance today. Perhaps we had it once; if so, we have lost it.

In the speech outline, each of the four key points would be followed by supporting, explanatory, or reinforcing points, as well as
notations about anecdotes, analogies, humor, quotations, examples,
statistics, transitions, visual aids, and other material to move the text
along.

To complete your outline, arrange all your points in the order
you wish to present them in the speech. This means not just the key
points but the supporting points and other material as well. By the
time you reach this stage, you should have begun to think of your
speech not as a collection of discussion points but as a coherent,
connected whole. In other words, your speech should be starting to
shape up in your mind.

Organizing the speech

A well-organized speech is the product of an orderly mind. No matter how compelling your thesis, how strong your arguments, how
interesting your material, the speech will not be a success if it is not
logically organized. There is no formula, no "right" or "wrong" way
to organize a speech. It depends on the material, the speaker, and the
audience.

If you're telling a story, chronological order might work, especially if there's an element of suspense and you want to build to a
climax. For most speeches, however, chronological order is not especially effective.

Some speakers like to start with a bang by stating the major
premise, or thesis, of the speech in the first minute or so. That can
be dramatic and effective—an attention getter—especially if the thesis is something startling or unexpected. The problem with that kind
of beginning is that if you're not careful, the speech goes downhill
from there.

Then there's the time-honored advice that almost every speech
writer gets at one time or another. It goes something like this: Use
the opening to tell the audience what you're going to tell them; use
the body of the speech to tell them what you said you were going to
tell them; and use the ending to tell them what you've told them.
(Or, as it is more often expressed: Tell 'em what you're gonna tell
'em. Then tell 'em. Then tell 'em what you've just told 'em.)

There may be some merit in that advice, but I wouldn't take it
too seriously. It's just a bit simplistic. Besides, it might be insulting

to some audiences or, at best, it might make the speaker seem condescending. I've never read a really good speech that followed that format.

It's not a bad idea, though, to tell the audience early what you're going to talk about and then to end with a brief summary.

One popular organizational form is based on cause-and-effect or problem-and-solution. That's where you state some problem that's pertinent to the speech thesis, give the cause of the problem, then describe its effect and suggest a solution. This does not necessarily imply a simplistic approach such as the following:

> *Government regulations increase the cost of doing business,*
> *which makes it difficult for businesses to make job-creating*
> *investments* [problem]. *This exacerbates the unemployment*
> *problem in the United States* [effect]. *Reducing the govern-*
> *ment regulatory burden on business would go a long way*
> *toward alleviating the unemployment problem* [solution].

In real life, the problem-solution will rarely be so straightforward. Most often, problems, causes, effects, and solutions will be commingled. For example, let's suppose that the imaginary speech we outlined above contained the following passage:

> *We will need to create ten million jobs in this country over*
> *the next few years just to provide employment for new work-*
> *ers coming into the workplace and, frankly, as a business*
> *executive, I can't see where these jobs are coming from. We*
> *already have an unacceptably high unemployment rate*
> *that, in my opinion, is due in large measure to burdensome*
> *government regulations. Government regulations increase*
> *the cost of doing business, which results in high prices for*
> *consumer goods and a shortage of expansion capital. This,*
> *in turn, expands the unemployment rolls, putting a serious*
> *strain on state and federal social systems. Costs of welfare,*
> *unemployment compensation, health care, and other bene-*
> *fits skyrocket, while tax collections drop.*

If you read the passage carefully, you see that it includes several problem statements: the need to create ten million jobs, unacceptably high unemployment, strained social systems, reduced tax collections. The main problem, based on the speech's thesis and statement of purpose, is government regulations. Some of the things mentioned as problems, then, become effects.

The suggested solution begins with a negative, a statement of what the solution *isn't*, and concludes with a simple, strong expression of your solution that ties directly to the thesis:

> *The government is attempting to stimulate the economy and create jobs. These efforts might alleviate the immediate situation, but government cannot provide a long-term solution. In the long term, only business can keep America at work. It is properly the responsibility of business to create the jobs we need. Government can help by providing a legislative and regulatory environment in which business is encouraged to grow and make job-creating investments.*
>
> *In short, what our government should do is get the hell out of the way.*

You could reverse the order and start with the solution. Begin with the speaker's advocacy of less government regulation of business, then discuss the problems that cause too much regulation.

The point here is not to provide you with a formula for organizing a speech; it is to suggest an approach to organizing that can be applied to both the whole speech and individual elements within the speech. I call these elements "thought modules."

Working in thought modules

Using thought modules is simply a way of breaking a speech down into small, manageable units. A thought module consists of a single idea and all necessary supporting material. For example, if you take the passage you've just read and add supporting material such as an interesting statistic, a pertinent quotation, or an anecdote, you have a thought module. I don't want to make this too complicated, but a whole speech can be considered a thought module, with the thesis as the single basic idea. Stated another way, every thought module is composed of smaller modules.

The idea behind constructing thought modules is to force yourself to think logically about what you write and to develop the habit of keeping related material together and arranged in logical order.

Word processing has made organizing a speech, or any written material, infinitely easier. If you have included a paragraph or sentence in one place and you decide you don't think it belongs there, you turn to that little user-friendly critter called a mouse. A flick of the mouse button is all it takes to try the paragraph somewhere else—or in any number of places until you find where it works best.

If time permits, put your outline aside for a few days before starting to write the speech. You'll carry it in your head, of course, and your subconscious mind will continue to work on it. I'm a great believer in the power of the subconscious. It can work miracles.

Finally, a caveat about outlines: Don't let your outline take over. It's a road map, as I've said, but that doesn't mean you have to follow it slavishly. You can always take a little side trip on your journey.

Podium Presence

Now let's consider our second "Podium Presence" tip:

In Chapter One we briefly discussed stage fright, or nervousness, or fear, or whatever you care to call it. Let me remind you that nervousness is something all speakers feel at one time or another. Its symptoms range from mild jitters to total, abject, irrational, disabling terror. Let's hope that what you feel is much closer to the first than the last.

Strangely enough, some speakers experience fear or nervousness before they rise to speak and lose it the moment they get started.

It's helpful to understand the nature of stage fright. It is often nothing more or less than a fear of failure. This being the case, thorough preparation may be the best way to control fear. We'll talk more about preparation later. For now, remember that exercising discretion in choosing which invitations to accept is part of your preparation. So are finding out about your audience and the occasion, selecting and researching your topic, writing the speech, and preparing the manuscript for use at the lectern. The better job you do on all these things, the less likely you will suffer from unreasonable fear. If you're really well prepared, you'll have no reason to worry about failing.

But, admittedly, there's more to it. Even a well-prepared speaker can suffer from stage fright to one degree or another.

Most people feel most nervous at the beginning of a speech. If that happens to you, try to concentrate on your audience. This will take your mind off yourself. You can't be nervous if you're not thinking of yourself. Allow your eyes to meet the eyes of some of the audience members. Chances are you'll see nothing but friendly faces. They want you to succeed. They expect you to succeed. If you see someone you know, acknowledge his presence with a smile or in some other way.

Two physical activities can help you overcome nervousness. One is breathing deeply; the other is stretching. Deep breathing draws more oxygen into your lungs, which clears your mind and helps you think and relax.

Certain stretching exercises can also help you relax. Of course, you can't stretch during a speech, but if you arrive for the speech early, which is something I highly recommend, you might have a few minutes to enjoy a private, relaxing stretch.

One of the best ways to relax is to use the well-known, highly effective progression method. This is something you can do in full view of the audience while you're waiting to speak. Start with the top of your head and relax your scalp. Then go to your facial muscles, then to your neck, shoulders, and on down through all your body parts. If you practice this technique, you'll be able to feel the tension flow out of your body. It's really a wonderful feeling. By the time you get to your toes, you'll be completely relaxed.

"A Celebration of Freedom"

Now, I want you to relax and experience President John F. Kennedy's inaugural address, delivered on January 20, 1961, which I mentioned previously. This is an uncommonly well-constructed speech, and it makes use of many of the rhetorical devices and techniques that we'll examine in later chapters.

This is arguably one of the finest speeches ever made by an American president. Whether you love John F. Kennedy or hate him, if it doesn't move you, bring a lump to your throat, you must be made of concrete:

We observe today not a victory of party but a celebration of freedom, symbolizing an end as well as a beginning, signifying renewal as well as change. For I have sworn before you and Almighty God the same solemn oath our forebears prescribed nearly a century and three-quarters ago.

The world is very different now. For man holds in his mortal hands the power to abolish all forms of human poverty and all forms of human life. And yet the same revolutionary belief for which our forebears fought is still at issue around the globe, the belief that the rights of man come not from the generosity of the state but from the hand of God.

We dare not forget today that we are the heirs of that first revolution. Let the word go forth from this time and place, to friend and foe alike, that the torch has been passed to a new generation of Americans, born in this century, tempered by war, disciplined by a hard and bitter peace, proud of our ancient heritage, and unwilling to witness or permit the slow undoing of these human rights to which this nation has always been committed, and to which we are committed today at home and around the world.

Let every nation know, whether it wishes us well or ill, that we shall pay any price, bear any burden, meet any hardship, support any friend, oppose any foe to assure the survival and the success of liberty.

This much we pledge and more.

To those old allies whose cultural and spiritual origins we share, we pledge the loyalty of faithful friends. United, there is little we cannot do in a host of co-operative ventures. Divided, there is little we can do, for we dare not meet a powerful challenge at odds and split asunder.

To those new states whom we welcome to the ranks of the free, we pledge our word that one form of colonial control shall not have passed away merely to be replaced by a far more iron tyranny. We shall not always expect to find them supporting our view. But we shall always hope to find them strongly supporting their own freedom, and to remember that, in the past, those who foolishly sought power by riding the back of the tiger ended up inside.

To those peoples in the huts and villages of half the globe struggling to break the bonds of mass misery, we pledge our best efforts to help them help themselves, for whatever period is required, not because the Communists may be doing it, not because we seek their votes, but because it is right. If a free society cannot help the many who are poor, it cannot save the few who are rich.

To our sister republics south of our border, we offer a special pledge: to convert our good words into good deeds, in a new alliance for progress, to assist free men and free governments in casting off the chains of poverty. But this peaceful revolution of hope cannot become the prey of hostile powers. Let all our neighbors know that we shall join with them to oppose aggression or subversion anywhere in the Americas. And let every other power know that this hemisphere intends to remain the master of its own house.

To that world assembly of sovereign states, the United Nations, our last best hope in an age where the instruments of war have far outpaced the instruments of peace, we renew our pledge of support: to prevent it from becoming merely a forum for invective, to strengthen its shields of the new and the weak, and to enlarge the area in which its writ may run.

Finally, to those nations who would make themselves our adversary, we offer not a pledge but a request: that both sides begin anew the quest for peace, before the dark powers of destruction unleashed by science engulf all humanity in planned or accidental self-destruction.

We dare not tempt them with weakness. For only when our arms are sufficient beyond doubt can we be certain beyond doubt that they will never be employed. But neither can two great and powerful groups of nations take comfort from our present course, both sides overburdened by the cost of modern weapons, both rightly alarmed by the steady spread of the deadly atom, yet both racing to alter that uncertain balance of terror that stays the hand of mankind's final war.

So let us begin anew, remembering on both sides that civility is not a sign of weakness, and sincerity is always subject to proof. Let us never negotiate out of fear, but let us never fear to negotiate.

Let both sides explore what problems unite us instead of belaboring those problems which divide us.

Let both sides, for the first time, formulate serious and precise proposals for the inspection and control of arms, and bring the absolute power to destroy other nations under the absolute control of all nations.

Let both sides seek to invoke the wonders of science instead of its terrors. Together let us explore the stars, conquer the deserts, eradicate disease, tap the ocean depths and encourage the arts and commerce.

Let both sides unite to heed in all corners of the earth the command of Isaiah to "undo the heavy burdens . . . [and] let the oppressed go free."

And if a beachhead of co-operation may push back the jungle of suspicion, let both sides join in creating a new endeavor, not a new balance of power, but a new world of law, where the strong are just and the weak secure and the peace preserved.

All this will not be finished in the first one hundred days. Nor will it be finished in the first one thousand days, nor in the life of this Administration, nor even perhaps in our lifetime on this planet. But let us begin.

In your hands, my fellow citizens, more than mine, will rest the final success or failure of our course. Since this country was founded, each generation of Americans has been summoned to give testimony to its national loyalty. The graves of young Americans who answered the call to service surround the globe.

Now the trumpet summons us again not as a call to bear arms, though arms we need; not as a call to battle, though embattled we are; but a call to bear the burden of a long twilight struggle, year in and year out, "rejoicing in hope, patient in tribulation," a struggle against the common enemies of man: tyranny, poverty, disease and war itself.

Can we forge against these enemies a grand and global alliance, North and South, East and West, that can assure a more fruitful life for all mankind? Will you join in that historic effort?

In the long history of the world, only a few generations have been granted the role of defending freedom in its hour of maximum danger. I do not shrink from this responsibility; I welcome it. I do not believe that any of us would exchange places with any other people or any other generation. The energy, the faith, the devotion which we bring to this endeavor will light our country and all who serve it, and the glow from that fire can truly light the world.

And so, my fellow Americans, ask not what your country can do for you; ask what you can do for your country.

My fellow citizens of the world, ask not what America will do for you, but what together we can do for the freedom of man.

Finally, whether you are citizens of America or citizens of the world, ask of us here the same high standards of strength and sacrifice which we ask of you. With a good conscience our only sure reward, with history the final judge of our deeds, let us go forth to lead the land we love, asking His blessing and His help, but knowing that here on earth God's work must truly be our own.

── Chapter Five ──

Beginning Well

"Well begun is well done."

So goes the old saying. Although speech writing is not quite that simple, it is certainly true that getting a speech off to a good start puts the speaker a lot closer to the time when "well done" can truly apply. In the next two chapters, the discussion will be about opening a speech. I'll cover the importance of crafting a good opening and give you numerous examples of openings of different kinds.

To have a good speech, you must have a good opening. If that seems too obvious to mention, think about this: The first minute or so of a speech is about the only time a speaker can be certain of having the undivided attention of the audience. Virtually every person in an audience is attentive at first. This brief period might be called the speaker's "grace period." After that, the speaker has to earn the audience's attention. If you lose the audience during this grace period, you might never regain their attention.

It's somewhat like the fabled first hundred days of a new president's term, except with a speaker it's more like a hundred seconds. During a president's first hundred days, tradition gives the president the benefit of the doubt . . . time to organize his administration . . . time to present his program to the nation. After a hundred days, the president, like the speaker in the first two or three minutes, runs out of automatic goodwill. Then the president has to earn the respect of the news media, the Congress, and the people. In the same way, the speaker has to earn the respect and attention of the audience after those first few minutes of grace.

In a sense, the opening is the time for the audience to get to know the speaker. Picture yourself in an audience. Except for what you might have learned from the introduction, you might know little or nothing about the person who's going to take up the next twenty or thirty minutes of your valuable time. Is he well qualified to speak on the subject? Is he a nice guy, someone you'd like to play a round of golf with? Is he funny? Smart? And so on. In the first couple of minutes, an audience can learn a lot about the speaker.

Conversely, the speaker can learn a thing or two about the audience during the opening. Do the people in the audience seem friendly and responsive? Do they share your sense of humor? Are they likely to be receptive to your views? The ability to use the opening to size up an audience can be very useful to a speaker.

Although a good opening does not guarantee a good speech, a bad opening almost always guarantees a bad speech.

Formal vs. informal

Now, we will take a look at some techniques and ideas for opening your speech. First, let's dispose of the question of the formal opening versus the informal opening.

In a formal opening, it's customary to address directly or acknowledge the key individuals and groups in the audience by mentioning each, usually starting with the most prominent or most senior. For example, if you're addressing the Southtown Rotary Club, a formal opening would begin something like this:

President Bennett.
Members and guests of the Southtown Rotary Club.

If the audience includes a distinguished guest, mention that person's name first. Let's say the mayor of Southtown is in the audience that day. Your acknowledgments should be:

Mayor Larson.
President Bennett.
Members of the Southtown Rotary Club.

If several distinguished people are in the audience, mentioning each one could be tedious, and you could lose your audience almost before you get started. In such a situation, your opening might be something like this:

Mayor Larson.
President Bennett.
Members of the Southtown Rotary Club.
Distinguished guests.

When you recognize people by name, you must be certain, to have the names and titles correct. If I were to be recognized by a speaker, I'd want my name pronounced correctly—DOWis, not DoWIS. Also, you must be careful not to leave out anyone who should be included.

Common sense is the only guideline for deciding whom to acknowledge at the beginning of a speech. Your decision will be affected by the program, the occasion, the content of your speech, the audience, and other factors.

Here is a very formal opening I wrote for the mayor of Atlanta to use in a short address to welcome a group of foreign dignitaries to the city:

> *Distinguished ambassadors and other officials of the United Nations, Officials of the United Nations Institute for Training and Research, Members of the Atlanta consular corps, Trustees and directors of the Atlanta Council for International Cooperation, Ladies and gentlemen.*
>
> *As mayor of the City of Atlanta and on behalf of Governor Zell Miller, who is unable to be with us this evening, I am honored to bring you greetings on the eve of what I consider to be an important and even historic occasion.*
>
> *And to our visitors from throughout the world, a very special welcome to the home of the 1996 Olympic Games.*

Many speakers and speech writers consider the formal opening stiff, old-fashioned, and out of sync with today's informality. Indeed, a formal style is reminiscent of an earlier, perhaps more gracious, era. In my opinion, acknowledgments still have a place in speeches, although they are not necessary for every speech and every occasion. In many of the speeches I have written, I have included acknowledgments, but I'm certain that many of my clients elected not to use them. Formal acknowledgments that sound perfectly natural coming from one speaker might seem hopelessly stilted from another.

Many fine speakers prefer to begin by saying something simple, such as "Good morning, ladies and gentlemen" or "Good evening, everyone," or simply, "Ladies and gentlemen." That's fine; I have no problem with that if it suits the occasion and the speaker's style and personality.

In addition to acknowledgments, thanking the organization for asking you to speak and thanking the person who has introduced you are customary and usually desirable. To me, this is just common courtesy. Even though more often than not you are doing the organization a favor by agreeing to speak, you should be both flattered and honored by the invitation.

I have heard some excellent speakers begin without any greeting, thank-yous, or acknowledgments.

In any case, acknowledgments, if any, and thank-yous are not the real speech opening. Let's just call them the opening of the opening.

On a very serious topic, a speaker might choose to get immediately to the point with few, if any, preliminaries that could be called an opening in the usual sense. When President Franklin D. Roosevelt asked Congress to declare war on Japan after Japanese forces attacked the U.S. Naval base at Pearl Harbor (see Chapter One), his only opening was the obligatory acknowledgment of the leaders of the House and Senate.

> *Mr. Vice President, Mr. Speaker, members of the Senate and the House of Representatives.*

Then he got right to the point:

> *Yesterday, December 7, 1941—a date which will live in infamy—the United States of America was suddenly and deliberately attacked by naval and air forces of the empire of Japan.*

Roosevelt's brief, simple speech was perfect for the occasion. It had a sort of lets-get-on-with-it tone, and the stirring phrase "a date which will live in infamy" will live as long as the memory of Pearl Harbor lives. He went on to recite the facts of the attack on Pearl Harbor and subsequent military moves by the Japanese. Not until the last paragraph did he ask for the declaration of war. It could be argued that the single-sentence last paragraph was the speech and that everything before it was the opening. For our purposes, however, I am defining the opening of a speech much more narrowly.

What an opening must accomplish

Constructing an effective opening is a challenge for the speech writer. An opening may, in a very short time, need to accomplish as many as half a dozen things:

• *First, the opening must establish a common ground, or a rapport, between the speaker and the audience.* There are many ways to do this. Presidents of the United States almost always establish a common ground by addressing the audience as "My fellow Americans." This, of course, is the president's way of saying, "You and I share this one great attribute. We are Americans. We may have differing ideas. We may be of different political parties. We may be of a different race or creed. But we are Americans. This is our common heritage; and this is the common meeting ground for this speech."

John F. Kennedy, speaking in the divided city of Berlin at the height of the Cold War, established rapport with his audience by saying "*Ich bin ein Berliner.*" Although Kennedy's use of the German idiom was flawed, the people loved it. The popular young president of the United States was expressing a sort of symbolic solidarity with the people of Berlin by saying "I am a Berliner."

In a comedy routine in the old TV show *Laugh-In,* Lily Tomlin, as a telephone operator, asks, "Have I reached the party to whom I'm speaking?" Establishing a common ground with the audience is the speaker's way of making sure he or she has reached the "party" to whom he or she is speaking.

At times, the common ground between speaker and audience might be inherent in the occasion. When Roosevelt asked Congress to declare war on Japan, there was certainly no need for additional common ground. Sorrow for the loss of young servicemen, concern for the country, and outrage at the surprise attack by the Japanese were the shared emotions that brought the president and his audience together.

• *An opening should set the tone for the speech.* Serious. Relaxed. Friendly. Formal. Informal. If you open with a joke or a humorous comment, you're telling the audience to relax, that although the topic may be an important one, your speech is not going to be without some lighter moments.

• *The opening might need to reinforce, or perhaps even establish, the speaker's credibility.* The degree to which this is important might depend upon how the speaker has been introduced or how the speech was publicized to members. And, of course, the speaker must be careful not to seem boastful.

• *The opening ought to arouse interest in the subject and lay the groundwork for the discussion.* Again, there's the matter of degree. It depends upon how much interest the audience already has, how much the speech has been promoted to the audience in advance, and the speaker's qualifications.

• *The opening should take advantage of what I think of as "the speaker's grace period."* This is the period in which the audience is most attentive. A weak opening might squander those precious minutes or seconds.

• *Finally, the opening should be used to segue smoothly into the topic.* It is a bit jarring to the audience, not to mention wasteful of their time, for a speaker to open with, let's say, a joke or an anecdote that has no relevance to the subject of the speech. As we continue the discussion of different kinds of openings, you will begin to see how good speakers use the opening to lead into the topic.

Not every opening accomplishes, or needs to accomplish, all six of the things I've mentioned, but most openings need to accomplish two, three, or more. Before you construct the opening for your speech, take a look at the list of things you want the speech to accomplish. Then, from the list above, consider what should be included in the mission of the speech opening to support the broad purpose of your speech.

Types of openings

Ways to begin a speech are almost unlimited, but they seem to me to fall into five main categories:

1. Novelty openings
2. Dramatic openings
3. Question openings
4. Humorous openings
5. Reference openings

Not every opening will fit neatly into one of these five categories, and some openings might have characteristics of more than one category.

Once you have decided on a topic for your speech and what you want the speech to accomplish, look at the five categories of openings to determine whether one or more will help you make a good beginning.

Now, let's take a look at some examples.

Novelty openings

Some years ago, I attended a meeting of a men's club at which the speaker was a businessman on a crusade. This man, who had survived a serious bout with cancer, was speaking under the auspices of the state chapter of the American Cancer Society. His mission was to persuade men to go to their physicians for rectal examinations.

He began his speech by tossing out to the audience several of the long plastic tubes used in that kind of exam. This was the prelude for telling his experience and for making a case for early detection.

Anyone seeing those long tubes and knowing what they were used for might not be thrilled with the idea of having such an examination. Nevertheless, tossing the tubes into the audience accomplished what the speaker intended: It got their attention. It was an effective beginning for an effective speech.

That opening could be called either a novelty opening or a dramatic opening. It was both—unquestionably novel and certainly dramatic. It was an attention-compeller and an ice-breaker.

In 1980, I wrote a speech for Jeff White, who was then executive vice president of Equifax Inc., the big credit-reporting and information services company, and who later was to become the company's chairman and chief executive officer. Mr. White was speaking to the 47th annual Credit Management Conference of the National Retail Merchants Association.

He wanted a very forward-looking speech in which he would predict a time when the relatively narrow field of consumer credit would have evolved into the much broader field of financial-transaction services.

To help him make that point in his speech, I constructed a novelty opening in which he would postulate the existence of a fictional organization called the National Consumer Financial Transaction Association, to which he would pretend to be speaking ten years in the future. Here is the opening:

> *Ladies and Gentlemen:*
>
> *It's an honor to have been invited to address the first annual conference of the National Consumer Financial Transaction Association on this beautiful September morning in 1990. I recall that it was just 10 years ago—September 22, 1980—that I spoke to the 47th annual Credit Management Conference of the National Retail Merchants Association.*

At first the audience was confused, but most soon realized what was happening. Mr. White continued the charade for perhaps a minute and a half before returning to the present in this way:

Enough of all that.

Time passes fast enough without my pretending that another decade has gone by in the twinkling of an eye.

Thank you, Mr. Chairman, for your very generous introduction. I'm happy to be back in 1980 and delighted at the opportunity to participate in this conference and to share my views—and a few of my personal prejudices—on the past and future of consumer credit. The purpose of my brief flight on the time machine was to dramatize my opinion about where this industry is heading.

The speech was very effective, and the opening was cited in a book on speech writing that was published some years later.

An opening of that type is not without danger for the speaker and the writer. Not every speaker could have pulled it off. I would not have written it if I had not been confident that Mr. White was one who could. I also knew that it was important not to allow the charade to continue too long, lest the audience become impatient or even resentful at being taken in.

Here is another example of an effective novelty opening. This one took the audience backward instead of forward. It's from a speech made by an executive of a Fortune 500 company:

Your overall theme for this meeting—"Dialog with Washington"—reminds me of something I read recently which seems appropriate for today's program:

"It is a gloomy moment in the history of our country. Not in the lifetime of most men has there been so much grave and deep apprehension; never has the future seemed so incalculable as at this time.

"Our dollar is weak throughout the world. Prices are so high, as to be utterly impossible.

"The political cauldron seethes and bubbles with uncertainty. Russia hangs like a cloud as usual, dark and silent upon the horizon. It is a solemn moment. Of our troubles, no man can see the end."

The audience assumed, as the speaker expected they would, that the quotation was of recent vintage—until he told them it was from the October 1857 issue of *Harper's Weekly*. This was an effective device to begin the speech. Most people are surprised to discover that many older recitations of the world's problems sound current.

Dramatic openings

Suspense is often an element in a dramatic opening. Here's a good example:

> *Let me warn you that what I am about to discuss is not for the faint of heart. By the end of this century, our way of doing business will have dramatically changed. Most executives, as we now know them, will be obsolete. And it is not because they will have been replaced by a computer or a robot.*

The speech was delivered by the chairman of a large international company. We can bet it got the attention of the executives in the audience. After all, the speaker was saying that most of them would be obsolete.

Here is an opening that combines suspense with a startling statement calculated to pique the audience's curiosity. The speech was designed to sell the controversial idea of deepening the harbor in Savannah, Georgia:

> *Today I want to talk with you about an issue of utmost importance to the economic well-being of Savannah and vicinity. Or, in plain English, what politicians sometimes call a pocketbook issue. The stakes are high: Hundreds of millions of dollars in economic benefits for businesses in the coastal area . . . thousands of jobs for local men and women . . . millions of dollars in state and local tax revenue.*
>
> *All this economic activity hinges on four feet of river bottom. Four feet. The difference between thirty-eight feet, the current depth of the harbor in Savannah, and forty-two feet, the minimum depth required for Savannah to hold on to its position as a world port of call over the next few years.*

Question openings

In a question opening, our third category, the speaker asks a question that may be either a rhetorical question, for which no answer is expected, or a real question that the speaker might be expected to answer. Here is an example of the latter:

> *It's a pleasure to visit with Town Hall of California, to talk about what we have all come to know as "the energy prob-*

lem." I think most people now recognize that the basic prob-
lem is America's overdependence on foreign oil.
The question is—What can we do about it?

That speech was delivered by an official of a major oil company in the days when the question, "What do we do about our energy problem?" was on just about everyone's mind. An oil-company executive might well have been expected to provide an answer.

Here is an example of a rhetorical question used as the opening of a speech to a group of business managers:

Good evening, ladies and gentlemen:

Thank you for inviting me to be a part of your program. This evening I want you to consider with me a question that is, or should be, on the mind of every person concerned with meeting a payroll: "Can business manage to survive government?" I cannot answer that question this evening. Neither can you. But by asking it, we take a first step in ensuring that business not only can, but will, survive the crushing burden of government regulation.

Humorous openings

The fourth category, humorous openings, can be quite effective if the humor is in good taste and is delivered with the right timing. A humorous opening can be an icebreaker; set the tone for the speech; and make, support, or illustrate a point related to the subject. We'll talk in more detail about humor in a later chapter, but let me give you a couple of examples of humorous openings. The first, from my own experience, requires a brief explanation:

During the 1970s I was a public-relations/public-affairs adviser to the Japanese consulate general for the southeastern United States. In that capacity, I once wrote a speech for a Japanese diplomat to deliver to an economic development forum in Columbia, South Carolina. To appreciate this example, you have to know that in South Carolina, stores that sell alcoholic beverages are not allowed to advertise the fact. They are, however, allowed to display a huge red ball, which tells people that they do, indeed, sell liquor. Just why the state chose that particular symbol for liquor stores remains a mystery, at least to me, but that's the way it is.

In any event, the similarity of the liquor symbol to the Japanese national symbol was too good to pass up. The red ball, in fact, looks *exactly* like the sun symbol on the Japanese flag.

Now, the Japanese diplomat who was to make the speech spoke

excellent English and had a fine sense of humor. He was puzzled, however, by the opening I wrote for his speech. I did not keep a copy of it, but as I recall, it went something like this:

> *I'm honored to be a part of this program, and I'm especially pleased to be here in Columbia, South Carolina. I must admit, however, that I'm overwhelmed by the welcome your city has prepared for me. Even though I have heard much about Southern hospitality, I was amazed upon my arrival here yesterday to see so many of your business establishments displaying the Japanese flag.*

The speaker was reluctant to use the opening because he had not been to South Carolina before and simply didn't understand. I persuaded him to use it anyway. He did and it had the desired effect. The audience loved it!

An important point is this: There were platitudes to be expressed about Japanese-American friendship and cooperation. The humorous opening led naturally into those platitudes and put the audience in the proper frame of mind to receive them.

Self-deprecating humor—that is, poking a bit of harmless fun at yourself—can be a good speech-opening device. One caveat, though: The speaker should be careful not to denigrate his qualifications or knowledge of the subject. The audience might believe him.

Here is an opening in which the president of a large public utility made a funny reference to his age:

> *As I was planning my remarks for today, I recalled the advice that a wise, old politician gave me some thirty years ago. He said a speech is something like a love affair. Almost any fool can start one, but ending it gracefully calls for considerable skill. This morning, my wife told me I was too old for a love affair, so she hoped I did well with the speech.*

That opening could very easily be used as a closing. In fact, it might be better as a closing.

Reference openings

Reference openings, category five, are by far the most common. In a reference opening, the speaker makes a reference of some sort and uses the reference as a kind of launching pad for the speech. You'll see how this is done in the next chapter as you examine some of my favorite reference openings.

"THIS BREED CALLED AMERICANS"

To close this chapter, I have selected President Ronald Reagan's masterful first inaugural address, January 20, 1981. Note especially the simple language, a characteristic of good speeches, and how each idea flows into another:

Thank you. Senator Hatfield, Mr. Chief Justice, Mr. President [Carter], Vice President Bush, Vice President Mondale, Senator Baker, Speaker O'Neill, Reverend Moomaw, and my fellow citizens:

To a few of us here today this is a solemn and most momentous occasion. And, yet, in the history of our nation it is a commonplace occurrence.

The orderly transfer of authority as called for in the Constitution routinely takes place as it has for almost two centuries and few of us stop to think how unique we really are. In the eyes of many in the world, this every-four-year ceremony we accept as normal is nothing less than a miracle.

Mr. President, I want our fellow citizens to know how much you did to carry on this tradition.

By your gracious cooperation in the transition process you have shown a watching world that we are a united people pledged to maintaining a political system which guarantees individual liberty to a greater degree than any other. And I thank you and your people for all your help in maintaining the continuity which is the bulwark of our republic.

The business of our nation goes forward.

These United States are confronted with an economic affliction of great proportions.

We suffer from the longest and one of the worst sustained inflations in our national history. It distorts our economic decisions, penalizes thrift and crushes the struggling young and the fixed-income elderly alike. It threatens to shatter the lives of millions of our people.

Idle industries have cast workers into unemployment, human misery and personal indignity.

Those who do work are denied a fair return for their labor by a tax system which penalizes successful achievement and keeps us from maintaining full productivity.

But great as our tax burden is, it has not kept pace with public spending. For decades we have piled deficit upon deficit, mortgaging our future and our children's future for the temporary convenience of the present.

To continue this long trend is to guarantee tremendous social, cultural, political and economic upheavals.

You and I, as individuals, can, by borrowing, live beyond our means, but for only a limited period of time. Why then should we think that collectively, as a nation, we are not bound by that same limitation?

We must act today in order to preserve tomorrow. And let there be no misunderstanding—we're going to begin to act beginning today.

The economic ills we suffer have come upon us over several decades. They will not go away in days, weeks or months, but they will go away. They will go away because we as Americans have the capacity now, as we have had in the past, to do whatever needs to be done to preserve this last and greatest bastion of freedom.

In this present crisis, government is not the solution to our problem; government is the problem.

From time to time we've been tempted to believe that society has become too complex to be managed by self-rule, that government by an elite group is superior to government for, by and of the people.

But if no one among us is capable of governing himself, then who among us has the capacity to govern someone else?

All of us together—in and out of government—must bear the burden. The solutions we seek must be equitable with no one group singled out to pay a higher price.

We hear much of special interest groups. Well, our concern must be for a special interest group that has been too long neglected.

It knows no sectional boundaries, or ethnic and racial divisions, and it crosses political party lines. It is made up of men and women who raise our food, patrol our streets, man our mines and factories, teach our children, keep our homes and heal us when we're sick.

Professionals, industrialists, shopkeepers, clerks, cabbies and truck drivers. They are, in short, "We the people." This breed called Americans.

Well, this Administration's objective will be a healthy, vigorous, growing economy that provides equal opportunities for all Americans with no barriers born of bigotry or discrimination.

Putting America back to work means putting all Americans back to work. Ending inflation means freeing all Americans from the terror of runaway living costs. All must share in the productive work of this "new beginning," and all must share in the bounty of a revived economy.

With the idealism and fair play which are the core of our system and our strength, we can have a strong, prosperous America at peace with itself and the world.

So as we begin, let us take inventory.

We are a nation that has a government, not the other way around. And this makes us special among the nations of the earth.

Our Government has no power except that granted it by the people. It is time to check and reverse the growth of government which shows signs of having grown beyond the consent of the governed.

It is my intention to curb the size and influence of the Federal establishment and to demand recognition of the distinction between the powers granted to the Federal Government and those reserved to the states or to the people.

All of us—all of us—need to be reminded that the Federal Government did not create the states; the states created the Federal Government.

Now, so there will be no misunderstanding, it's not my intention to do away with government.

It is rather to make it work—work with us, not over us; to stand by our side, not ride on our back. Government can and must provide opportunity, not smother it; foster productivity, not stifle it.

If we look to the answer as to why for so many years we achieved so much, prospered as no other people on earth, it was because here in this land we unleashed the energy and individual genius of man to a greater extent than has ever been done before.

Freedom and the dignity of the individual have been more available and assured here than in any other place on earth. The price for this freedom at times has been high, but we have never been unwilling to pay that price.

It is no coincidence that our present troubles parallel and are proportionate to the intervention and intrusion in our lives that result from unnecessary and excessive growth of Government.

It is time for us to realize that we are too great a nation to limit ourselves to small dreams. We're not, as some would have us believe, doomed to an inevitable decline. I do not believe in a fate that will fall on us no matter what we do. I do believe in a fate that will fall on us if we do nothing.

So, with all the creative energy at our command let us begin an era of national renewal. Let us renew our determination, our courage and our strength. And let us renew our faith and our hope. We have every right to dream heroic dreams. Those who say that we're in a time when there are no heroes—they just don't know where to look. You can see heroes every day going in and out of factory gates. Others, a handful in number, produce enough food to feed all of us and then the world beyond.

You meet heroes across a counter—and they're on both sides of that counter. There are entrepreneurs with faith in themselves and faith in an idea, who create new jobs, new wealth and opportunity.

There are individuals and families whose taxes support the Government and whose voluntary gifts support church, charity, culture, art and education. Their patriotism is quiet but deep. Their values sustain our national life.

Now, I have used the words "they" and "their" in speaking of these heroes. I could say "you" and "your" because I'm addressing the heroes of whom I speak—you, the citizens of this blessed land.

Your dreams, your hopes, your goals are going to be the dreams, the hopes and the goals of this Administration, so help me God.

We shall reflect the compassion that is so much a part of your makeup. How can we love our country and not love our countrymen? And loving them reach out a hand when they fall, heal them when they're sick and provide opportunity to make them self-sufficient so they will be equal in fact and not just in theory?

Can we solve the problems confronting us? Well, the answer is an unequivocal and emphatic yes.

To paraphrase Winston Churchill, I did not take the oath I've just taken with the intention of presiding over the dissolution of the world's strongest economy.

In the days ahead I will propose removing the roadblocks that have slowed our economy and reduced productivity.

Steps will be taken aimed at restoring the balance between the various levels of government. Progress may be slow "measured in inches and feet, not miles" but we will progress.

It is time to reawaken this industrial giant, to get government back within its means and to lighten our punitive tax burden.

And these will be our first priorities, and on these principles there will be no compromise.

On the eve of our struggle for independence a man who might've been one of the greatest among the Founding Fathers, Dr. Joseph Warren, president of the Massachusetts Congress, said to his fellow Americans, "Our country is in danger, but not to be despaired of. On you depend the fortunes of America. You are to decide the important questions upon which rest the happiness and the liberty of millions yet unborn. Act worthy of yourselves."

Well, I believe we the Americans of today are ready to act worthy of ourselves, ready to do what must be done to ensure happiness and liberty for ourselves, our children and our children's children.

And as we renew ourselves here in our own land we will be seen as having greater strength throughout the world. We will again be the exemplar of freedom and a beacon of hope for those who do not now have freedom.

To those neighbors and allies who share our freedom, we will strengthen our historic ties and assure them of our support and firm commitment.

We will match loyalty with loyalty. We will strive for mutually beneficial relations. We will not use our friendship to impose on their sovereignty, for our own sovereignty is not for sale.

As for the enemies of freedom, those who are potential adversaries, they will be reminded that peace is the highest aspiration of the American people. We will negotiate for it, sacrifice for it; we will not surrender for it—now or ever.

Our forbearance should never be misunderstood. Our reluctance for conflict should not be misjudged as a failure of will.

When action is required to preserve our national security, we will act. We will maintain sufficient strength to prevail if need be, knowing that if we do we have the best chance of never having to use that strength.

Above all we must realize that no arsenal or no weapon in the arsenals of the world is so formidable as the will and moral courage of free men and women.

It is a weapon our adversaries in today's world do not have.

It is a weapon that we as Americans do have.

Let that be understood by those who practice terrorism and prey upon their neighbors.

I am told that tens of thousands of prayer meetings are being held on this day; for that I am deeply grateful. We are a nation under God, and I believe God intended for us to be free. It would be fitting and good, I think, if on each inaugural day in future years it should be declared a day of prayer.

This is the first time in our history that this ceremony has been held, as you've been told, on this West Front of the Capitol.

Standing here, one faces a magnificent vista, opening up on this city's special beauty and history.

At the end of this open mall are those shrines to the giants on whose shoulders we stand.

Directly in front of me, the monument to a monumental man, George Washington, father of our country. A man of humility who came to greatness reluctantly. He led America out of revolutionary victory into infant nationhood.

Off to one side, the stately memorial to Thomas Jefferson. The Declaration of Independence flames with his eloquence.

And then beyond the Reflecting Pool, the dignified columns of the Lincoln Memorial. Whoever would understand in his heart the meaning of America will find it in the life of Abraham Lincoln.

Beyond those monuments to heroism is the Potomac River, and on the far shore the sloping hills of Arlington National Cemetery with its row upon row of simple white markers bearing crosses or Stars of David. They add up to only a tiny fraction of the price that has been paid for our freedom.

Each one of those markers is a monument to the kind of hero I spoke of earlier.

Their lives ended in places called Belleau Wood, the Argonne, Omaha Beach, Salerno and halfway around the world on Guadalcanal, Tarawa, Pork Chop Hill, the Chosin Reservoir, and in a hundred rice paddies and jungles of a place called Vietnam.

Under such a marker lies a young man, Martin Treptow, who left his job in a small town barber shop in 1917 to go to France with the famed Rainbow Division.

There, on the Western front, he was killed trying to carry a message between battalions under heavy artillery fire.

We are told that on his body was found a diary.

On the flyleaf under the heading, "My Pledge," he had written these words:

"America must win this war. Therefore I will work, I will save, I will sacrifice, I will endure, I will fight cheerfully and do my utmost, as if the issue of the whole struggle depended on me alone."

The crisis we are facing today does not require of us the kind of sacrifice that Martin Treptow and so many thousands of others were called upon to make.

It does require, however, our best effort and our willingness to believe in ourselves and to believe in our capacity to perform great deeds; to believe that together with God's help we can and will resolve the problems which now confront us.

And after all, why shouldn't we believe that? We are Americans.

God bless you and thank you. Thank you very much.

— CHAPTER SIX —

The Best of References

In Chapter Five, we discussed six things that a good opening might need to accomplish:

1. Establish a common ground between speaker and audience
2. Set the tone for the speech
3. Reinforce or establish the speaker's qualifications
4. Arouse interest in the subject
5. Take advantage of the speaker's "grace period"
6. Segue smoothly into the subject

Then we discussed four of the five categories of speech openings—the novelty opening, the dramatic opening, the humorous opening, and the question opening—leaving the fifth category, reference openings, for a longer discussion in this chapter.

In a reference opening, the reference can be to any number of things. It often, but not always, has some relation to the speech or the event. A list of possible references would include the date, the location, the subject, the organization, a historical event, a recent or current event, the introduction, the speaker's topic, the speech title, the speaker himself, and so on. An opening might make use of more than one reference and might be combined with elements of openings in one or more of the other four categories.

Here is an example of an opening that refers to the introduction and a literary figure and uses a bit of self-deprecating humor:

Thank you, Bob, for that much too generous introduction.
Mark Twain once said that a person could live for a month on one compliment. That being the case, you have just assured me of immortality. I'm afraid, however, that some of my colleagues who know me a lot better than you do might look upon your introduction the way one politi-

cian described a speech by his opponent. He called it a Burger King speech—just one whopper after another.

From there the speaker eased into the topic this way:

I promise you, though, that you've heard all the whoppers you're going to hear this morning, because I'm going to give you the straight skinny on my subject.

Here's a humorous opening that I wrote for an executive of a Georgia company who was speaking in New York, his home town. The references are to himself and to the city:

I'm very happy to be in New York. This is where I grew up, and I'm always glad to have a reason to come home. I'll have to say, however, that I've been with a Georgia-based company for so long that when I get back to New York, I think you guys up here talk funny. I want you to know that I've been practicing for this meeting for two weeks. No, not rehearsing my speech. Practicing my accent. I'm trying to sound like a New Yorker again. You know what they say: If you don't use it, you lose it.

This afternoon I'm going to use my newly recovered New York accent to talk with you briefly about one segment of our business.

In the next example, the speaker used a reference to John F. Kennedy's famous "Ich bin ein Berliner" remark to make a complimentary reference to the Kiwanis Club audience:

Whenever I make a talk to a service club, I recall John F. Kennedy's famous opening for a speech in West Berlin. To dramatize American solidarity with the people of West Berlin, who are isolated in Communist East Germany from the rest of their countrymen, Kennedy began his speech by declaring: "Ich bin ein Berliner." So I was tempted to begin my talk this afternoon by saying, I am a Kiwanian, to symbolize my agreement with the principles and the work of this fine organization. But, in truth, I am a Rotarian.

A reference to other speakers on the program or panel often works well. For example, a member of a panel discussion at a meeting of young business leaders began his remarks this way:

Thank you and good evening. I'm honored to be here. I'm sure that my fellow speakers, Col. Locurcio and Mr. Davis, would agree that the subject we will discuss is one of utmost importance, not only to Savannah but also to Georgia and the Southeast.

Continuing the opening, the speaker refers to the audience and directly addresses one segment of the audience:

It's especially appropriate, I think, that such a discussion take place before an audience that includes so many of Savannah's young leaders. Because you are in positions of leadership today, you no doubt will be in even more important leadership positions tomorrow. For this reason, you are the men and women most concerned with the issues that we will raise in this discussion.

Here is an opening I wrote for an executive who was participating in a forum sponsored by the J.C. Penney Company:

I'm honored to have been invited to represent the credit-reporting industry in this discussion of consumer credit. At the outset, I want to commend the J. C. Penney organization for its sponsorship of this forum. I can recall many years ago reading about the late J. C. Penney. He was a dynamic man whose success in building one of the great retail enterprises of all time is testimony to the enormous potential of a free economic system. Mr. Penney was also a man whose concern for people and society was apparent throughout his long and productive life.

Location references

In a talk to a group of public affairs people at a North Carolina mountain resort, I used an opening in which I referred to the location and to several topics that were on people's minds at the time:

I'm very happy to be here this morning. There's something about these magnificent mountains in June—or any other time for that matter—that makes me confident that things are going to turn out okay no matter how bad they might seem to be. When I'm up here I have no trouble forgetting about such things as the Los Angeles riots, Murphy Brown's baby, the federal budget deficit, and the fact that the Atlanta Braves are under .500.

One of my favorite location-reference openings comes from a speech by an Atlanta-based executive to a business group in Chicago, which has long prided itself on being "the city that works." The opening combined humor and a knowledge of the host city to establish a common meeting ground between the speaker and the audience:

> *It's good to be here in the company of such distinguished men and women in the great city of Chicago. Back in Atlanta, we refer to Chicago as "the other city that works." Chicago and Atlanta do have a great deal in common, quite aside from being the economic and cultural capitals of their respective regions of the country. Atlanta was burned in 1864 by a Yankee general named Sherman; Chicago was burned in 1871 by Mrs. O'Leary's cow.*

Personal references

Personal references can be quite effective if they serve the speaker's purpose. Care must be taken, though, that such a reference does not make the speaker sound as if he is on an ego trip. The late Roberto Goizueta had more reason than most of us to be egotistical. He was a Cuban who escaped the Castro regime and came to the United States as a young man with only $20 in his pocket. He rose to become chairman, president, and chief executive of The Coca-Cola Company. In a speech delivered on the campus of Yale University, his alma mater, he used a powerful personal reference:

> *Returning to Yale is always a thought-provoking experience for me. I have often emphasized the importance of education by telling the story of how my family left Cuba when the Castro regime took control. I always point out that the only property I was allowed to bring with me into this country was my education. And that property, I carried in my head. It is a powerful and uniquely American idea that a young immigrant could come to this country with nothing but a good education and eventually have the opportunity to lead one of the world's best enterprises.*

The purpose of Mr. Goizueta's speech was to announce the establishment of a fund to promote interdisciplinary study among three academic fields. His opening reference to his own education was an excellent lead-in.

It's not uncommon for a good speaker to open a speech with a reference to speaking. Here is such an opening, from a speech by the chairman of one of the big oil companies. It combines the speaking reference with self-deprecating humor and a mention of a celebrity:

> *I thank you for that kind introduction. I only hope that when I've finished speaking, you won't echo the famous actress Tallulah Bankhead, who once said: "There is less here than meets the eye."*

Literary references

References to literature can be effective openers, but the speaker must consider whether the audience is likely to be familiar with the work referred to. For example, this opening, from a speech by an executive of a forest-products company to his company's shareholders, might be lost on many audiences:

> *Dr. Pangloss, a character in Voltaire's* Candide, *was fond of the statement, "All's for the best in the best of all possible worlds."*
> *Well, in the field of for-sale residential construction, in finance, and in many of the other areas for which I have responsibility, we are close to, if not in, the best of all possible worlds.*

Whether it was lost on the shareholders may be problematic, but the lead-in from the quotation to the point of the speech seemed to work well.

Everybody talks about the weather

Reference to weather can be effective, but even the best weather forecasters sometimes fail to take their umbrella and end up with a soaking. When a top-level executive of a major industrial corporation scheduled a speech at the University of Chicago's Graduate School of Business, he (or his speech writer) anticipated springlike weather for the event and wrote the speech opening accordingly. What actually happened was that the speaker encountered a rare April snowstorm. Here is how he handled the opening:

> *I barely made it here from New York, flying through a blinding April snowstorm. Many of you barely made it across town, but I'm delighted you are here. You won't believe the opening paragraph of the speech I wrote for you last week. It certainly proves that the best laid plans of mice and men go oft astray. Listen:*
>
> *"It's great to be in Chicago. While I love Michigan Avenue in December, with all the white lights on, I must admit it feels a lot better in April."*
>
> *The trauma of this unseasonable weather has an accidental relevance to the subject of my remarks. Snowstorm or not, I'm particularly pleased to be here at the Business School of this distinguished University, close to the cradle of monetarism—a subject on which, you'll be relieved to hear, I have no pronouncements.*

New twists

Good speech writers seem to have a knack for taking a fresh look at an old subject. Here is an opening in which the speaker first mentioned the topic to be discussed, then put a new twist on a couple of hoary clichés:

> *This afternoon I want to share with you some observations about what's happening in world trade, and in the process I'll try to bring you up to date on what's happening with Georgia's seaports, which handle at least 95 percent of the state's international trade.*
>
> *Someone recently described our ports in Savannah and Brunswick as Georgia's "best-kept secret." In this regard, it occurs to me that there were only seven wonders of the ancient world, but today there must be a million things that have been called "the eighth wonder of the world."*
>
> *And there never seems to be a whole lot going on in the here and now. Everything is "just around the corner." By the same token, Georgia must have a million best-kept secrets—from the wild beauty of north Georgia's Chattooga River to the unbeatable taste of Ogeechee River shad.*
>
> *So, I'm not going to say the ports are Georgia's best-*

kept secret. There's just too much competition in that category. I'll just say they're the second-best secret.

Even if our ports are merely number two in the secret category, they've been a secret too long. It's time we let the rest of the people of Georgia in on it.

Celebrities, past and present, are often very quotable and thus provide plenty of material for openings. Here is an example of an opening in which the speaker took a different tack by referring to a person who was not very quotable. In an address titled "A Sunbelt Growth Strategy," the head of a large corporation mentioned the theme of the conference and a quotation attributed to Calvin Coolidge. He tied them both very nicely to the subject:

It's a pleasure to be with you this morning. I'm honored to have been asked to participate in this discussion of a Sunbelt growth strategy. The topic is interesting to me for a number of reasons, not the least of which is my conviction that such a strategy is essential and that my company and other corporate citizens have a role to play in helping to formulate and carry it out.

President Calvin Coolidge was best known for never having said much of anything. But he did say something worthwhile on a subject that is closely related to what we are here to discuss: "Prosperity," Coolidge said, "is only an instrument to be used, not a deity to be worshiped."

Today we can and should make the same observation about growth—an instrument to be used, not a deity to be worshiped.

Wisdom in the funnies

Comic strips are a rich source of ideas for speech openings. I have written or read speech openings quoting "Peanuts," "Pogo," "Ziggy," "Calvin and Hobbes," and "Dilbert." Here is an opening in which the speaker ties the subject to one of Charlie Brown's sage pronouncements:

In thinking about what I might say to you this morning, I recalled a "Peanuts" comic strip that I saw several years ago. In the strip, Charlie Brown and his pal Linus are talking. Linus, the younger and more optimistic of the two, says, "I guess it's wrong to always be worrying about tomorrow.

Maybe we should think only about today." And good old Charlie Brown, who is usually a gloomy sort of guy, says, "No; that's giving up. I'm still hoping yesterday will get better."

Now, of course, the only way yesterday can get better is for tomorrow to be so bad it makes yesterday look good by comparison. As far as our company is concerned, that's just not going to happen.

Every day is special

References to the date or time of year are an old standby. Here is an opening for a speech in which a company president delivered a sort of annual report to employees shortly after January 1:

This is a wonderful way to start the new year—to spend an hour or so with old friends and familiar faces, to talk about our company, look back over the past year, and maybe take a peek into the future.

One evening during the Christmas holiday my wife and I were watching one of those year-end rehashes in which some television commentator tells us everything that happened during the year and then solemnly explains what it all meant. When it was over my wife said, "Well, nothing is going to happen in 1992, because everything that can happen, did happen in 1991."

Well, it was an eventful year. It began with the mother of all battles and ended with the grandfather of all recessions.

The reference to the recession provided a lead-in to a discussion of economic conditions that affected the company's performance.

Speech writers know that every day of the year is a day set aside to commemorate something or other. Every day is the anniversary of various historical events and every day is the birth date of celebrities past and present. For example, I share my birth date with Jonas Salk, developer of the polio vaccine; Bruce Morton, the TV commentator; Bruce Jenner, the Olympic decathlon medalist; Evelyn Waugh, the brilliant English novelist; and others. Also, on my birth date in 1886, the Statue of Liberty was unveiled; on the same date in 1954, Ernest Hemingway received the Nobel Prize; and in 1962, Nikita Krushchev bowed to pressure from John F. Kennedy and removed Soviet missiles from Cuba. The month in which I was born is Consumer Information Month, Liver Awareness Month, Car Care Month, Roller Skating Month, Adopt-a-Dog Month, Family Sexuality Education Month, Microwave Month, Pizza Month, and the month in which we have to set our watches back an hour for the end of daylight saving time.

I could easily provide a similar list for every day and every month of the year. A speech writer with imagination can often use such seemingly useless trivia, which is readily available from a variety of sources, to develop a speech opening tied to the day, week, or month of a speech.

Imagine that you're writing a speech for an executive on the subject of corporate takeovers and their effect on business. Let's say the date of the speech is August 30. You check on historical events, commemoratives, and birthdays for August 30 and learn that the novelist Mary Shelley was born on that date in 1797. A lightbulb comes on in your head. Mary Shelley . . . Frankenstein . . . monster . . . conglomerate . . . takeover. Aha! Suddenly you have an idea for the speech opening: Takeovers create conglomerates, which may be the Frankenstein's monsters of the business world. Not bad.

Here is an opening I wrote for a client who was making a speech on October 12. The speech was a defense of the profit motive as an essential part of the free enterprise system:

> *If I remember my history correctly, today—October 12—is the four hundred and eighty-fourth anniversary of the landing of Christopher Columbus. Before our Federal government in its infinite wisdom decided that we needed more long weekends, October 12 was observed as Columbus Day. Now, I enjoy long weekends as much as anyone. But I cannot help feeling that too much tampering of that type weakens our sense of history and lessens our understanding and appreciation of the important events that made our nation what it is.*
>
> *It was the profit motive that brought Columbus to the shores of the New World. His voyage across uncharted waters gained him the fame and fortune he sought and for which he was willing to risk his life.*

Reference openings are limited only by the speech writer's imagination. I could easily provide many more examples. Ideas are everywhere—sports, current affairs, history, entertainment. The possibilities are endless.

The most important point to remember about reference openings is that the reference should be something the audience is familiar with or can relate to. You would not want to refer to baseball pitcher Don Larson's World Series perfect game in a speech to a ladies' garden club. Conversely, you would not want to tell an anecdote about Beverly Sills in a speech at the annual gridiron dinner. The tie-in with the subject should be clear and credible, and the reference opening should flow smoothly and naturally into the subject.

Podium Presence

In my "Podium Presence" suggestion in Chapter Four, I mentioned that arriving early at the site of a speech would give you a chance for a private, relaxing stretch. True, but that's not the only reason for arriving early. If circumstances permit, visit the site a day or two ahead and even consider visiting it more than once. The main reason for doing this is to become familiar with your surroundings. If you're in familiar surroundings, you're less likely to be nervous.

Stand at the lectern and imagine there's an audience in front of you. Read a few paragraphs from your speech. If possible, have someone stand near the back of the room and tell you how well your voice carries.

Even if you visit the room days in advance, you'll still want to arrive early on the day of the speech. You'll need to check out the physical facilities—the sound system, microphone, projector, and other equipment. If you arrive just in time, you won't be able to correct anything that might not be right. Arriving early will also give you a chance to meet other people on the program, if any. Knowing your fellow participants will help you overcome self-consciousness.

"Remember How Futures Are Built"

On July 16, 1984, New York Governor Mario Cuomo electrified the nation with his keynote address to the Democratic Convention in San Francisco, in which he stated what he called the credo of the Democratic Party. Many observers thought the speech would launch a run for the presidency. That never happened, but the speech is still cited as a fine example of political oratory. In this excerpt, notice how often Governor Cuomo begins successive sentences with the same phrase, such as "We believe." That is a technique called anaphora, which we will discuss later:

We Democrats still have a dream. We still believe in this nation's future.

And this is our answer, our credo:

We believe in only the government we need, but we insist on all the government we need.

We believe in a government characterized by fairness and reasonableness, a reasonableness that goes beyond labels, that doesn't distort or promise to do what it knows it can't do.

A government strong enough to use the words "love" and "compassion" and smart enough to convert our noblest aspirations.

We believe in encouraging the talented, but we believe that while survival of the fittest may be a good working description of the process of evolution, a government of humans should elevate itself to a higher order, one which fills the gaps left by chance or a wisdom we don't understand.

We would rather have laws written by the patron of this great city, the man called the "world's most sincere Democrat," St. Francis of Assisi, than laws written by Darwin.

We believe, as Democrats, that a society as blessed as ours, the most affluent democracy in the world's history, that can spend trillions on instruments of destruction, ought to be able to help the middle class in its struggle, ought to be able to find work for all who can do it, room at the table, shelter for the homeless, care for the elderly and infirm, hope for the destitute.

We proclaim as loudly as we can the utter insanity of nuclear proliferation and the need for a nuclear freeze, if only to affirm the simple truth that peace is better than war because life is better than death.

We believe in firm but fair law and order, in the union movement, in privacy for people, openness by government, civil rights, and human rights.

We believe in a single fundamental idea that describes better than most textbooks and any speech what a proper government should be. The idea of family. Mutuality. The sharing of benefits and burdens for the good of all. Feeling one another's pain. Sharing one another's blessings. Reasonably, honestly, fairly, without respect to race, or sex, or geography or political affiliation.

We believe we must be the family of America, recognizing that at the heart of the matter we are bound one to another, that the problems of a retired school teacher in Duluth are our problems. That the future of the child in Buffalo is our future. The struggle of a disabled man in Boston to survive, to live decently is our struggle. The hunger of a woman in Little Rock, our hunger. The failure anywhere to provide what reasonably we might, to avoid pain, is our failure.

For 50 years we Democrats created a better future for our children, using traditional democratic principles as a fixed beacon, giving us direction and purpose, but constantly innovating, adapting to new realities; Roosevelt's alphabet programs; Truman's NATO and the GI Bill of Rights; Kennedy's intelligent tax incentives and the Alliance For Progress; Johnson's civil rights; Carter's human rights and the nearly miraculous Camp David peace accord.

Democrats did it—and Democrats can do it again.

We can build a future that deals with our deficit.

Remember, 50 years of progress never cost us what the last four years of stagnation have. We can deal with that deficit intelligently, by shared sacrifice, with all parts of the nation's family contributing, building partnerships with the private sector, providing a sound defense without depriving ourselves of what we need to feed our children and care for our people.

We can have a future that provides for all the young of the present by marrying common sense and compassion.

We know we can, because we did it for nearly 50 years before 1980. We can do it again. If we do not forget. Forget that this entire nation has profited by these progressive principles. That they helped lift up generations to the middle class and higher: gave us a chance to work, to go to college, to raise a family, to own a house, to be secure in our old age and, before that, to reach heights that our own parents would not have dared dream of.

That struggle to live with dignity is the real story of the shining city. It's a story I didn't read in a book, or learn in a classroom. I saw it, and lived it. Like many of you.

I watched a small man with thick calluses on both hands work 15 and 16 hours a day. I saw him once literally bleed from the bottoms of his feet, a man who came here uneducated, alone, unable to speak the language, who taught me all I needed to know about faith and hard work by the simple eloquence of his example. I learned about our kind of democracy from my father. I learned about our obligation to each other from him and from my mother. They asked only for a chance to work and to make the world better for their children and to be protected in those moments when they would not be able to protect themselves. This nation and its government did that for them.

And that they were able to build a family and live in dignity and see one of their children go from behind their little grocery store on the other side of the tracks in south Jamaica (NY) where he was born, to occupy the highest seat in the greatest state of the greatest nation in the only world we know, is an ineffably beautiful tribute to the democratic process. And on Jan. 20, 1985, it will happen again. Only on a much grander scale. We will have a new President of the United States, a Democrat born not to the blood of kings but to the blood of immigrants and pioneers.

We will have America's first woman Vice President, the child of immigrants, a New Yorker, opening with one magnificent stroke a whole new frontier for the United States.

It will happen, if we make it happen.

I ask you, ladies and gentlemen, brothers and sisters—for the good of all of us, for the love of this great nation, for the family of America, for the love of God. Please make this nation remember how futures are built.

—— Chapter Seven ——

Watch Your Language

When the philosopher Aristotle described man as "a language-using animal," he was saying that one of the things that distinguish humans from lower orders of animals is the ability to use language.

Without language, we couldn't pass on our knowledge to others, and the advance of civilization would cease. We couldn't express our thoughts because without language, we couldn't think, except on the most rudimentary level.

It stands to reason, then, that the greater our skill with language, the more clearly we think and the better we express our thoughts. In his famous essay, "Politics and the English Language," George Orwell used an analogy to make the connection between language and thought. "A man may take to drink," Orwell wrote, "because he thinks himself a failure, and then fail all the more completely because he drinks. It is rather the same thing that is happening to the English language. It becomes ugly and inaccurate because our thoughts are foolish, but the slovenliness of our language makes it easier for us to have foolish thoughts."

Good speakers and writers usually have many, many words at their command. But having them and using them with discretion are different matters. A mechanic might have hundreds of tools, but he doesn't feel the need to use all of them for every job, and he doesn't always reach for the most sophisticated tool in his box just because it's there.

The power of simplicity

Using the language well in a speech often means using the strong, simple words that compose our everyday language. To illustrate the power of simplicity, I want to share with you something I composed for use in the Members' Handbook of the Society for the Preservation of English Language and Literature (SPELL):

> *You don't have to use long words when you speak or write. Most of the time, you can make your points quite well with short ones. In fact, big words may get in the way of what you want to say. And what's more, when you use short words, no one will need to look them up to learn what they mean.*
>
> *Short words can make us feel good. They can run and jump and dance and soar high in the clouds. They can kill the chill of a cold night and help us keep our cool on a hot day. They fill our hearts with joy, but they can bring tears to our eyes as well. A short word can be soft or strong. It can sting like a bee or sing like a lark. Small words of love can move us, charm us, lull us to sleep. Short words give us light and hope and peace and love and health—and a lot more good things. A small word can be as sweet as the taste of a ripe pear, or tart like plum jam.*
>
> *Small words make us think. In fact, they are the heart and the soul of clear thought.*
>
> *When you write, choose the short word if you can find one that will let you say what you want to say. If there is no short word that does the job, then go ahead and consider the utilization of a sesquipedalian expression as a viable alternative, but be cognizant of the actuality that it could conceivably be incumbent upon many of your perusers to expend, by consulting a dictionary or perhaps an alternative lexicon of particularized patois, copious amounts of their invaluable time in attempting to determine the message you are endeavoring to impart to them through the instrumentality of your missive.*

The passage you've just read contains 310 words. The first 231 are all words of a single syllable. The first word that has more than one is *ahead*. After that, I packed into the passage as many long, fuzzy words as I could think of.

Contrary to what some people seem to believe, the ability to use language well does not mean the ability to come forth with long words like *cognizant, incumbent,* and *instrumentality*. Now, I'm all for having a large working vocabulary. Learning words can be very satisfying and life enriching, but . . .

Good writers and speakers know the power and grace and eloquence of simplicity. Some of the most eloquent and powerful words ever written are some of the simplest. Consider, for example, this well-known passage from the Book of Ecclesiastes:

> *I returned, and saw under the sun, that the race is not to the swift, nor the battle to the strong, neither yet bread to the wise, nor yet riches to men of understanding, nor yet favor to men of skill; but time and chance happeneth to them all.*

Orwell rendered that Biblical passage in what he facetiously called "modern English" to show how power, grace, and even meaning can be lost through unnecessarily complex language:

> *Objective consideration of contemporary phenomena compels the conclusion that success or failure in competitive activities exhibits no tendency to be commensurate with innate capacity, but that a considerable element of the unpredictable must invariably be taken into account.*

Notice how the strong, simple, concrete words and phrases of the original passage have become vague concepts in Orwell's "modern English" version. "I saw" in the original has become "objective consideration of contemporary phenomena" in Orwell's revision. "Race," "bread," and "battle" are "competitive activities," and "time and chance" has become "a considerable element of the unpredictable."

The most memorable lines from the great speeches, some of which you have read in this book, or will have read by the end of the book, are often the simplest. For example:

- General Douglas MacArthur's "Old soldiers never die."
- William Jennings Bryan's "You shall not crucify mankind on a cross of gold."
- Abraham Lincoln's "I do not believe this government can endure, permanently half slave and half free."
- Franklin D. Roosevelt's "The only thing we have to fear is fear itself."
- John F. Kennedy's "The torch has passed to a new generation of Americans."
- Martin Luther King, Jr.'s "I have a dream."
- And Ronald Reagan's "How can we not believe in the greatness of America?"

Ralph Waldo Emerson wrote, "An orator or author is never successful until he has learned to make his words smaller than his ideas." Compare the size of Churchill's ideas with the size of his words in this passage from one of his speeches:

> *We shall not flag or fail. We shall go on to the end. We shall fight in France. We shall fight on the seas and oceans. We shall fight with growing confidence and growing strength in the air. We shall defend our island, whatever the cost may be. We shall fight on the beaches. We shall fight on the landing grounds. We shall fight in the fields and in the streets. We shall fight in the hills. We shall never surrender.*

Of eighty-one words in that excerpt, only nine have more than one syllable. Only four have more than two.

Make language work for you

Good speakers are not afraid to use simple language. They have confidence in their ideas and don't feel they need to couch them in flowery or pretentious language. Pretentious language draws attention to itself and away from the idea it is supposed to express. This doesn't mean that the language of a speech ought to be simplistic or that every speaker should talk like Dick and Jane. The language in the examples I've cited is simple, but it's far from simplistic.

Here are some suggestions for making language work for you when you write or deliver a speech.

• *Be yourself.* Use the language that is natural to you. If you're not a folksy person, don't try to sound like one of the guys down at the barbershop. On the other hand, if you are the folksy type, don't try to sound like William F. Buckley. Your speech will sound phony. It will be phony. If you rarely tell jokes, don't open your speech with a joke just because you think people expect it. If you're a mature adult talking to a teenage audience, don't try to show your mastery of teen slang. Chances are, you'll sound foolish. Reserve *like* for something you like and *cool* for the evening breeze.

• *Talk* with *the audience, not* to *them, not* at *them.* Speak as if you're carrying on a conversation, not delivering a lecture. You can achieve this effect by using personal pronouns, contractions, and other conversational speech, as I've done throughout this book. Notice that I have often addressed you the reader directly. For example, just a moment ago, you read, "If you're not a folksy person," "If you rarely tell jokes," and "You can achieve this effect." What if I had been unwilling to use such references? What if I had felt that in each case I would have to say things like "If the speaker is not a folksy person," "If the speaker rarely tells jokes," and "One can achieve this effect"? You'd probably get the idea that I didn't have a lot of interest in you and didn't really care about your desire to become a better speaker or speech writer.

• *Don't hesitate to use personal references when they seem appropriate for the subject and the audience.* Here is an excerpt from a speech by William Sessions, who was at the time head of the FBI. He was addressing the American Academy of Achievement:

> *I was born in 1930, and as the older folks here remember, we were in the midst of the Great Depression. So I was a child who understood that things were very dear and times were very tough. As I began to grow, I began to worry about those things that were happening all around me over which I seemed to have no control. When I was eleven years old, my father departed for Southeast Asia and World War II. So I had no father for a while and didn't think I would have a father again—but I did, four years later. So when I was fifteen, I then resumed my relationship with my father. The concerns I had at that time are issues that might concern you today.*

Sometimes, personal references can have strong emotional appeal. On May 12, 1962, General Douglas MacArthur bade a memorable and emotional farewell to the Corps of Cadets at West Point. Here is an excerpt:

> *The shadows are lengthening for me. The twilight is here. My days of old have vanished—tone and tints. They have gone glimmering through the dreams of things that were. Their memory is one of wondrous beauty, watered by tears and coaxed and caressed by the smiles of yesterday. I listen, then, but with thirsty ear, for the witching melody of faint bugles blowing reveille, of far drums beating the long roll.*
>
> *In my dreams I hear again the crash of guns, the rattle of musketry, the strange, mournful chatter of the battlefield. But in the evening of my memory I come back to West Point. Always there echoes and re-echoes: duty, honor, country.*

A cynic might call that a tear-jerker. But I'm willing to bet there were no cynics among the assembled cadets that day.

• *Use strong, active verbs and vivid nouns.* I call such words "gut words" because they seem to come from the gut rather than the brain. The strongest verbs are those that express everyday actions: Verbs such as *run, cry, spring, jump, ooze, leak, roar, stink,* and *burst* evoke images of flesh-and-blood creatures doing things. Verbs like *represent, indicate, transpire, postulate, cogitate, surmise, ascertain,* and *fabricate,* although they have their uses, are lifeless and colorless. They denote *concepts* rather than *action.* Notice also that of the examples I cited, the strong verbs are all short; the concept verbs have two or more syllables each.

Suppose I'm describing the reaction of baseball fans on that unforgettable evening when Henry Aaron hit the home run that broke Babe Ruth's lifetime record. I might say, "Aaron was given a standing ovation by fifty thousand fans. The tribute continued for at least five minutes." That's accurate. It's what happened. No doubt about it.

But compare that description with this, "Fifty thousand fans sprang to their feet, clapping, screaming, cheering wildly in a pandemonium that went on for a full five minutes." That's also what happened. Is there a difference?

You bet there is. The first version tells what happened all right, but it doesn't involve the listener. There's no fire, no passion. It's like saying, "I went to the store and bought a loaf of bread." So what? Big deal?

The second version paints a word picture that puts the listeners right in the stadium, making them part of that clapping, cheering crowd.

"Standing ovation" is a concept. It's essentially lifeless and colorless. "Sprang to their feet" is action. "Tribute" is a concept. "Clapping," "cheering," "screaming," and "pandemonium" are vividly descriptive. "Continued" is less vigorous than "went on."

• *Prefer the active voice to the passive.* In case you've forgotten your basic grammar, *voice* refers to the relationship of a subject to its verb. If the subject is *acting,* the sentence is in the active voice. If the subject is *acted upon,* the sentence is in the passive voice. For example, "Barbara threw the pie at Charles" is active because the subject (Barbara) is acting (throwing the pie). "The pie was thrown at Charles by Barbara" is passive because the subject (pie) is acted upon (thrown). In either case, Charles gets a face full of pie, but the active-voice sentence is stronger, more vigorous, and more interesting. Good writers and speakers tend to prefer the active voice. This does not mean that the passive voice is never appropriate. On the contrary, it is often appropriate and sometimes preferable.

• *Use specific, concrete language rather than generalities.* No, let me amend that. Use specific language if you want to be completely understood. In *The Write Way* (Pocket Books, 1995), a book that I co-wrote with linguist Richard Lederer, concrete language is called "the language of control." That's because using concrete language enables the speaker to control the message rather than cede control to the listener.

To illustrate this point, let me give you a little test. Read the three statements below and answer the question about each:

1. I went to visit my friend in mid-January. It was very cold that day.
2. Within a month after leaving the army, I went to work for a five-figure salary.
3. Joe is of average height.

Now for the questions: How cold was it on the day I visited my friend? How much money did I earn on the job I took a month after leaving the army? How tall is Joe?

If you happen to live in northern Minnesota, "very cold" could be minus twenty degrees. If you live in south Florida, thirty-five degrees might be "very cold."

The job I took right after I left the army did, indeed, pay a five-figure salary—$10,000 a year. But, of course, my wife and I would have preferred the higher end of the "five-figure salary" range—$99,999.

Joe is, well, who knows what "average height" is? Average for what? An NBA basketball team? Members of the Bolshoi Ballet? A Boy Scout troop?

Am I suggesting that you never speak in generalities? Of course not. I'm saying that you need to be conscious of how generalities affect your messages and the impressions you want to leave. The more concrete the word, the more precise its meaning. Moreover, concrete language is more interesting. Generalities are often dull.

• *Use jargon sparingly, if at all.* Jargon is vocabulary peculiar to a particular trade, profession, or group. Lawyers, doctors, teachers, and other professionals have their own ways of speaking when they talk to each other. The word *jargon* comes from a middle French word that originally meant "meaningless chatter," and at least one dictionary calls it "strange, outlandish, or barbarous language." Some of it *is* strange, outlandish, or barbarous, but not all jargon is bad. Used properly and at the proper time, it can serve as a sort of shorthand that makes communication more efficient. The problem is that jargon, like crabgrass, often shows up where it's neither wanted nor needed. When jargon escapes its boundaries and creeps into general usage, it may be confusing to people who don't "talk the talk." Moreover, some jargon is essentially meaningless even to those who do understand it. I recall reading a letter from an art studio that described a particular form of art as "a very accelerated mode of transport of harmonial movement that balances the personal requirement for centeredness." I defy anyone to translate that nonsense into plain English.

The main point about jargon is this: If you're speaking to members of your own profession, go ahead and use the language you use in everyday conversation with your colleagues. They'll understand you. But do not use professional jargon when you're addressing a lay audience. The chances of miscommunicating are unacceptably high. And do not attempt to use the jargon of another profession. The chances of sounding foolish are unacceptably high. Finally, if you use jargon, use it correctly and don't overdo it, no matter what audience you're addressing.

• *Be aware that words have meanings, or connotations, that sometimes go beyond their dictionary definitions.* To demonstrate this, I ask you to read the following list of words, pausing for two or three seconds after each. During the pause, close your eyes and allow a picture to form in your mind.

- thin
- slender
- skinny
- underweight
- reedy

Okay. What image came to mind when you read the word *slender*? How about *thin*? Or *skinny*? All the words in the list are closely related in meaning, but the images they evoke are quite different. Most people would like to be slender, but few want to be skinny. So, when you choose your words, think what pictures they conjure up in people's minds.

• *Set the right tone.* Back in the 1950s, psychiatrist Eric Berne developed a concept called transactional analysis, which he introduced in his book, *Games People Play.* A decade or so later, Dr. Thomas A. Harris, a protégé of Dr. Berne, came out with another book on the subject, *I'm O.K., You're O.K.* The theory behind transactional analysis is that the human personality comprises three elements, or behavioral states, called "child," "parent," and "adult." At any given time, one of the three might be dominant in a person. Any "transaction," which is to say any contact between individuals, will be affected by whichever personality element is dominant in each person at the time. A transaction can be a written contact as well as a face-to-face contact.

Now, obviously, the behavioral state that is dominant in the speaker can affect what is said, how it is said, and how the audience receives the message. In other words, it can affect the tone of the speech.

To understand the three behavioral states, compare these three statements:

1. *If the people in the office weren't so noisy, I could get my work done without having to stay late every day.*
2. *If you would just plan your work a little better, you could get your work done on time and wouldn't have to stay late every day.*
3. *When there's a distraction in the hall, you might consider closing your office door so you won't be disturbed.*

In the first statement the speaker is simultaneously making excuses for not completing the work on time, pointing the finger of blame at colleagues, and seeking sympathy for having to work late. The statement is whiny and childlike.

In the second statement, the speaker could be a mother or father admonishing a wayward child. The "parent" is the speaker's dominant behavioral state.

The third statement suggests a reasonable solution to the problem; the "adult" is clearly in control.

Transactional analysis was designed to explain and improve interpersonal relationships. In a speech, a speaker's dominant behavioral state of the moment can affect the tone of the speech. Needless to say, the tone should always be "adult."

• *Get to the point.* Abraham Lincoln might have begun his Gettysburg Address by saying, "A long time ago, I think it must have been in the neighborhood of 86 or 87 years ago—anyway, it was before my time—some of our ancestors, which is to say our forefathers, got together for a little meeting and . . ."

Well, if Abe had spoken like that, the South might have won the war. But he didn't. He got straight to the point, said what he wanted to say, and stopped. If you will do likewise when you speak, your words will have power and your ideas will be well-received.

• *Whatever you say, say it right.* This suggestion might also be expressed as "follow the rules." Some speakers and writers today seem determined to ignore basic standards of grammar and correct word use. Although acceptable standards for speaking are somewhat more flexible than for writing, a speaker who is sloppy in his grammar, usage, and pronunciation may have less than the total respect of his audience and may even find his credibility is suspect. Such a speaker might make a bad impression on the audience and never know why.

Not long ago I heard a speech by a United States senator who repeatedly used the word *infer* when *imply* was clearly required. Another high official is often heard to say things like "for my wife and I." A former president habitually pronounces *nuclear* as if it were spelled "nucular." A respected college professor of my acquaintance often uses *laying*, as in "the book is laying on the table," instead of the correct word, *lying*. Even nationally known television personalities pollute the airways with inexcusable errors in grammar, syntax, usage, and pronunciation.

Your diction may be perfect, but if you're like most of us, you do make errors now and then. Although it is beyond the scope of this book to provide instruction in grammar and usage, I feel it's worthwhile to devote a little time in a discussion of some of the most common errors that I hear and read. And that is the subject of the next chapter.

"My Last Good Night to You"

Meanwhile, let's read an excerpt from a speech by President Dwight D. Eisenhower. The date is January 17, 1961. The occasion is President Eisenhower's gracious farewell to the nation upon leaving office after his second term and "passing the torch" to John Kennedy's "new generation of Americans." President Eisenhower will not go down in history as one of the great presidential orators, but he did have a speaking style that made him seem to be a decent, down-to-earth sort of guy. It was just impossible not to like him:

Good evening, my fellow Americans: First, I should like to express my gratitude to the radio and television networks for the opportunities they have given me over the years to bring reports and messages to our nation. My special thanks go to them for the opportunity of addressing you this evening.

Three days from now, after half a century in the service of our country, I shall lay down the responsibilities of office as, in traditional and solemn ceremony, the authority of the Presidency is vested in my successor.

This evening I come to you with a message of leave-taking and farewell, and to share a few final thoughts with you, my countrymen.

Like every other citizen, I wish the new President, and all who will labor with him, Godspeed. I pray that the coming years will be blessed with peace and prosperity for all.

Our people expect their President and the Congress to find essential agreement on issues of great moment, the wise resolution of which will better shape the future of the nation. . . .

So, in this, my last good night to you as your President, I thank you for the many opportunities you have given me for public service in war and in peace. I trust that, in that service, you find some things worthy. As for the rest of it, I know you will find ways to improve performance in the future.

You and I, my fellow citizens, need to be strong in our faith that all nations, under God, will reach the goal of peace with justice. May we be ever unswerving in devotion to principle, confident but humble with power, diligent in pursuit of the nation's great goals.

To all the peoples of the world, I once more give expression to America's prayerful and continuing aspiration:

We pray that peoples of all faiths, all races, all nations, may have their great human needs satisfied; that those now denied opportunity shall come to enjoy it to the full; that all who yearn for freedom may experience its spiritual blessings, those who have freedom will understand, also, its heavy responsibility; that all who are insensitive to the needs of others, will learn charity, and that the scourges of poverty, disease and ignorance will be made to disappear from the earth; and that in the goodness of time, all peoples will come to live together in a peace guaranteed by the binding force of mutual respect and love.

Now, on Friday noon, I am to become a private citizen. I am proud to do so. I look forward to it.

Thank you and good night.

—— Chapter Eight ——

Write It Right, Say It Right

In the previous chapter, I gave you eleven suggestions for making language work for you:

1. Be yourself.
2. Talk with, not to or at, the audience.
3. Don't hesitate to use personal references.
4. Use strong, active verbs and vivid nouns.
5. Prefer the active to the passive voice.
6. Use specific, concrete language.
7. Use jargon sparingly, if at all.
8. Be aware of word connotations that go beyond their actual meanings.
9. Set the right tone for your speech.
10. Get to the point.
11. Follow the rules.

That brings us to the subject of this chapter: proper word use. As I have said, it is beyond the scope of this book to instruct you completely in grammar and usage. However, I have selected some commonly misused words and pairs of words that you might want to be especially aware of when you write or speak. With each word or pair of words is a brief discussion of right and wrong usage.

Advise/inform

Advise means to give advice or counsel. *Inform* means to provide information. It is incorrect to say "Please keep me advised of your progress." Instead, say, "Please keep me informed of your progress."

Affect/effect

To *affect* something is to exert influence on it; to *effect* something is to make it happen. *Effect* can also be a noun meaning a result or outcome. Here are examples of the correct use of each word:

"How will our earnings report *affect* the price of the company's stock?"

"What *effect* will the earnings report have on the price of the company's stock?"

"What can we do to *effect* a smooth transition?"

Aggravate/irritate

To *aggravate* something is to make it worse; to *irritate* is to create a new condition. Example: "Mary was irritated because John was late for the wedding, and the fact that he forgot the ring aggravated the situation." *Exacerbate* is a synonym for *aggravate*; *annoy* is a synonym for *irritate*.

Alternate/alternative

These words are often used interchangeably, but they shouldn't be. *Alternative* is a noun meaning a choice, preferably between *two* possibilities, not several. *Alternate* is the adjective that's related to the noun *alternative*. *Alternative* should not be used as an adjective, as in "alternative choice." Here is an example of the correct use of each word:

"We have the alternative of taking the train or driving."
"The alternate method of transportation is the train."

Amount/number

Amount is used for bulk quantities; *number* is used for countable quantities. Thus, a large number of dollars makes a large amount of money. We should not say, as many people do, "A large amount of people [*dollars*, *miles*, or whatever]."

Appraise/apprise

To *apprise* means to inform; to *appraise* means to evaluate. Do not say "Keep me appraised of your progress." "Keep me apprised" is correct.

Aren't I?

This questioning expression represents a real dilemma. The English language lacks a contraction of *am not*. Logically, we would say "am't" for *am not*, but for a reason unknown to me, that hasn't caught on. This creates no problem except in questions, such as "Am I not invited to the party?" Some writers and speakers use the illogical expression *aren't I?* presumably to avoid the ungrammatical *ain't I?* In my opinion, *aren't I?* is as bad as *ain't I?* I prefer *am I not?* To some, however, *am I not?* sounds like an affectation.

Given a choice of "Ain't I a handsome devil?" "Aren't I a handsome devil?" or "Am I not a handsome devil?" I'd take the third choice without a doubt. My advice is, don't use *ain't* unless you're trying to be funny. Don't use *am I not?* if you're uncomfortable with it. Don't use *aren't I?* at all.

Assure/ensure/insure

To *assure* is to promise someone, as in "John assured Mary he would be on time." To *ensure* means to make certain, as in "Mary gave John an alarm clock to ensure that he would be on time." To *insure* means to safeguard, as in "I have my home insured against fire." Although *ensure* and *insure* are pronounced alike, you should make the distinction in your written speech.

Averse/adverse

These two similar words are often confused. To be *averse* to something is to oppose it, as in "The congresswoman was averse to a tax increase." *Averse* can apply only to a person. *Adverse* means unfavorable and usually applies to conditions. Thus, we may say that the congresswoman was averse to a tax increase because it might cause adverse business conditions.

Bad/badly

Bad is usually an adjective and thus describes a noun; *badly* is an adverb and thus tells how something is done. It is incorrect to say "I feel badly" unless you are referring to the act of feeling. If you want to describe your physical condition, say "I feel bad."

Between/among

Generally, *between* should be used with two persons or things, and *among* should be used with more than two. It is incorrect to say, "Between the three of us, we have enough money to buy the property." Say "Among the three of us . . ."

Compare to/compare with

Use *compare to* when discussing things that are dissimilar. Use *compare with* when discussing things of the same category. For example, a company's profits for one year may be compared *with* its profits for the previous year, but a pretty girl should be compared *to*, not *with*, a melody.

Comprise/compose

It is unclear why or when the phrase *comprised of* crept into the language and began to be used interchangeably with *composed of*, as in "the company is comprised of four divisions." Although the use of *comprised of* is increasingly accepted, careful writers and speakers insist on holding to the traditional meaning of *to comprise*, which is to include or contain. I recommend that you do likewise. It makes no more sense to say "comprised of" than to say "included of." Think of it this way: The whole *comprises* (includes) the parts; the parts *compose* (constitute) the whole. Thus, "The company is composed of four divisions" or "The company comprises four divisions."

Consensus

Consensus means agreement, but not necessarily unanimous agreement. The word often appears in the redundant phrase, "consensus of opinion." Don't let that redundancy creep into your speech.

Convince/persuade

These words are often used interchangeably, but the distinction between them is worth preserving. To *convince* someone is to bring the person to your point of view. To *persuade* someone is to induce the person to do something. For example, "Now that I have convinced you of the importance of a well-written speech, I hope I can persuade you to engage me as your speech writer."

Could care less

We often hear someone say, "I could care less," meaning something like "I'm indifferent to the matter." That absurd expression is a corruption of the cliché *couldn't care less*, which means that you don't care at all so caring less would be impossible. If you're inclined to use the expression, use it correctly and say "I couldn't care less," or, as Rhett said to Scarlett, "Frankly, my dear, I don't give a damn."

Criterion/criteria

Criterion is singular. Its plural is *criteria*. The error I hear most often is the use of *criteria* as singular. It's just as wrong to say "This is the criteria" as it is to say "This is the books."

English has a number of words taken intact from Greek or Latin that have plurals not formed as are plurals of most English words. The most commonly misused plural is *media*. *Media* is the plural of *medium*, but *media* is widely used as a singular noun when it refers collectively to the news media. I often hear something like "The news media *is* acting irresponsibly because *they* have not covered the story thoroughly." Illogical as it may be, the speaker who says that uses *media* as both singular and plural in the same sentence. The true singular, *medium*, is rarely used in reference to the news media. It sounds a bit awkward, probably because *medium* has so many other meanings. If "news medium" sounds awkward to you, I suggest you say "one of the news media." In any case, avoid using *media* as singular.

How about *data*? Technically, *data* is plural. Its singular is *datum*, which means an item of information. *Datum*, however, is rarely used in the United States, except in scientific or academic writing. That being the case, *data*, for all practical purposes, has no singular. Although many speakers and writers—including me—prefer *data* as plural, as in "The data *are* all recorded," others accept *data* as a synonym for information, as in "The data *is* all recorded."

My advice is to use *data* as plural if you want to be always beyond reproach. If you're not comfortable with it as plural, use it as singular. No one is likely to criticize you except perhaps a hopeless pedant.

While I'm on the subject, I want to mention some words that are especially troublesome to those of us who have forgotten their high school Latin.

If I said, "My wife is an *alumnus* of Georgia State College for Women," the Latin scholars among us would give me a strange look. That's because *alumnus* is a masculine word. The feminine word is *alumna* (pronounced *a-LUM-nuh*). The plural of *alumnus* is *alumni* (pronounced *a-LUM-ni,* with the *i* being long as in *like*); the plural of *alumna* is *alumnae* (pronounced *a-LUM-ni,* with the *i* being short, as in *little*). *Alumni* can also refer to either men or women and is always used when both are part of a compound subject.

If this all sounds confusing, here are some examples:

"Alice is an *alumna* of Princeton."
   "Alice and Brenda are *alumnae* (or *alumni*) of Princeton."
      "Humphrey is an *alumnus* of Princeton."
         "Humphrey and Bruce are *alumni* of Northwestern."
            "Humphrey, Bruce, Alice, and Brenda are all *alumni* of Northwestern."

Different from/different than

Than ordinarily is used with comparative adjectives. For example, *better than, stronger than.* But *different* is not a comparative. Therefore, statements such as "Her cake is different than mine" are not considered good usage. "Her cake is different *from* mine" is preferred. Use *different than* when a clause is to follow. For example, "This house is different than it was when I lived here."

Disinterested/uninterested

Disinterested means impartial; *uninterested* means unconcerned. A trial judge should be *disinterested* but not *uninterested.*

Enormity/enormousness

The most common misuse of these words is to use *enormity* to describe something of very large physical size. *Enormity* refers to something that is monstrous or appalling; *enormousness* refers to size, either figurative or physical. We may speak of the *enormity* of a crime but we must say *enormousness* when we're talking about the vastness of the desert.

Feasible/possible/viable

An undertaking may be *possible*, but it might not be *feasible* if the cost is too high. *Viable* has become one of the great buzzwords of modern business. How often have you heard someone speak of "viable alternatives"? *Viable* means "capable of independent life." The use of *viable* as a synonym for *feasible* is jargony at best and should be avoided. It leads to such absurdities as "Suicide is a viable option."

Few/less

Use *few* (or *fewer*) for things that are counted; *less* for things that are measured in other ways. Thus, fewer dollars, less money; fewer hogs, less pork; less food, fewer calories; less hay, fewer bales.

Flaunt/flout

Flaunt means to show off, usually ostentatiously; *flout* means to ignore contemptuously. Thus, conspicuous consumption is *flaunting* one's wealth. Reckless driving is *flouting* the traffic laws.

Founder/flounder

Founder means to sink or fall. It is often, but not always, a nautical term. *Flounder* means to struggle or thrash around.

Further/farther

Use *farther* for physical distance and *further* for figurative distance, time, or a continuation of something other than distance. The choice is not always clear-cut, but the distinction is made by most good speakers most of the time. For example, "This subject will be examined further in a later chapter"; "The climber went farther up the mountain than anyone had gone before"; "The police decided not to investigate the matter further."

Graduated/graduated from/was graduated

It is incorrect to say "My son graduated high school last year." Either "My son graduated from high school" or "My son was graduated" is okay.

Hopefully

Hopefully is an adverb meaning "in a hopeful manner." It should not be used to mean "I hope" or "it is hoped," as in "Hopefully, Congress will decide not to enact the bill." In that sentence there is nothing for *hopefully* to modify. The only verb is *decide* and certainly the sentence is not meant to say that Congress will decide "in a hopeful manner." As another example, "Hopefully, she looked at the numbers on her lottery ticket" is not the same as "She looked hopefully at the numbers on her lottery ticket."

Imply/infer

Imply means to convey an impression by what you say or do; *infer* means to draw a conclusion from what you hear or see. You do not *infer* while speaking; nor do you *imply* while listening.

For example:

> "In his speech, the senator implied that he would vote for the legislation."
> "From what the senator said, I inferred that he would vote for the legislation."

Important/importantly

Importantly is an adverb and should not be used except to modify a verb. In a sentence such as "Most importantly, we completed the project on time," the only verb is *completed*. Because "importantly completed" is nonsensical, it is obvious there is no verb for *importantly* to modify. Although some authorities do accept either word in such sentences, *important* is the better choice. Some speakers and writers, even experienced ones, use *importantly* rather than *important*, perhaps because they imagine it sounds more important—not importantly.

In behalf of/on behalf of

To speak *in behalf of* someone is to plead that person's case. To speak *on behalf of* someone is to speak in the person's stead. These two sentences illustrate the correct usage: "I was about to be fired, but Myrna spoke to the boss in my behalf," and "Addressing the shareholders, the chairman spoke on behalf of all the company's employees."

Liable/likely

If you are *liable,* something unpleasant might result. For example, if you damage someone's property, you may be liable. *Likely* expresses simple probability with no unpleasant connotation. *Liable* should not be used as a synonym for *likely,* as in "I'm liable to see Robert tomorrow." Think of *liable* as being related to *liability.*

Lie/lay

These might be the most misused words in the English language. *Lie* is an intransitive verb, which means it does not take an object; *lay* is transitive. The main reason for confusion is that *lay* is also the past tense of *lie.* The past tense of the transitive *lay* is *laid.* The past participle of *lie* is *lain,* and the past participle of *lay* is *laid.* The present participle of *lie* is *lying;* the present participle of *lay* is *laying.*

If all this seems too technical, consider the following sentences as examples of correct usage:

"I often *lie* down for a nap after lunch."
"Yesterday I *lay* down for a nap after lunch."
"I have *lain* here for an hour."
"Please *lay* the book on the table."
"I *laid* the book on the table."
"I have *laid* the book on the table."
"I am *lying* down for a nap."
"The book is *lying* on the table."
"I am *laying* the book on the table."
"The chicken was *laying* an egg on the ground."

And here are a couple that are *not* correct.

"The man was *laying* on the ground." [The correct usage is
lying.]
     "He *laid* there for an hour." [The correct usage is *lay*.]

Literally/figuratively

Many a good figure of speech is ruined by being preceded by
literally. "I literally laughed myself to death" is an absurdity because
literally means "actually; without exaggeration," and a person who
literally laughed himself to death wouldn't be around to tell the tale.
A person who says "I literally laughed myself to death" really means
"I figuratively laughed myself to death." Of course, there's no need
to use *figuratively* with a figure of speech. If it's a good one, the listener will know and won't have to be reminded. "I laughed myself
to death" is sufficient.

Loathe/loath

What a difference a little *e* makes. To *loathe* is to feel intense
dislike or even hatred. *Loath* is an adjective meaning "reluctant."
Example: "I loathe my job, but I am loath to leave all my friends in
the company." Their pronunciations are slightly different. In *loathe*,
the *th* is pronounced as the *th* in *clothe*; in *loath* the *th* is pronounced as the *th* in *worth*.

Mobile/movable

If something is *mobile,* it can *move.* If the thing is *movable,* it
can be moved. Thus, a badly damaged automobile might be *movable*
but not *mobile.* A badly injured person is almost certainly not *mobile*, and may not be *movable* if the injury is too severe.

None is/none are

Traditionalists have long insisted that *none* must take a singular
verb form. Their argument is based on the obvious fact that zero cannot be plural. This argument has always seemed foolish to me. Zero
can be neither singular nor plural. Whether *none is* or *none are* is
correct depends on the sense intended. In "None of us *is* going to the
meeting," *none* means "not one." In "None of us are going to the
meeting, *none* means "not any." This distinction is subtle and may
not always be worth making. In most instances, the one that sounds
right is correct.

Prescribe/proscribe

These two words are almost opposites. To *prescribe* is to dictate a course of action; to *proscribe* is to prohibit. If your physician *prescribes* Viagra, it's okay to take it. If he or she *proscribes* it, find another solution to your problem.

Sewerage/sewage

Sewerage is a system for disposing of *sewage.* If an adjective is needed, use *sewage* rather than *sewerage.* Thus, "Sewage lines [not sewerage lines] are being installed in the area." "Sewerage is being installed" is okay.

Shall/will

Except in such expressions as "Shall we dance?" and in legal documents, *shall* has almost disappeared from American English. *Shall* and *should* have been replaced by *will* and *would.* If you want to say "I shall be coming home soon" or "I should like to have a cup of coffee," go ahead, but you'll sound a bit odd to most ears. In legal documents, *shall* connotes a mandate. "The seller shall deliver a clear title to the property" means the seller *must deliver a clear title.*

Tandem/parallel

Some people use *tandem* when they mean *parallel.* Statements like "The advertising and public relations programs proceeded in tandem" are common. Usually, the speaker means the programs proceeded together. *In tandem* means one after the other; *parallel* means side by side. Rails on a train track are parallel, but the cars of the train are in tandem.

That/which

As relative pronouns, these words are often used interchangeably. Careful writers and speakers, however, use *that* to introduce restrictive (defining) clauses and *which* to introduce nonrestrictive (nondefining) clauses. So used, *which* should always be preceded by a comma (or a pause); *that,* never. In "This is the book that my son gave me for Christmas," *that my son gave me for Christmas* is a restrictive clause that (not *which*) defines the book. In "This book, which is by Richard Lederer, was given to me by my son," *which is by Richard Lederer* is nonrestrictive. It gives additional information about the book without defining it as a particular book.

Those kinds/that kind

Where *these* or *those* is used as a demonstrative adjective, it must modify a plural noun. When a singular noun is needed, the singular form of the demonstrative adjective is required. Thus, *these* (or *those*) *kinds,* and *this* (or *that*) *kind* are correct. *Those kind* is not.

Ultimate/penultimate

Ultimate means last and it often connotes superiority, especially when it appears in advertising copy, as in "The ultimate [the last word] in men's clothing." *Penultimate* means next-to-last, nothing more. It carries no connotation of superiority. So the actress who won an Oscar and gushed, "This is the *penultimate* experience of my life," surely was not to be taken literally.

Whom/who

Grammarians have been predicting the doom of *whom* for a long time, but it survives today in the speech and writing of educated people. It is not really difficult to learn when to use *whom*, and when to use *who* if you understand the grammatical principle involved. *Whom* is the objective form of the pronoun *who*. It is the correct form for the object of a verb or a preposition. Most people have no trouble knowing when to use *whom* if the pronoun is preceded immediately by a preposition, as in "To whom will you give the money?" But certain constructions can be troublesome. A sentence like "Give the message to whoever answers the telephone" often comes out "Give the message to whomever answers the telephone." That's because we tend to select the objective case for a word immediately after the preposition *to*. A quick analysis of the sentence tells us that *whoever* is required because it is the subject of *answers*, not the object of *to*.

Here are some examples of the correct use of *who* and *whom*:

"I went to see Dr. Epstein, who I heard was the best physician in town."
　　"Who did you say was on the telephone?"
　　"Whom was the telephone call for?"

Some people are self-conscious about using *whom* in speaking even though they may be quite comfortable with it in writing. If you're in that number, there's no problem with using *who* most of the time. The more egregious error is to use *whom* when *who* is required. That makes a speaker sound as if he's trying to be correct but doesn't know how.

I cannot stress enough the importance of using words correctly when you speak or when you write a speech for someone else. The words and phrases discussed above constitute a lexicon of words and phrases that should raise red flags in your mind because they're so often misused. I urge you to acquire, in addition to a good standard dictionary, at least one of several good usage handbooks that are readily available. You'll find yourself referring to your usage handbook often. The best usage manual available is probably Bryan A. Garner's *Dictionary of Modern American Usage*, but some of the old standbys are also good. They include H. W. Fowler's classic *Modern English Usage*, Theodore Bernstein's *The Careful Writer*, and Bergen and Cornelia Evans's *A Dictionary of Contemporary American Usage*.

Podium Presence

Have you ever listened to a speaker who seemed to be afraid to look anyone in the eye? It's an almost-painful experience. Good speakers use eye contact to connect with their audiences. They don't keep their eyes glued to their notes, and they don't stare off into space. Maintaining good eye contact accomplishes two things: One, it helps keep your mind off yourself and thus helps you control self-conscious nervousness; two, it keeps the audience in play, so to speak. It makes them feel you're talking to them individually and collectively.

It is important to develop the habit of looking at people when you talk to them. In a later chapter we will discuss eye contact as part of an overall discussion of nonverbal communications.

"The Name American Must Always Exalt Pride"

Some 165 years before President Eisenhower delivered his "last goodnight," another president, George Washington, bade his farewell. In that speech, delivered in March 1797, President Washington announced that he would not serve a third term and offered some advice that our political leaders of today would do well to follow. The antiquated language sounds stilted to modern ears, but the speech is well worth reading and studying:

Friends and fellow citizens: The period for a new election of a citizen to administer the executive government of the United States being not far distant, and the time having actually arrived when your thoughts must be employed in designating the person who is to be clothed with that important trust, it appears to me proper, especially as it may conduce to a more distinct expression of the public voice, that I should now apprise you of the resolution I have formed, to decline being considered among the number of those out of whom a choice is to be made.

I beg you at the same time to do me the justice to be assured that this resolution has not been taken without a strict regard to all the consideration appertaining to the relation which binds a dutiful citizen to his country; and that in withdrawing the tender of service which silence in my situation might imply, I am influenced by no diminution of zeal for your future interest, no deficiency of grateful respect for your past kindness, but am supported by a full conviction that the step is compatible with both.

The acceptance of and continuance hitherto in the office to which your suffrages have twice called me have been a uniform sacrifice of inclination to the opinion of duty and to a deference for what appeared to be your desire. I constantly hoped that it would have been much earlier in my power, consistently with motives which I was not at liberty to disregard, to return to that retirement from which I had been reluctantly drawn. The strength of my inclination to do this, previous to the last election have even led to the preparation of an address to declare it to you; but mature reflection on the then perplexed and critical posture of our affairs with foreign nations and the unanimous advice of persons entitled to my confidence, impelled me to abandon the idea. I rejoice that the state of your concerns, external as well as internal, no longer renders the pursuit of inclination incompatible with the sentiment of duty or propriety, and am persuaded, whatever partiality may be retained for my services, that in the present circumstances of our country you will not disapprove of my determination to retire.

The impressions with which I first undertook the arduous trust were explained on the proper occasion. In the discharge of this trust I will only say that I have, with good intentions contributed towards the organization and administration of the government the best exertions of which a very fallible judgment was capable. Not unconscious, in the outset, of the inferiority of my qualification, experience, in my own eyes, perhaps still more in the eyes of others, has strengthened the motives to diffidence of myself; and every day the increasing weight of years admonishes me more and more that the shade of retirement is as necessary to me as it will be welcome. Satisfied that if any circumstances have given peculiar value to my services they were temporary, I have the consolation to believe that, while choice and prudence invite me to quit the political scene, patriotism does not forbid it.

In looking forward to the moment which is intended to terminate the career of my public life, my feelings do not permit me to suspend the deep acknowledgment of that debt of gratitude which I owe to my beloved country for the many honors it has conferred upon me; still more for the steadfast confidence with which it has supported me; and for the opportunities I have thence enjoyed of manifesting my inviolable attachment by services faithful and persevering, though in usefulness unequal to my zeal. If benefits have resulted to our country from these services, let it always be remembered to your praise, and as an instructive example in our annals that under circumstances in which the passions agitated in every direction, were liable to mislead; amidst appearances sometimes dubious, vicissitudes of fortune often discouraging; in situations in which not infrequently want of success has countenanced the spirit of criticism, the constancy of your support was the essential prop of the efforts and the guarantee of the plans by which they were effected. Profoundly penetrated with this idea, I shall carry it with me to my grave as a strong incitement to unceasing wishes that heaven may continue to you the choicest tokens of its beneficence; that your union and brotherly affection may be perpetual; that the free constitution which is the work of your hands may be sacredly maintained; that its administration in every department may be stamped with wisdom and virtue; that, in fine, the happiness of the people of these States, under the auspices of liberty, may be made complete by so careful a preservation and so prudent a use of this blessing as will acquire to them the glory of recommending it to the applause, the affection and adoption of every nation which is yet a stranger to it. . . .

The unity of government which constitutes you one people is also now dear to you. It is justly so, for it is a main pillar in the edifice of your real independence, the support of your tranquillity at home, your peace abroad, of your safety, of your prosperity, of that very liberty which you so highly prize. . . .

The name of American, which belongs to you in your national capacity, must always exalt the just pride of patriotism more than any appellation derived from local discrimination. With slight shades of difference, you have the same religion, manners, habits, and political principles. You have in a common cause fought and triumphed together. The independence and liberty you possess are the work of joint councils and joint efforts, of common dangers, sufferings, and successes. . . .

The basis of our political systems is the right of the people to make and to alter the constitutions of government. But the constitution which at any time exists until changed by an explicit and authentic act of the whole people is sacredly obligatory upon all. . . .

It is, indeed, little else than a name where the government is too feeble to withstand the enterprises of faction, to confine each member of society within the limits prescribed by the laws, and to maintain all in the secure and tranquil enjoyment of the rights of person and property.

It is important . . . that the habits of thinking in a free country should inspire caution in those entrusted with its administration to confine themselves within their respective constitutional spheres, avoiding, in the exercise of the powers of one department to encroach upon another. The spirit of encroachment tends to consolidate the powers of all the departments in one, and thus to create, whatever the form of government, a real despotism. . . .

Of all those dispositions and habits, which lead to political prosperity, religion and morality are indispensable supports. In vain would that man claim the tribute of patriotism who should labor to subvert these great pillars of human happiness—these firmest props of the destinies of men and citizens. . . . Let it simply be asked, Where is the security for property, for reputation, for life, if the sense of religious obligation desert the oaths, which are the instruments of investigation in courts of justice? And let us with caution indulge the supposition that morality can be maintained without religion. Whatever may be conceded to the influence of refined education on minds of peculiar structure, reason and experience both forbid us to expect that national morality can prevail in exclusion of religious principles.

It is substantially true that virtue or morality is a necessary spring of popular government. The rule indeed extends with more or less force to every species of free government. Who that is a sincere friend to it can look with indifference upon attempts to shake the foundation of the fabric? Promote, then, as an object of primary importance, institutions for the general diffusion of knowledge. In proportion as the structure of a government gives force to public opinion, it is essential that public opinion should be enlightened.

As a very important source of strength and security, cherish public credit. One method of preserving it is to use it as sparingly as possible; avoiding occasions of expense by cultivating peace, but remembering also that timely disbursements to prepare for danger frequently prevent much greater disbursements to repel it; avoiding likewise the accumulation of debt, not only by shunning occasions of expense, but by vigorous exertions in time of peace to discharge the debts which unavoidable wars may have occasioned, not ungenerously throwing upon posterity the burden which we ourselves ought to bear. The execution of these maxims belongs to your representatives; but it is necessary that public opinion should co-operate. To facilitate to them the performance of their duty it is essential that you should practically bear in mind that towards the payment of debts there must be revenue; that to have revenue there must be taxes. . . .

Observe good faith and justice towards all nations. Cultivate peace and harmony with all. Religion and morality enjoin this conduct and can it be that good policy does not equally enjoin it? It will be worthy of a free, enlightened, and at no distant period a great nation, to give to mankind the magnanimous and too novel example of a people always guided by an exalted justice and benevolence. . . .

The great rule of conduct for us, in regard to foreign nations is, in extending our commercial relations to have with them as little political connection as possible. . . .

Taking care always to keep ourselves, by suitable establishments on a respectable defensive posture, we may safely trust to temporary alliances for extraordinary emergencies.

Harmony, liberal intercourse with all nations are recommended by policy, humanity, and interest. But even our commercial policy should hold an equal and impartial hand, neither seeking nor granting exclusive favors or preferences; consulting the natural course of things; diffusing and diversifying by gentle means the streams of commerce, but forcing nothing. . . . There can be no greater error than to expect to calculate upon real favors from nation to nation. It is an illusion, which experience must cure, which a just pride ought to discard.

In offering to you, my countrymen, these counsels of an old and affectionate friend I dare not hope they will make the strong and lasting impression I could wish, that they will control the usual current of the passions or prevent our nation from running the course which has hitherto marked the destiny of nations. But if I may even flatter myself that they may be productive of some partial benefit, some occasional good—that they may now and then recur to moderate the fury of party spirit, to warn against the mischiefs of foreign intrigues, to guard against the impostures of pretended patriotism—this hope will be a full recompense for the solicitude for your welfare, by which they have been dictated.

How far in the discharge of my official duties I have been guided by the principles which have been delineated the public records and other evidences of my conduct must witness to you and to the world. To myself the assurance of my own conscience is that I have at least believed myself to be guided by them. . . .

Though, in reviewing the incidents of my Administration, I am unconscious of intentional error, I am nevertheless too sensible of my defects, not to think it probable that I may have committed many errors. Whatever they may be, I fervently beseech the Almighty to avert or mitigate the evils to which they may tend. I shall also carry with me the hope that my country will never cease to view them with indulgence, and that, after forty-five years of my life dedicated to its service with an upright zeal, the faults of incompetent abilities will be consigned to oblivion, as myself must soon be to the mansions of rest.

Relying on its kindness in this as in other things, and actuated by that fervent love towards it which is so natural to man who views in it the native soil of himself and his progenitors for several generations, I anticipate with pleasing expectations that retreat in which I promise myself to realize without alloy the sweet enjoyment of partaking in the midst of my fellow citizens the benign influence of good laws under a free government—the ever favorite object of my heart, and the happy reward, as I trust, of our mutual cares, labors, and dangers.

—— Chapter Nine ——

"Secrets" of the Pros

Today we are bombarded with offers of "secrets" that are guaranteed to help us live longer, play a musical instrument, hit a golf ball farther, lose weight, pick winning lottery numbers, get rich in real estate, beat the stock market, or restore sexual vigor to a 98-year-old great grandfather. Always there's the implication that we'll be "let in on" inside information, good stuff heretofore known to a few cognoscenti who have selfishly kept the information to themselves. Now, so goes the advertising copy, one of the chosen few has broken ranks and will make the miracle-working secrets available to you— for only $19.95, $39.95, or $99.95, plus shipping and handling and sales tax where applicable, allow six to eight weeks for delivery.

In this chapter I'm going to share with you some "secrets" of professional speech writing—immediate delivery, no charge for shipping and handling. Well, actually, the things I'll be discussing are not secrets at all. They're proven techniques that speech writers use to make their speeches more interesting, more meaningful, and more dramatic. You can find them not only in well-written speeches but in many kinds of writing, from ad copy to fiction. This chapter will tell you what these techniques are and how to use them in a speech.

The rule of three

Churchill's famous "blood, toil, tears, and sweat" has been widely misquoted as "blood, sweat, and tears." Although I would never presume to edit the writing of Churchill, I must admit that the misquoters have a point in their favor. There's something almost mystical about the number three. It's as if two are not enough and four are too many. Writers, especially speech writers, have long

recognized this phenomenon and often use a rhetorical device called
a triad. Or, as some prefer to express it, "the rule of three."

"The Rule of Three" is something of a misnomer because there's
no rule involved, just a principle. That principle is that the human
ear has a peculiar affinity for triplets. Writers with a good ear for
cadence use triads routinely.

A triad is the expression of related thoughts or ideas in a group
of three, often with the initial words or sounds the same for all three,
and almost always with each element of the triad using the same
grammatical form. The elements of a triad can be single words—
nouns, adjectives, adverbs, or verbs. They can also be phrases,
clauses, even sentences. Some examples will serve better than my
definition. Here are some well-known triads:

> *From the Bible: And now abideth faith, hope, and charity,
> but the greatest of these is charity.*
>
> *From the Declaration of Independence: . . . [W]e mutu-
> ally pledge to each other our lives, our fortunes, and our
> sacred honor.*
>
> *Julius Caesar: Veni, vidi, vici (I came, I saw, I con-
> quered).*
>
> *Franklin Delano Roosevelt; I see one-third of a nation
> ill-housed, ill-clad, ill-nourished.*
>
> *Sir Walter Scott: Unwept, unhonored, unsung.*
>
> *Abraham Lincoln: . . . [T]hat government of the people,
> by the people, for the people, shall not perish from the
> earth.*
>
> *And here's one of my own that's not yet famous but a
> triad can give force to our ideas, eloquence to our words,
> and rhythm to our sentences.*

If you read the examples carefully, you probably noticed that
with the exception of *faith, hope, and charity*, each has words or
sounds that are repeated in each element of the triad, but not always
the initial sounds. If that didn't register at first, reread the examples.

In the quotation from the Declaration of Independence, *our* appears as the first word in each element: "*our* lives, *our* fortunes, *our*
sacred honor." It's worth noting also that the last part of the triad is
"our sacred *honor*." Writers know that the end of a sentence, not
the beginning, is the point of greatest emphasis. The authors of the
Declaration, being men who placed the highest value on honor, put
honor above, which is to say *after*, both life and fortune. If they had
said, "our sacred honor, our lives, our fortunes," the emphasis
would have shifted and the effect diminished. It would have left the

impression that their fortunes were more important than their sacred honor.

In the Julius Caesar triad, the repeated sounds are the *w* sound at the beginning of each element and long-*e* sound at the end—*WAYnee, WEEdee, WEEkee.* In the FDR quotation, there's the repetition of *ill,* in *ill-housed, ill-clad, ill-nourished.* In the Sir Walter Scott quotation, it's the prefix *un-* that repeats—*unwept, unhonored, unsung.* In the Lincoln quotation, the repeated words are *the people* at the end of each prepositional phrase—*of the people, by the people, for the people.* The three parallel grammatical forms give the triad its wonderful cadence. (In my triad about triads, the repeated phrase comes in the middle of each element—*to our,* as in *force to our ideas.*)

General Douglas MacArthur was a fine orator and rhetorician. You will recall that in an earlier chapter we quoted from his speech delivered to the Cadet Corps at West Point on May 12, 1962. In that speech, MacArthur used two triads to play on "Duty, Honor, Country," the motto, also a triad, that appears on the West Point coat of arms:

> *"Duty . . . honor . . . country"—those three hallowed words reverently dictate what you want to be, what you can be, what you will be. They are your rallying point to build courage when courage seems to fail, to regain faith when there seems to be little cause for faith, to create hope when hope becomes forlorn.*

Notice how effectively the Old Soldier uses contrast to build up to his main point in the triad "what you *want* to be, what you *can* be, what you *will* be." In the second triad, he begins each element with an infinitive—*to build . . . to regain . . . to create.* The effect is heightened by repetition of the object of each infinitive—"to build *courage* when *courage* seems to fail" . . . "to regain *faith* when there seems little cause for *faith*" . . . "to *hope* when *hope* becomes forlorn."

I'm not sure anybody really knows why triads have such ear appeal. Possibly it's for the same reason that a musical triad, a three-note chord, pleases the ear. Of course, a chord cannot be composed of just any three notes. The three notes of the chord must blend in the right way. The same is true of a speech triad. The elements of the triad must follow a certain pattern to create the desired tone and cadence. Unfortunately, there's no formula for creating a speech triad as there is for a musical one.

One point is certain: Ideas grouped in threes are more memorable, which may explain why the Churchillian phrase is so often mis-quoted. No matter how many times we hear "blood, toil, tears, and sweat," we tend to remember it as "blood, sweat, and tears." Such is the unique power of the triad.

As I've already noted, a triad can be composed of single words, phrases, sentences, or even paragraphs. Here is one composed of complete sentences. It's from a speech I wrote on the challenges facing American business:

> *We don't need protectionism.*
> *We don't need central economic planning.*
> *We don't need a so-called industrial policy.*

To again use a musical analogy, that triad seems to cry out for resolution. The thrice-repeated negative phrase "we don't need," like a suspended chord, leaves listeners unsatisfied. I resolved the suspense in the next sentence, closing the circle, so to speak, by using a positive phrase, "what we do need":

> *What we do need is the will to make our system function as*
> *it has in the past and as we know it can function in the*
> *future.*

If you harbor any doubt about the effectiveness of triads, take a couple of the examples and remove or add one element. In the Biblical quotation, instead of "faith, hope, and charity," say "Now abideth faith and charity" or "Now abideth faith, love, hope, and charity." The first has too few elements, the second too many. Drama and rhythm are gone from both.

Now let's take another one and alter the repeated sounds. Suppose that Roosevelt, instead of saying "ill-clad, ill-housed, ill-nourished" had said, "ill-clad, poorly housed, and undernourished." Quite a difference, don't you agree?

And, as another example, try removing the parallel grammatical construction from the selection from the Lincoln quotation. Make it, "That government of the people, which the people themselves created, and which is intended to serve the people, shall not vanish from the earth." A bit jarring to the ear, no? The sentiment expressed is the same as in the original, but the drama is missing.

So, in summary, well-constructed triads add drama, interest, and rhythm to a speech. They also emphasize important points and make them stick in the minds of listeners.

Anaphora: repetition that doesn't bore

My triad that begins with "We don't need" provides an example of
anaphora, another device professional speech writers use often.
Anaphora is nothing more than the repetition of a word or words at
the beginning of successive phrases, clauses, or sentences. Speech
writers often combine triads with anaphora, but anaphora is also
used when more than three elements are needed. For example, the
keynote speaker at the 1928 Democratic convention used a sort of
double anaphora very effectively to compare the philosophy of Alex-
ander Hamilton with that of Thomas Jefferson, whose philosophy
was said to have been the foundation for the ideals of Democrats.
This was the convention, by the way, that nominated New York Governor Al Smith to face Republican Herbert Hoover in a contest to
succeed Calvin Coolidge.

The keynoter, one Claude Bowers, stated his thesis this way:

> *To understand the conflicting views of these two men on the
> functions of government is to grasp the deep significance of
> this campaign.*

Then he supported it with no fewer than six sentences in which
he repeated the name *Hamilton* at the beginning of each and the
name *Jefferson* at the beginning of a second clause in each.

> *Now, Hamilton believed in the rule of an aristocracy of
> money; and Jefferson in a democracy of men.*
> *Hamilton believed that governments are created for the
> domination of the masses; and Jefferson that they are cre-
> ated for the service of the people.*
> *Hamilton wrote to Morris that governments are strong
> in proportion as they are made profitable to the powerful;
> and Jefferson knew that no government is fit to live that does
> not conserve the interest of the average man.*
> *Hamilton proposed a scheme for binding the wealthy
> to the government by making government a source of reve-
> nue to the wealthy; and Jefferson unfurled his banner of
> equal rights.*
> *Hamilton would have concentrated authority remote
> from the people; and Jefferson would have diffused it
> among them.*
> *Hamilton would have injected governmental activities
> into all the affairs of men; and Jefferson laid it down as an*

axiom of freedom that government is best which governs least.

The effectiveness of the keynote speech evidently did not carry forward into the campaign, for Hoover and the Republicans prevailed in the election.

Here is another fine example of anaphora:

Today, twenty-seven million Americans, one in five—more than the entire population of Canada—are functional illiterates. That means, basically, they can exist. Like turtles on the beach. They are there. Period.

They can write their names   maybe.
They can't read a street sign.
They can't look up a phone number.
They can't count change.
They can't follow directions on a medicine bottle.
They can't fill out a job application, to say nothing of reading a newspaper or Huckleberry Finn.
They are lost, just lost.

The speaker began eight consecutive sentences with *they.* The last one, "They are lost, just lost" gives the listener the feeling of despair that an illiterate person must feel being unable to do all those things.

In his most famous speech, Martin Luther King, Jr. began eight sentences with "I have a dream." Not only did the phrase echo and re-echo throughout the speech, it continues to echo throughout American society today. For good reason, "I have a dream" is the most remembered part of the speech.

Although anaphora is defined as repetition at the beginning of *successive* phrases, clauses, or sentences, I have heard speeches in which key phrases are repeated with several sentences or even several paragraphs between them. This device was used to good effect in a commencement address at the Southwest Texas State University several years ago. The inspirational speech was titled "Living With Abandon." The speaker used "If you would live with abandon, you must . . ." five times during her speech—for example, "If you would live with abandon, you must have a self you respect," and "If you would live life with abandon, you must learn to enjoy life's processes, not just life's rewards." Each such use introduced a related discussion ranging in length from a half to more than one full page of typewritten text.

Tongue-twisting repetition

Repetition in various forms can be effective if used with reasonable restraint. Alliteration is one form of repetition that ought to be used with special care. Alliteration is the repetition of several similar sounds in sequence, which is itself an example of alliteration. The late Spiro Agnew, who was Richard Nixon's first vice president, was famous for a speech in which he criticized pessimists for being "nattering nabobs of negativism."

New York Times columnist William Safire, who at that time was a speech writer in the Nixon White House, claims to have originated that phrase, and I assume it served its purpose. Alliteration, however, is difficult to read and may cause even a seasoned speaker to stumble. Occasional alliteration included on purpose is fine, but alliteration that is accidental can be troublesome. I might have said that a good speech writer will "always avoid any accidental alliteration." Try reading that aloud.

Even the best speakers can sound as if they need speech therapy when they come unexpectedly upon some tongue-twisting phrase and sometimes even when they know the phrase is there. A line in a speech to the Democratic Convention in 1984 by the Rev. Jesse Jackson was "I am not a *perfect* servant; I am a *public* servant." When Mr. Jackson delivered the line, he almost committed a spoonerism by transposing the first syllables of *perfect* and *public*. He said, "I am not a pu- . . ." Then he caught himself and said it right.

If he hadn't stopped himself, the line might have come out "I am not a *pufect* servant, I am a *perblic* servant"; or, perhaps worse, "I am not a public servant, I am a perfect servant."

Jackson, incidentally, is a master of rhyme, alliteration, and other rhetorical devices. He speaks with the fervor, color, and richness of an old-time country preacher. Whether you agree with his positions or not, you can learn much from listening to or reading his speeches.

Antithesis

Antithesis, another common and useful device, is simply placing an idea next to one to which it is sharply contrasted or directly opposed. Technically, the first idea is called the thesis; the opposing one is called the antithesis, or antithetic statement. But in the study of rhetoric, the device is usually referred to as antithesis. Again, some examples make the definition clear. Patrick Henry's famous "Give me liberty or give me death" is a classic one.

The main function of antithesis in a speech is to give emphasis to an idea by placing it next to a contrasting idea. The often-quoted lines from Tennyson's poem, "The Charge of the Light Brigade," illustrate this point:

> *Theirs not to reason why,*
> *Theirs but to do or die*

So does John F. Kennedy's memorable dictum from his inaugural address:

> *Ask not what your country can do for you. Ask what you*
> *can do for your country.*

Incidentally, the opening line of that speech was a triad of antithesis:

> *We observe today not a victory of a party, but a celebration*
> *of freedom—symbolizing an end as well as a beginning, sig-*
> *nifying renewal as well as change.*

Think for a moment about how powerful and appropriate those ideas were, and how much more effective they were because of the juxtaposition of contrasting ideas—"not a victory but a celebration," "an end as well as a beginning," "renewal as well as change." Imagine the passage without the contrast: "We observe today a celebration of freedom, symbolizing an end, signifying renewal." Not a bad triad, but not to be compared with the original.

Articulate speakers and writers throughout history have used antithesis to great effect. Shakespeare often used the device in the speech of his characters. In the play *Julius Caesar*, Cassius said, "Not that I loved Caesar less, but that I loved Rome more," and then "I come to bury Caesar, not to praise him."

The philosopher Socrates, condemned to death in a highly politicized trial, said this in a statement to his judges:

> *To die is one of two things: for either the dead may be anni-*
> *hilated and have no sensation of anything whatever, or, as*
> *it is said, there are a certain change and passage of the soul*
> *from one place to another.*

And Lincoln, in his annual address to Congress, on December 1, 1852, used antithesis combined with an anaphoral triad when he said:

*Our national strife springs not from our permanent part, not
from the land we inhabit, not from our national homestead.
Our strife pertains to ourselves.*

Antithesis is conflict, and like any conflict, it ought to be resolved when it can be. Drawing again from a speech by Jesse Jackson,
here is an example from his speech to the Democratic Convention in
Atlanta on July 20, 1988. Mr. Jackson was comparing his background
with that of Michael Dukakis, the nominee who eventually lost to
George Bush. Here is the antithesis:

*His parents came to America on immigrant ships; my par-
ents came to America on slave ships.*

And here is how the two contrasting ideas are reconciled:

*But whatever the original ships, we're in the same boat to-
night.*

One of the finest examples of antithesis in a speech comes from
an address delivered in Boston more than a century ago by Henry W.
Grady, the esteemed editor of *The Atlanta Constitution*. The speech
dramatized the economic plight of the South, which then was still
largely agrarian. Mr. Grady describes the funeral of a poor farmer:

*They buried him in the midst of a marble quarry . . . and
yet the little tombstone they put above his head was from
Vermont. They buried him in a pine forest, and yet the pine
coffin was imported from Cincinnati . . . The nails in his
coffin and the iron in the shovel that dug his grave were
imported from Pittsburgh. . . . The wool in the coffin bands
and the bands themselves were brought from the North. The
South didn't furnish a thing on earth for that funeral but
the corpse and the hole in the ground.*

The last sentence was the dramatic highlight that brought the
antithesis points into sharp focus.

Similes tell it "like" it is

A simile is the comparison of one thing to another, usually something of an entirely different category—in other words, a *figurative*

comparison. For example, "Honesty is like pregnancy; either you is or you ain't" or "My love is like a red, red rose." A simile almost always uses the word *like.* But a simple comparison does not make a simile. If you said that the Kennedy tax cuts of the 1960s were like the Reagan tax cuts of the 1980s, that would not be a simile.

To be effective, a simile must strike a responsive chord in the audience or make a point relevant to the subject. The honesty-pregnancy comparison is humorous, if a bit gray-bearded, but it does make a point: You cannot be "a little bit honest" any more than you can be "a little bit pregnant." Although similes are often humorous, a simile does not have to be funny to be good.

Often a good simile evokes a mental picture. The Bible tells us that a righteous person is "like a tree planted by the water." That brings forth an image of a tall, sturdy tree.

Like many good speakers, Ronald Reagan knew how to use similes. In a proclamation for Education Day 1986, President Reagan said:

> *Education is like a diamond with many facets: It includes the basic mastery of numbers and letters that give us access to the treasury of human knowledge, accumulated and refined through the ages; It includes technical and vocational training as well as instruction in science, higher mathematics, and humane letters.*

Metaphors evoke powerful images

A metaphor is also a comparison of one thing to another, but it differs from a simile in that it describes the thing being compared as if it actually were the other. For example, "When it came to standing firm, he was the Rock of Gibraltar." The comparison can be made also by attributing characteristics or actions of one thing to another. "In his resolve, he was solid as the Rock of Gibraltar." Here is an excerpt from a speech by a bank executive in which the financial markets are given the attributes of a life-support apparatus:

> *To one degree or another, the financial markets reflect just about everything that is occurring—or is expected to occur—throughout the world economy. As the economy's life-support system, they provide measures of the blood pressure, heart rate, brain waves, and general health of the system.*

Sometimes an entire speech, or a large part of it, is built on a metaphor. An executive of a high-tech company concerned about an impending recession and growing competition from foreign producers of electronics began a speech by announcing that he would be speaking on herpetology, the study of snakes:

> *The snake I would like to talk about this morning is the boa constrictor. Now . . . some of you may have labored in the past under the impression that the boa constrictor drops out of a tree on its victims and quickly crushes them in the powerful folds of its body. That is not how it operates. On the contrary, extensive research on the part of my staff, which consisted of my secretary looking up "boa constrictor" in the* Encyclopedia Americana, *has revealed the true modus operandi of this dangerous reptile. Let me read it to you:*
>
> *"Ordinarily the snake places two or three coils around the chest of its prey. Then, each time the victim relaxes and exhales its breath, the snake simply takes up the slack. After three or four breaths, there is no more slack. The prey quickly suffocates and is swallowed by the boa."*
>
> *This deadly phenomenon of a victim becoming a willing accomplice in its own destruction is not confined to the animal world.*
>
> *The big boa we are facing—or rather failing to face—is the aggressive . . . hungry . . . efficient offshore competition, and each coil of the snake is another recession.*

The speaker continues the boa-constrictor metaphor by talking about what happens when economic conditions improve and the industry breathes a sigh of relief. Then, he says, "the boa constrictor smiles as we relax again."

This metaphor creates some powerful images, especially the one of the boa smiling and tightening its grip. The boa metaphor slithers along for several paragraphs.

Unless you're trying for a laugh, be careful not to mix your metaphors. I once heard a CEO say, "Our company is at a crossroads today, and we are going to have to navigate some stormy seas in the next few months."

Analogies help explain

An analogy is another type of comparison. Analogies usually compare real similarities—for example, the functioning of the human heart to that of an automobile fuel pump—but an analogy might also have metaphorical characteristics.

Analogies are especially useful in explaining something that is difficult for an audience to grasp. It is easier to understand a concept if it is explained in terms of something you're already familiar with. When I was learning how to use a computer, my mentor suggested that I think of the computer's hard drive as an office with filing cabinets and shelves containing various equipment and material I would need to work with, and the RAM as a desktop where the work would take place. This helped me to understand some things that had been confusing.

A fine example of an analogy that's part metaphor is found in a speech by Daniel Webster, one of the greatest orators of all times. This is the opening of a speech he delivered to the United States Senate on January 26, 1830:

> Mr. President: When the mariner has been tossed for many days, in thick weather, and on an unknown sea, he naturally avails himself of the first pause in the storm, the earliest glance of the sun, to take his latitude, and ascertain how far the elements have driven him from his true course. Let us imitate this prudence, and, before we float farther on the waves of this debate, refer to the point from which we departed, that we may at least be able to conjecture where we now are.

As you have no doubt inferred from the examples, similes, metaphors, and analogies have characteristics in common. At times they seem to overlap. The terms themselves, however, are unimportant. What is important is their effects. The use of good figures of speech can help make your points clear and your speech dramatic and interesting.

Telling it like it isn't

Hyperbole, or exaggeration for the sake of emphasis, is another useful device. You must be careful, however, not to make your hyperbole sound like an advertiser's phony claims of product superiority. Hyperbole used for dramatic effect should be an obvious exaggeration, such as "He was as big as a grizzly bear and twice as mean." Or, "She ran so fast she left her shadow ten yards behind." Or, "This guy has a 500-megabyte memory; and that's 100 megs more than his computer." Or, "My memory is terrible. I went to an Easter egg hunt for senior citizens. They let me hide my own eggs, and I never found a single one of them."

And, on the opposite end, don't forget the value of understatement. The late Senator Everett Dirksen is famous for having said, in reference to an extravagant spending bill being considered by Congress, "A billion here, a billion there. Pretty soon it adds up to real money."

Surprise! Surprise!

Some speakers like to spring dramatic surprises on their audiences. Here, as an example, is a quotation from a speech delivered at a Loyola University graduation banquet. The subject is "In Search of Heroes":

> *I was fortunate to have had a friend and business partner who I believe was a hero. His upbringing was probably less promising than yours. His name was Marion Morrison. He was born of simple surroundings in a small Iowa town. His father was a druggist; his mother a telephone operator. He moved to California when he was young. He went to Glendale High School, then to USC. He took a summer job at a movie studio in the late 1920s and later started acting in movies for Raoul Walsh, who changed his [the young actor's] name to John Wayne.*

Had he been less skillful at constructing a speech, the speaker might have started that little story by saying something like, "Let me tell you about my friend and business partner, John Wayne." Instead, he gave the Duke's real name first and saved the kicker until last with a sort of matter-of-fact statement that Marion Morrison's employer had changed the young actor's name to John Wayne. It's not hard to imagine the surprise and delight the audience felt upon learning that the hero Marion Morrison was really the big guy who later dispatched hundreds of assorted train robbers, cattle rustlers, and other bad guys. It seems likely that the audience listened with anticipation to the rest of the speech.

Here's another example of dramatic surprise. It's excerpted from a speech I wrote for delivery by a Japanese government official at a conference in Orlando, Florida:

> *It is especially appropriate that we find ourselves here in Orlando, the gateway to Disney World, and in time to help*

celebrate the birthday of one of the best-known and most-admired of all Americans—one who is loved throughout the world, and most especially in Japan—[LONG PAUSE] Mickey Mouse. Let us hope that this association will be as youthful and vigorous in its fiftieth year as Mickey is today.

Commentator Paul Harvey uses a similar technique in his commentaries titled "The Rest of the Story." The difference is, Harvey's audiences are expecting a surprise ending and therefore the effect of the surprise is blunted somewhat.

From here to there

One of the marks of a professional writer is the ability to move smoothly from one subject to another—in other words, to use transitions effectively.

Good transitions are important in any kind of writing, but especially in speeches. If you're writing an article or a book, you can use subheads, bullets, or other typographical devices to tell the reader you're changing subjects—as I have done throughout this book.

In a speech, you must find other ways to make your transitions. Sometimes a slightly exaggerated pause or emphasis of a word or phrase serves as a transition. Pauses and emphases are the punctuation of speech: A short pause is a comma, a longer pause is a period. An even longer one might be equated with a typographical bullet. In writing speeches, I often skip extra lines or even write the word *PAUSE* in parentheses to indicate a pause used as a transition.

Without transitions, your speech can seem choppy or jarring. Transitions help ensure clarity by helping the listener shift mental gears. They are used to connect major parts of a speech—for example, the opening to the body and the body to the ending—and points to subpoints. They also signal the listener that a change of position, a contradiction, or an example is coming.

A transition can be a single sentence, a phrase, a word, or even a number, as in a list of numbered points.

Some common and simple transitions are *nevertheless . . . for example . . . let's examine that . . . however. . . .* The list is almost endless.

The repetition of a word, sentence, or phrase can be a transition. In the discussion of rhetorical devices I gave several examples of anaphora, the repetition of initial words at the beginning of successive phrases, clauses, sentences, or paragraphs. In one of the examples, the keynote speaker at the 1928 Democratic convention began six consecutive sentences with the name *Hamilton*. He was, you will recall, comparing Hamilton with Jefferson, and each repetition was, in effect, a transition to another comparison point.

Here is a good example from a speech by the executive director of the Georgia Ports Authority in which he is delivering a progress report of port improvements:

> *This project, plus the new Savannah River Bridge, which is opening this spring, will catapult the Savannah harbor into the modern era of shipping—at least so far as channel width and height requirements are concerned. Channel depth, however, is another matter.*

The last sentence, "Channel *depth*, however, is another matter," is a transition. It leads to a several-paragraph discussion of the need to deepen the channel in order to accommodate modern cargo vessels. The use of *however* and the stress on the word *depth* make the transition especially effective.

A question can sometimes serve as a transition. An executive of a company involved heavily in international trade spends several minutes discussing developments in recent years that have turned the world into a global marketplace. Then, abruptly, he asks, "What does all this mean to our company?"

The question is a transition that moves the discussion from the general—world events—to the specific, the practical effects of those events on his own company.

In reading and listening, we are barely conscious of transitions, but they are there, nevertheless, in all good writing. We usually become conscious of them only when they are not there.

As you continue to refine your speech-writing and speaking skills, you will find yourself becoming more conscious of transitions and how they contribute to ease of understanding.

In the next chapter, we'll continue the discussion of rhetorical devices and other professional speech-writing techniques. Incidentally, many of the techniques we've discussed, and will be discussing in the next chapter, can be found in writing other than speeches. Watch for them as you read newspapers, magazines, and books, and, of course, listen for them in any speeches you might hear. As you become more conscious of the techniques, you'll become more adept at using them.

"Common Ground and Common Sense"

Few orators can turn a phrase as Reverend Jesse Jackson can. Even his political detractors agree on that. Reverend Jackson's speeches often reflect his training as a minister and draw from his experience with the Civil Rights Movement. The following speech, slightly abridged, was delivered at the Democratic National Convention in July 1988, but he was clearly addressing a larger audience and attempting to put his stamp on the upcoming presidential campaign.

The term "common ground" permeates the text and is used anaphorically to emphasize key points. Metaphors, analogies, antithesis, and numerous personal references are used to good effect. The simple statement, "You must not," makes a dramatic closing:

Tonight we pause and give praise and honor to God for being good enough to allow us to be at this place at this time. When I look out at this convention, I see the face of America, red, yellow, brown, black and white, we're all precious in God's sight—the real rainbow coalition. All of us, all of us who are here and think that we are seated. But we're really standing on someone's shoulders. Ladies and gentlemen, Mrs. Rosa Parks, the mother of the civil rights movement. . . .

My right and my privilege to stand here before you has been won—in my lifetime—by the blood and the sweat of the innocent. Twenty-four years ago, the late Fanny Lou Hamer and Aaron Henry—who sits here tonight from Mississippi—were locked out on the streets of Atlantic City, the head of the Mississippi Freedom Democratic Party. But tonight, a black and white delegation from Mississippi is headed by Ed Cole, a black man, from Mississippi, 24 years later.

Many were lost in the struggle for the right to vote. Jimmy Lee Jackson, a young student, gave his life. Viola Luizzo, a white mother from Detroit, called nigger lover, and brains blown out at point blank range.

Schwerner, Goodman and Chaney—two Jews and a black—found in a common grave, bodies riddled with bullets in Mississippi. The four darling little girls in the church in Birmingham, Alabama. They died so that we might have a right to live. Dr. Martin Luther King, Jr. lies only a few miles from us tonight.

Tonight he must feel good as he looks down upon us. We sit here together, a rainbow, a coalition—the sons and daughters of slave masters and the sons and daughters of slaves sitting together around a common table, to decide the direction of our party and our country. His heart would be full tonight.

As a testament to the struggles of those who have gone before; as a legacy for those who will come after; as a tribute to the endurance, the patience, the courage of our forefathers and mothers: as an assurance that their prayers are being answered, their work has not been in vain, and hope is eternal; tomorrow night my name will go into nomination for the presidency of the United States of America.

We meet tonight at a crossroads, a point of decision. Shall we expand, be inclusive, find unity and power; or suffer division and impotence.

We come to Atlanta, the cradle of the old South, the crucible of the new South.

Tonight there is a sense of celebration because we are moved, fundamentally moved, from racial battlegrounds by law, to economic common ground, tomorrow we will challenge to move to higher ground.

Common ground!

Think of Jerusalem—the intersection where many trails met. A small village that became the birthplace for three great religions—Judaism, Christianity, and Islam.

Why was this village so blessed? Because it provided a crossroads where different people met, different cultures, and different civilizations could meet and find common ground.

When people come together, flowers always flourish and the air is rich with the aroma of a new spring. Take New York, the dynamic metropolis. What makes New York so special?

It is the invitation of the Statue of Liberty—give me your tired, your poor, your huddled masses who yearn to breathe free.

Not restricted to English only.

Many people, many cultures, many languages—with one thing in common, they yearn to breathe free.

Common ground!

Tonight in Atlanta, for the first time in this century we convene in the South. A state where governors once stood in school house doors. Where Julian Bond was denied his seat in the state legislature because of his conscientious objection to the Vietnam War. A city that, through its five black universities, has graduated more black students than any city in the world.

Atlanta, now a modern intersection of the new South.

Common ground!

That is the challenge to our party tonight.

Left wing. Right wing. Progress will not come through boundless liberalism nor static conservatism, but at the critical mass of mutual survival. It takes two wings to fly.

Whether you're a hawk or a dove, you're just a bird living in the same environment, in the same world. The Bible teaches that when lions and lambs lie down together, none will be afraid and there will be peace in the valley. It sounds impossible. Lions eat lambs. Lambs sensibly flee from lions. But even lions and lambs find common ground. Why? Because neither lions nor lambs want the forest to catch on fire. Neither lions nor lambs want acid rain to fall.

Neither lions nor lambs can survive nuclear war. If lions and lambs can find common ground, surely, we can as well, as civilized people.

The only time that we win is when we come together. In 1960, John Kennedy, the late John Kennedy, beat Richard Nixon by only 112,000 votes—less than one vote per precinct. He won by the margin of our hope. He brought us together. He reached out. He had the courage to defy his advisors and inquire about Dr. King's jailing in Albany, Georgia. We won by the margin of our hope, inspired by courageous leadership.

In 1964, Lyndon Johnson brought both wings together. The thesis, the antithesis and to create a synthesis and together we won.

In 1976, Jimmy Carter unified us again and we won. When we do not come together, we never win.

In 1968, division and despair in July led to our defeat in November.

In 1980, rancor in the spring and the summer led to Reagan in the fall. When we divide, we cannot win. We must find common ground as a basis for survival and development and change and growth.

Today when we debated, differed, deliberated, agreed to agree, agreed to disagree, when we had the good judgment to argue our case and then not self-destruct, George Bush was just a little further away from the White House and a little closer to private life.

Tonight, I salute Governor Michael Dukakis.

He has run a well-managed and a dignified campaign. No matter how tired, he always resisted the temptation to stoop to demagoguery. I've watched a good mind fast at work, with steel nerves, guiding his campaign out of the crowded field without appeal to the worst in us. I've watched his perspective grow as his environment has expanded. I've seen his toughness and tenacity close up. I know his commitment to public service.

Mike Dukakis's parents were a doctor and a teacher; my parents, a maid, a beautician and a janitor. There's a great gap between Brookline, Massachusetts and Haney Street, the Fieldcrest Village housing projects in Greenville, South Carolina. He studied law; I studied theology. There are differences of religion, region, and race; differences in experiences and perspectives. But the genius of America is that out of the many, we become one.

Providence has enabled our paths to intersect. His foreparents came to America on immigrant ships; my foreparents came to America on slave ships. But whatever the original ships, we're in the same boat tonight.

Our ships could pass in the night if we have a false sense of independence, or they could collide and crash. We would lose our passengers. But we can seek a higher reality and a greater good apart. We can drift on the broken pieces of Reaganomics, satisfy our baser instincts, and exploit the fears of our people. At our highest, we can call upon noble instincts and navigate this vessel to safety. The greater good is the common good.

As Jesus said, "Not my will, but thine be done." It was his way of saying there's a higher good beyond personal comfort or position.

The good of our nation is at stake—its commitment to working men and women, to the poor and the vulnerable, to the many in the world. With so many guided missiles, and so much misguided leadership, the stakes are exceedingly high. Our choice, full participation in a Democratic government, or more abandonment and neglect. And so this night, we choose not a false sense of independence, not our capacity to survive and endure.

Tonight we choose interdependency in our capacity to act and unite for the greater good. The common good is finding commitment to new priorities, to expansion and inclusion. A commitment to expanded participation in the Democratic Party at every level. A commitment to a shared national campaign strategy and involvement at every level. A commitment to new priorities that ensure that hope will be kept alive. A common ground commitment for a legislative agenda by empowerment for the John Conyers bill, universal, on-site, same-day registration everywhere—and commitment to D.C. statehood and empowerment—D.C. deserves statehood. A commitment to economic set-asides, a commitment to the Dellums bill for comprehensive sanctions against South Africa, a shared commitment to a common direction.

Common ground.

Easier said than done. Where do you find common ground at the point of challenge? This campaign has shown that politics need not be marketed by politicians, packaged by pollsters and pundits. Politics can be a marvel arena where people come together, define common ground.

We find common ground at the plant gate that closes on workers without notice. We find common ground at the farm auction where a good farmer loses his or her land to bad loans or diminishing markets. Common ground at the school-yard where teachers cannot get adequate pay, and students cannot get a scholarship and can't make a loan. Common ground, at the hospital admitting room where somebody tonight is dying because they cannot afford to go upstairs to a bed that's empty, waiting for someone with insurance to get sick. We are a better nation than that. We must do better.

Common ground.

What is leadership if not present help in a time of crisis? And so I met you at the point of challenge in Jay, Maine where paper workers were striking for fair wages; in Greenfield, Iowa, where family farmers struggle for a fair price; in Cleveland, Ohio, where working women seek comparable worth; in McFarland, California, where the children of Hispanic farm workers may be dying from poison land, dying in clusters with cancer; in the AIDS hospice in Houston, Texas, where the sick support one another, 12 are rejected by their own parents and friends.

Common ground.

America's not a blanket woven from one thread, one color, one cloth. When I was a child growing up in Greenville, South Carolina, and grandmother could not afford a blanket, she didn't complain and we did not freeze. Instead, she took pieces of old cloth—patches, wool, silk, gabardine, crockersack on the patches—barely good enough to wipe off your shoes with.

But they didn't stay that way very long. With sturdy hands and a strong cord, she sewed them together into a quilt, a thing of beauty and power and culture.

Now, Democrats, we must build such a quilt. Farmers, you seek fair prices and you are right, but you cannot stand alone. Your patch is not big enough. Workers, you fight for fair wages. You are right. But your patch labor is not big enough. Women, you seek comparable worth and pay equity. You are right. But your patch is not big enough. Women, mothers, who seek Head Start and day care and pre-natal care on the front side of life, rather than jail care and welfare on the back side of life, you're right, but your patch is not big enough.

Students, you seek scholarships. You are right. But your patch is not big enough. Blacks and Hispanics, when we fight for civil rights, we are right, but our patch is not big enough. Gays and lesbians, when you fight against discrimination and a cure for AIDS, you are right, but your patch is not big enough. Conservatives and progressives, when you fight for what you believe, right-wing, left-wing, hawk, dove you are right, from your point of view, but your point of view is not enough.

But don't despair. Be as wise as my grandmama. Pool the patches and the pieces together, bound by a common thread. When we form a great quilt of unity and common ground we'll have the power to bring about health care and housing and jobs and education and hope to our nation.

We the people can win. We stand at the end of a long dark night of reaction. We stand tonight united in a commitment to a new direction. For almost eight years, we've been led by those who view social good coming from private interest, who viewed public life as a means to increase private wealth. They have been prepared to sacrifice the common good of the many to satisfy the private interest and the wealth of a few. We believe in a government that's a tool of our democracy in service to the public, not an instrument of the aristocracy in search of private wealth.

We believe in government with the consent of the governed of, for, and by the people. We must not emerge into a new day with a new direction. Reaganomics, based on the belief that the rich had too much money—too little money, and the poor had too much.

That's classic Reaganomics. It believes that the poor had too much money and the rich had too little money.

So, they engaged in reverse Robin Hood—took from the poor, gave to the rich, paid for by the middle class. We cannot stand four more years of Reaganomics in any version, in any disguise.

How do I document that case? Seven years later, the richest 1 percent of our society pays 20 percent less in taxes; the poorest 10 percent pay 20 percent more. Reaganomics.

Reagan gave the rich and the powerful a multibillion-dollar party. Now, the party is over. He expects the people to pay for the damage. I take this principled position convention, let us not raise taxes on the poor and the middle class, but those who had the party, the rich and the powerful, must pay for the party!

I just want to take common sense to high places. We're spending $150 billion a year defending Europe and Japan 43 years after the war is over. We have more troops in Europe tonight than we had seven years ago, yet the threat of war is ever more remote. Germany and Japan are now creditor nations that means they've got a surplus. We are a debtor nation it means we are in debt.

Let them share more of the burden of their own defense, and use some of that money to build decent housing!

Use some of that money to educate our children!

Use some of that money for long-term health care!

Use some of that money to wipe out these slums and put America back to work!

I just want to take common sense to high places. If we can bail out Europe and Japan, if we can bail out Continental Bank and Chrysler and Mr. Iacocca makes $8,000 an hour, we can bail out the family farmer.

I just want to make common sense. It does not make sense to close down 650,000 family farms in this country while importing food from abroad subsidized by the U.S. government.

Let's make sense. It does not make sense to be escorting oil tankers up and down the Persian Gulf paying $2.50 for every $1.00 worth of oil we bring out while oil wells are capped in Texas, Oklahoma and Louisiana. I just want to make sense.

Leadership must meet the moral challenge of its day. What's the moral challenge of our day? We have public accommodations. We have the right to vote. We have open housing.

What's the fundamental challenge of our day? It is to end economic violence. Plant closing without notice, economic violence. Even the greedy do not profit long from greed. Economic violence. Most poor people are not lazy. They're not black. They're not brown. They're mostly white, and female and young.

But whether white, black or brown, the hungry baby's belly turned inside out is the same color. Call it pain. Call it hurt. Call it agony. Most poor people are not on welfare.

Some of them are illiterate and can't read the want-ad sections. And when they can, they can't find a job that matches their address. They work hard every day, I know. I live amongst them. I'm one of them.

I know they work. I'm a witness. They catch the early bus. They work every day. They raise other people's children. They work every day. They clean the streets. They work every day. They drive vans with cabs. They work every day. They change the beds you slept in these hotels last night and can't get a union contract. They work every day.

No more. They're not lazy. Someone must defend them because it's right, and they cannot speak for themselves. They work in hospitals. I know they do. They wipe the bodies of those who are sick with fever and pain. They empty their bedpans. They clean out their commode. No job is beneath them, and yet when they get sick, they cannot lie in the bed they made up every day. America, that is not right. We are a better nation than that. We are a better nation than that.

We need a real war on drugs. You can't just say no. It's deeper than that. You can't just get a palm reader or an astrologer; it's more profound than that. We're spending $150 billion on drugs a year. We've gone from ignoring it to focusing on the children. Children cannot buy $150 billion worth of drugs a year. A few high profile athletes—athletes are not laundering $150 billion a year—bankers are.

I met the children in Watts who are unfortunate in their despair. Their grapes of hope have become raisins of despair, and they're turning to each other and they're self-destructing but I stayed with them all night long. I wanted to hear their case. They said, "Jesse Jackson, as you challenge us to say no to drugs, you're right. And to not sell them, you're right. And to not use these guns, you're right."

And, by the way, the promise of CETA—they displaced CETA. They did not replace CETA. We have neither jobs nor houses nor services nor training—no way out. Some of us take drugs as anesthesia for our pain. Some take drugs as a way of pleasure—both short-term pleasure and long-term pain. Some sell drugs to make money. It's wrong, we know. But you need to know that we know. We can go and buy the drugs by the boxes at the port. If we can buy the drugs at the port, don't you believe the federal government can stop it if they want to?

They say, "We don't have Saturday night specials any more." They say, "We buy AK-47s and Uzis, the latest lethal weapons. We buy them across the counter on Long Beach Boulevard." You cannot fight a war on drugs unless and until you are going to challenge the bankers and the gun sellers and those who grow them. Don't just focus on the children, let's stop drugs at the level of supply and demand. We must end the scourge on the American culture.

Leadership. What difference will we make? Leadership can not just go along to get along. We must do more than change presidents. We must change direction. Leadership must face the moral challenge of our day. The nuclear war build-up is irrational. Strong leadership cannot desire to look tough, and let that stand in the way of the pursuit of peace. Leadership must reverse the arms race.

At least we should pledge no first use. Why? Because first use begat first retaliation, and that's mutual annihilation That's not a rational way out. No use at all—let's think it out, and not fight it out, because it's an unwinnable fight. Why hold a card that you can never drop? Let's give peace a chance.

Leadership—we now have this marvelous opportunity to have a breakthrough with the Soviets. Last year, 200,000 Americans visited the Soviet Union. There's a chance for joint ventures into space, not Star Wars and the war arms escalation but a space defense initiative. Let's build in space together, and demilitarize the heavens. There's a way out.

America, let us expand. When Mr. Reagan and Mr. Gorbachev met, there was a big meeting. They represented together one-eighth of the human race. Seven-eighths of the human race was locked out of that room. Most people in the world tonight half are Asian, one-half of them are Chinese. There are 22 nations in the Middle East. There's Europe; 40 million Latin Americans next door to us the Caribbean; Africa—a half-billion people. Most people in the world today are yellow or brown or black, non-Christian, poor, female, young, and don't speak English—in the real world.

This generation must offer leadership to the real world. We're losing ground in Latin America, the Middle East, South Africa, because we're not focusing on the real world, that real world. We must use basic principles, support international law. We stand the most to gain from it. Support human rights: we believe in that. Support self-determination; we'll build on that. Support economic development; you know it's right. Be consistent, and gain our moral authority in the world.

I challenge you tonight, my friends, let's be bigger and better as a nation and as a party. We have basic challenges. Freedom in South Africa we've already agreed as Democrats to declare South Africa to be a terrorist state. But don't just stop there. Get South Africa out of Angola. Free Namibia. Support the front-line states. We must have a new, humane human rights assistance policy in Africa.

I'm often asked, "Jesse, why do you take on these tough issues? They're not very political. We can't win that way."

If an issue is morally right, it will eventually be political. It may be political and never be right. Fannie Lou Hamer didn't have the most votes in Atlantic City, but her principles have outlasted every delegate who voted to lock her out. Rosa Parks did not have the most votes, but she was morally right. Dr. King didn't have the most votes about the Vietnam War, but he was morally right. If we're principled first, our politics will fall in place.

Jesse, why did you take these big bold initiatives? A poem by an unknown author went something like this: We mastered the air, we've conquered the sea, and annihilated distance and prolonged life, we were not wise enough to live on this earth without war and without hate.

As for Jesse Jackson, I'm tired of sailing by little boat, far inside the harbor bar. I want to go out where the big ships float, out on the deep where the great ones are. And should my frail craft prove too slight, the waves that sweep those billows o'er, I'd rather go down in a stirring fight than drown to death in the sheltered shore.

We've got to go out, my friends, where the big boats are.

And then, for our children, young America, hold your head high now. We can win. We must not lose you to drugs and violence, premature pregnancy, suicide, cynicism, pessimism and despair. We can win.

Wherever you are tonight, I challenge you to hope and to dream. Don't submerge your dreams. Exercise above all else, even on drugs, dream of the day you're drug-free. Even in the gutter, dream of the day that you'll be up on your feet again. You must never stop dreaming. Face reality, yes. But don't stop with the way things are; dream of things as they ought to be. Dream. Face pain, but love, hope, faith, and dreams will help you rise above the pain.

Use hope and imagination as weapons of survival and progress, but you keep on dreaming, young America. Dream of peace. Peace is rational and reasonable. War is irrational in this age and unwinnable.

Dream of teachers who teach for life and not for living. Dream of doctors who are concerned more about public health than private wealth. Dream of lawyers more concerned about justice than a judgeship. Dream of preachers who are concerned more about prophecy than profiteering. Dream on the high road of sound values.

And in America, as we go forth to September, October and November and then beyond, America must never surrender to a high moral challenge.

Do not surrender to drugs. The best drug policy is a no first use. Don't surrender with needles and cynicism. Let's have no first use on the one hand, or clinics on the other. Never surrender, young America.

Go forward. America must never surrender to malnutrition. We can feed the hungry and clothe the naked. We must never surrender. We must go forward. We must never surrender to illiteracy. Invest in our children. Never surrender; and go forward.

We must never surrender to inequality. Women cannot compromise ERA or comparable worth. Women are making 60 cents on the dollar to what a man makes. Women cannot buy meat cheaper. Women cannot buy bread cheaper. Women cannot buy milk cheaper. Women deserve to get paid for the work that you do. It's right and it's fair.

Don't surrender, my friends. Those who have AIDS tonight, you deserve our compassion. Even with AIDS you must not surrender in your wheelchairs. I see you sitting here tonight in those wheelchairs. I've stayed with you. I've reached out to you across our nation. Don't you give up. I know it's tough sometimes. People look down on you. It took you a little more effort to get here tonight.

And no one should look down on you, but sometimes mean people do.

The only justification we have for looking down on someone is that we're going to stop and pick them up. But even in your wheelchairs, don't you give up. We cannot forget 50 years ago when our backs were against the wall, Roosevelt was in a wheelchair. I would rather have Roosevelt in a wheelchair than Reagan and Bush on a horse. Don't you surrender and don't you give up.

Don't surrender and don't give up. Why can I challenge you this way? Jesse Jackson, you don't understand my situation. You be on television. You don't understand. I see you with the big people. You don't understand my situation. I understand. You're seeing me on TV but you don't know the me that makes me, me. They wonder why does Jesse run, because they see me running for the White House. They don't see the house I'm running from.

I have a story. I wasn't always on television. Writers were not always outside my door. When I was born late one afternoon, October 8th, in Greenville, South Carolina, no writers asked my mother her name. Nobody chose to write down our address. My mama was not supposed to make it. And I was not supposed to make it. You see, I was born to a teen-age mother who was born to a teen-age mother.

I understand. I know abandonment and people being mean to you, and saying you're nothing and nobody, and can never be anything. I understand. Jesse Jackson is my third name. I'm adopted. When I had no name, my grandmother gave me her name. My name was Jesse Burns until I was 12. So I wouldn't have a blank space, she gave me a name to hold me over. I understand when nobody knows your name. I understand when you have no name. I understand.

I wasn't born in the hospital. Mama didn't have insurance. I was born in the bed at home. I really do understand. Born in a three-room house, bathroom in the backyard, slop jar by the bed, no hot and cold running water. I understand. Wallpaper used for decoration? No. For a windbreaker. I understand. I'm a working person's person, that's why I understand you whether you're black or white.

I understand work. I was not born with a silver spoon in my mouth. I had a shovel programmed for my hand. My mother, a working woman. So many days she went to work early with runs in her stockings. She knew better, but she wore runs in her stockings so that my brother and I could have matching socks and not be laughed at school.

I understand. At 3 o'clock on Thanksgiving Day we couldn't eat turkey because mama was preparing someone else's turkey at 3 o'clock. We had to play football to entertain ourselves and then around 6 o'clock she would get off the Alta Vista bus; then we would bring up the leftovers and eat our turkey leftovers, the carcass, the cranberries around 8 o'clock at night. I really do understand.

Every one of these funny labels they put on you, those of you who are watching this broadcast tonight in the projects, on the corners, I understand. Call you outcast, low down, you can't make it, you're nothing, you're from nobody, subclass, underclass—when you see Jesse Jackson, when my name goes in nomination, your name goes in nomination.

I was born in the slum, but the slum was not born in me. And it wasn't born in you, and you can make it. Wherever you are tonight you can make it. Hold your head high, stick your chest out. You can make it. It gets dark sometimes, but the morning comes. Don't you surrender. Suffering breeds character. Character breeds faith. In the end faith will not disappoint.

You must not.

— CHAPTER TEN —

Wisdom of the Ages

Chapter Nine began a discussion of rhetorical devices and techniques that professional speech writers use to make their speeches more rhythmic, more dramatic, and more memorable. Remember triads and anaphora? You've just read a triad that is also an example of anaphora—*more rhythmic, more dramatic, more memorable.*

Now I want you to do a little practice exercise. Read the list of techniques below. For each one, think about what the technique is and try to recall, either from the text or from your own experience, at least one example. Then choose a subject that you might like to write a speech about and write a few sentences or paragraphs in which you apply some or all of the techniques to your subject:

- Alliteration
- Antithesis
- Hyperbole
- Understatement
- Dramatic surprise
- Anaphora
- Triad
- Metaphor
- Analogy
- Simile

If you don't feel you're ready for this exercise, continue reading, but please come back to it when you feel you are ready. The practice will serve you well.

In this chapter, you'll learn how to put the wisdom of the ages into your speech. It's really quite simple; you just quote somebody. Quoting is one of the most commonly used and most effective devices to enliven a speech.

In others' words

Read the following three quotations and try to identify the source of each. Here's the first:

> *We pause to ask what our country has done for each of us and to ask ourselves what we can do for our country in return.*

Sound familiar? How about this one?:

> *In the great fulfillment, we must have a citizenship less concerned with what the government can do for it and more anxious about what it can do for the nation.*

Now the third:

> *And so, my fellow Americans, ask not what your country can do for you. Ask what you can do for your country.*

The third one, of course, is from John F. Kennedy's inaugural address on January 20, 1961. You've no doubt heard or read that memorable line often, and of course it has been referred to previously in this book. The first is from a speech by Justice Oliver Wendell Holmes Jr., May 30, 1884. The second is from a speech by Warren G. Harding, delivered at the Republican national convention on June 7, 1916.

The messages are virtually identical, although Kennedy's is by far the most eloquently expressed. Is it possible that Kennedy's speech writer paraphrased either Harding's or Holmes's all-but-forgotten line and turned it into Kennedy's most memorable one?

It's not only possible, it's likely. But this is not to say that Kennedy or his speech writer was a plagiarist. The idea is much the same in each of the three quotations, but the words are quite different. Some sources, incidentally, attribute that idea to Frederick I, King of Prussia, who lived some three hundred years ago. Maybe Kennedy borrowed it from Harding who borrowed it from Holmes who borrowed it from Frederick. Where did old Freddy get it? Who knows? Who cares? The point now is that Kennedy "owns" it because he made the most effective use of it.

Every American is familiar with Patrick Henry's ringing declaration, "Give me liberty or give me death." But few know that the fiery British suffragette Emmeline Pankhurst echoed strikingly similar sentiments in a speech in 1913:

We can't do it ourselves, but we will put the money in the position whereto they will have to choose between giving us freedom or giving us death.

The words of both Patrick Henry and Mrs. Pankhurst were very close in meaning to those of the Greek poet Aeschylus, who died almost five hundred years before the birth of Christ. He wrote, "Better to die on your feet than live on your knees."

The truth is, nothing under the sun is really new. I recall writing a speech in which I used the line "The only constant is change." To be certain I wasn't stealing anyone's line; I checked several sources. I learned that the idea of change being the only constant has been used several times and goes back at least to 513 B.C. and the Greek philosopher Heraclitus.

So if you have an idea that's been used before, you need not hesitate to use it in your own speech provided you put it in your own words. The paraphrase must be substantial. Just changing a word or two words isn't enough. Paraphrasing is useful also because it enables you to adapt the thought to the context of your speech rather than trying to make your speech fit a particular quotation that you happen to like. So the various and numerous sources of quotations can be sources of ideas. And, by the way, *inspiration.*

Credit where credit is due

If you use a quotation word-for-word, or substantially word-for-word, you must give full credit to the originator. Not to give credit is to be dishonest and to hold yourself up for well-deserved criticism. Of course, you can and should also give credit for a closely paraphrased quotation. For example, if a speaker said something like, "We have nothing to be afraid of except the consequences of being afraid," most audiences would recognize that as a clumsy knockoff of FDR's "We have nothing to fear but fear itself." If for some reason the speaker did not want to use Roosevelt's exact words, it would be appropriate to say, "As Franklin D. Roosevelt once observed, fear is the only thing we have to fear."

When you use a well-selected quotation, you put authority on your side and give credibility to your words. If you're speaking on, say, women's rights, what could be better than to have Susan B. Anthony join you at the lectern and help you make your points? You can have her, though she has been long a-moldering in her grave, by using her words to reinforce your own. It was she who pricked the nation's conscience by saying:

> *It was we, the people; not we, the white male citizens; nor yet we, the male citizens; but we the whole people who formed the Union. And we formed it, not to give the blessings of liberty, but to secure them; not to the half of ourselves and the half of our postery, but to the whole people—women as well as men.*

Could you say it better? If not, let Susan B. give you a hand.

Or, if you're speaking on leadership, you can get some help from General Stormin' Norman Schwarzkopf?

> *You can manage* a business, but you *lead* people. People go to work to succeed, and it is the duty of a leader to help the succeed.

Sources aplenty

As a speaker or speech writer, you can, by using quotations, tap into an almost unlimited source of ideas. Quotations are effective as openings, endings, and everywhere between. No matter what subject you're speaking on, you'll find scores of appropriate quotations, if you just know where to look.

The first thought that comes to mind when quotations are mentioned is that old standby, Bartlett's. But *Bartlett's Familiar Quotations* is just one of many compilations of quotes—familiar and unfamiliar. For a serious writer, one book of quotations is not enough. I have several. My favorite is *The Home Book of Quotations*, compiled by Burton Stevenson. I also like *The Oxford Dictionary of Modern Quotations*, by Tony Augarde. A good source for light quotes is *1,911 Best Things Anybody Ever Said*, compiled by Robert Byrne. And a good source for business quotes is *The Ultimate Book of Business Quotations*, edited by Stuart Crainer.

I also have a computer program that has a database of ten thousand quotations. It is incredibly fast and easy to use. I can search by topic, author, or source, or I can just browse and see what turns up. I can even add my own favorite quotations to the program so I'll always be able to find one when I need it. And, of course, I can use the "copy and paste" feature to put a quote into the document I'm working on. Although ten thousand quotes might seem like a lot, it really isn't. My *Home Book of Quotations* has almost three thousand pages, and each page has fifteen, twenty, or more quotations.

In addition, I have a CD-ROM, entitled *World's Greatest Speeches,* with the full texts of four hundred of the world's best speeches. If I need a quote on the subject of, say, leadership, I can quickly find every speech in which the word *leadership* appears, and the word will be highlighted in every use. To give you an idea of how this works, I did just that. The computer program listed ninety-nine speeches in which *leadership* was used in any context. The first happened to be Franklin D. Roosevelt's first inaugural address, March 4, 1933. The first time *leadership* was mentioned was in this sentence:

> *In every dark hour of our national life, a leadership of frankness and vigor has met with the understanding and support of the people themselves.*

Not a bad quote, for a five-minute search. If I had been working on a speech when I found it, it might not have been appropriate, but there are plenty more where it came from.

Various anthologies compiled especially for speakers include many quotations and anecdotes. Books on speech writing often have lists of eloquent quotations selected by the authors of the books. *Reader's Digest* publishes quotes frequently. Several newsletters for speech writers include quotes that often are too new to be included in any of the other sources and for that reason may be especially valuable.

Books, newspapers, magazines, and television—even comic strips—are excellent sources. The Bible and the works of Shakespeare are especially rich in quotable material.

How to use quotes

When you are looking for someone to quote, you want to be certain the one you select will be familiar to your audience. You might find a wonderful quote by Joe MacSnerd, but if the people in your audience have never heard of MacSnerd, the quote won't do much for your credibility. Of course, you can always tell your audience who MacSnerd is, but that can be awkward. Better leave him to wallow in obscurity.

On the other hand, don't carry familiarity so far that you select tired old quotes that have been used over and over. With all the thousands available, you should, without too much effort, be able to come up with a reasonably fresh one.

Sometimes you can find a new twist or a new wrinkle for an overused quote. For example, this quote from Ralph Waldo Emerson, has had more than its share of exposure in one form or another:

If a man write a better book, preach a better sermon, or make a better mousetrap than his neighbor, tho' he build his house in the woods, the world will make a beaten path to his door.

I once used it this way in a speech for a marketing executive:

Emerson said that if you build a better mousetrap, the world will beat a path to your door . . . or words to that effect. That's only half true. If you build a better mousetrap, the world will beat a path to your door—if the world knows about it. That's what marketing is all about. Telling the world about our mousetrap. It's not enough to have a good product and good service, we have to let our potential customers know it.

I thought that use was sufficiently different to justify giving Emerson's mousetrap metaphor another turn in the spotlight.

Some speakers seem to have trouble getting into a quote. Resist the temptation to say things like "I believe it was Emerson who said . . ." And avoid the expression "quote unquote." The best way to let the audience know when the quote begins and ends is to use pauses and a different tone of voice. Be certain the audience knows when the quote ends and when the speaker resumes. Some speakers who use reading glasses will put them on when they begin a quote and remove them when they end it. This is effective even when the speaker doesn't really need the specs to read. Another good device is to pick up the paper you're reading from and let the audience see that you're reading. Either of these devices works well and might even add credibility.

Ronald Reagan often used quotes in his speeches. Speaking to students at Oxford University, December 4, 1992, he quoted Winston Churchill:

At the height of World War II, Sir Winston Churchill reminded Britons that, "These are not dark days; these are great days—the greatest days our history has ever lived; and we must thank God that we have been allowed, each of us according to our stations, to play a part in making these days memorable in the history of our race."

You can be sure that Reagan did not say, "At the height of World War II, Sir Winston Churchill reminded Britons that, and I quote . . ."

No doubt he accomplished the same purpose by a slight pause and a slight change of tone.

The most important thing to remember about using quotations effectively is that a quotation should lead smoothly and logically into a point that you want to make. Resist the temptation to twist your thoughts around to accommodate a quote that you happen to like. And, of course, the tie-in to the subject must be made clear quickly. Otherwise, your audience will be thinking, *Okay, so what's the point?*

And, by the way, don't make your quotation too long. The audience might have trouble following it. If the quote you want to use seems too long, use part of it verbatim and paraphrase or summarize the rest.

Let's examine some different ways in which quotations have been used in speeches. In each example, note how the quotation ties in with the subject of the speech or the point the speaker wants to make. Our first example is from a speech by a business executive to a Kiwanis Club. He quotes the great American philosopher Charlie Brown, of the "Peanuts" comic strip:

> *Whenever I speak to a service club I'm reminded of a "Peanuts" comic strip that appeared several years ago. In the first panel of the strip, good old Charlie Brown is on the pitcher's mound. He is saying to himself, "It's the last of the ninth. The bases are loaded. There are two outs and the count is three balls and two strikes on the batter."*
>
> *The second panel shows one of those "meetings on the mound" that baseball is famous for. Charlie is surrounded by his teammates, who are shouting, "Throw him a fastball, Charlie Brown." "Throw him a curve." And so on.*
>
> *In the last panel, there is Charlie Brown, all alone on the mound, knowing that he's the guy who holds the game in the palm of his hand, knowing that it's his game to win or lose. He is saying to himself, "The world is filled with people who are anxious to serve in an advisory capacity."*

The speaker uses the quote as a lead-in to compliment the Kiwanians:

> *What I like about the Kiwanis and other service clubs is that you're willing to do a lot more than just serve in an advisory capacity. You go out and make things happen in this community and this nation. You know that the ball game is in your hands.*

In the next example, the speaker uses a quotation from a well-known literary classic to draw a vivid analogy:

> *Dr. Frankenstein, in Mary Shelley's famous novel, described his first look at his creation this way: "I beheld the wretch—the monster whom I had created." Today we can look at our national healthcare system in much the same way—a monster, dangerous, out of control, a creature of our own making. And like Dr. Frankenstein's monster, our monster is a product of good intentions. Yet it has the potential to destroy us.*

Speakers often quote from Lewis Carroll's *Alice in Wonderland*, and many of the best-known lines from that classic are overused. Here is an example of one that has not been overused. The speaker uses it effectively to lead into the subject:

> *You're familiar with the story of Alice in Wonderland. And you may recall after falling down that fateful hole, Alice encountered a large blue caterpillar who, upon seeing her, inquired, "Who are you?"*
>
> *To which Alice replied, rather shyly, "I-I hardly know, sir, just at present—at least I knew who I was when I got up this morning, but I think I must have been changed several times since then."*
>
> *Our business has changed so rapidly that sometimes we're like Alice. We hardly know who we are just at present.*

A corporate executive speaking about the National Alliance of Business, an organization that works to secure pledges of private-sector jobs and training for the disadvantaged, reached back in memory for the words of an old song:

> *You read the morning paper from the front to the back,*
> *But every job that's open needs a man with a knack.*
> *So put it right back in the rack, Jack.*

The executive ties the song to the subject neatly:

> *That old song pretty well expresses the frustration that some men and women might feel when they can't get a job because they have no experience and can't get experience because no one will hire them without experience.*

An executive of one of the Big-3 automakers used a profound quotation from George Bernard Shaw to open a speech to the Michigan Freedom Foundation. He preserves the drama of the opening by beginning with the quotation—no preliminaries:

The reasonable man adapts himself to the world. The unreasonable one persists in trying to adapt the world to himself. Therefore all progress depends on the unreasonable man." Good morning. Those were the words of the famous British writer George Bernard Shaw. This morning I want to ask you to be unreasonable people.

The speaker follows the opening with an inspirational story about Vic Wertz, a pro baseball player whom he called "an unreasonable man" because he returned to his career after fighting polio.

Sometimes it's effective to make a point first, then use a quotation to support it. Here, for example, is an excerpt from a speech on the importance of research and development, delivered by an executive of General Electric:

You want to invent and develop the best technology, to hone, to refine, to improve. But you also want to get into production fast, to get to market fast. The Japanese have resolved this conflict by moving rapidly into markets with adequate, but not forefront, technology, while we take time to perfect a more advanced technology. They've been tremendously successful with this old, but effective, strategy, which can be traced back at least to the British radar pioneer of the 1930s, Sir Robert Watson Watt, who expressed it this way: "Give me the third best technology. The second best won't be ready in time. The best will never be ready."

A speech I wrote some years ago for a bank executive makes good use of a quotation from the late Dean Rusk, as reported in *Reader's Digest*:

A couple of years ago, Reader's Digest *published an anecdote about a speech to the graduating class at the University of Southern California by Dean Rusk, who was Secretary of State under Presidents Kennedy and Johnson and who is now a highly respected professor of International Law and Diplomacy at the University of Georgia. Mr. Rusk told the USC graduates that they should be grateful to members of past generations. "They have gone to special pains," he said, "to save some interesting problems for you to solve."*

Well, after I have finished my speech, you'll have reason to be grateful to me, because I have no intention of solving all your interesting problems.

Indirect quotes

A quotation may be used as either a direct quote or an indirect quote. If you use a quote, even if it's indirect rather than direct, don't mangle it. A couple of years ago, an actor doing a TV commercial for an Atlanta bank solemnly intoned something like this: "Shakespeare said life is divided into seven stages." The Bard said nothing of the kind. As the copywriter would have known had he taken the trouble to look it up, Shakespeare wrote, "All the world's a stage and all the men and women merely players; they have their exits and their entrances; and one man in his time plays many parts, his acts being seven ages." Nothing there about stages.

Indirect quotations are sometimes preferable to direct quotations. An indirect quotation is more easily shortened and therefore can be snappier and more pithy. Here are some examples of indirect quotations. The first is from a speech about banking regulations:

> *Art Buchwald said in a recent speech in Atlanta that 1980 would go down in history as the year in which it was cheaper to borrow money from the Mafia than from the local bank. Of course, what Mr. Buchwald didn't say was that the Mafia has an unfair competitive advantage. It doesn't have to worry about federal regulations. And the Mafia doesn't have any collection problems, either.*

The next example was used by a company president in a speech congratulating employees on a good year for their company:

> *Now . . . having said all those good things, I have to recall what the late Adlai Stevenson had to say about praise: Praise is like perfume; it's fine as long as you don't swallow it.*

This one is from an introduction of a speaker who was a person of great accomplishment:

Thomas Edison once said that if we did all the things we are capable of doing, we would astonish ourselves. Looking at the résumé of our speaker makes me wonder if I am about to introduce a very astonished fellow.

And here is an indirect quote from a speech about developing mutually profitable business partnerships:

Andrew Carnegie, who knew a thing or two about making money, once said that no one can become rich without enriching others.

The speaker then uses the quotation to lead to points about how a business can prosper only by helping its customers to prosper.

*   *   *

Quotations put the wisdom of the ages at your disposal. As long as you can use quotations when you deliver a speech, you don't have to be at the lectern alone. You can take with you just about anybody you like to help you get your message across.

In the next chapter, we conclude our discussion of techniques and rhetorical devices that you can use, as professional writers do, to improve your speeches.

Podium Presence

For the fifth and final "Podium Presence" tip, let me answer a question that's often asked: "What, if anything, should I eat and drink before I make a speech?"

Well, of course, everyone's body is different. What would be bad for one person might not bother another. There are, however, some useful, if rather general, guidelines about eating and drinking.

First and most important, eat lightly. A heavy meal can make you mentally and physically sluggish. For some time after you eat, your body's resources are hard at work in the process of digesting your food. Some speakers don't eat at all before they speak, but most need at least some food to sustain them, so a light meal is probably best for most people. Don't eat hot or spicy foods or foods that may be hard to digest, especially if such foods tend to cause you problems.

Second, don't drink a lot of liquids if you have a tendency to experience nature's call frequently. The best thing to drink is plain water, which helps lubricate your vocal cords. It's a good idea to have a pitcher of water handy while you're speaking. Stopping to take a sip of water now and then, whether you're thirsty or not, forces you to slow down and helps you relax. Coffee isn't bad if you don't overdo it. But remember, caffeine acts as a short-term stimulant but long-term depressant. It also causes dry mouth in some people. Carbonated drinks generate gas and might cause you to belch at an inopportune time.

Finally, don't take pills, alcohol, or anything else to help you relax or reduce your inhibitions. They are self-defeating.

Much of this advice on eating and drinking is common sense, but common sense is strangely uncommon at times.

"The Battle Has Been Joined"

President George Bush will not be remembered as a great orator. His voice had a sort of nasal twang, and his delivery tended to be flat and boring. His syntax was often mangled. But his speeches were well-crafted and quite substantive. He was at his best when dealing with foreign affairs. Below is his report to the nation on the beginning of the bombing of Iraq, January 16, 1991. Notice how effectively he bolstered his case with quotations from four military men involved in the Gulf War—a general, a corporal, a master sergeant, and a lieutenant. The technique of using references to "ordinary people" in speeches is reminiscent of the speeches of Mr. Bush's former boss, Ronald Reagan. Each quotation in Mr. Bush's speech is introduced anaphorically with "Listen to . . ." He also uses anaphora by several times repeating "While the world waits," which he changes on the final use to "While the world prays":

Just two hours ago, allied air forces began an attack on military targets in Iraq and Kuwait. These attacks continue as I speak. Ground forces are not engaged. This conflict started August 2, when the dictator of Iraq invaded a small and helpless neighbor. Kuwait, a member of the Arab League and a member of the United Nations, was crushed, its people brutalized. Five months ago, Saddam Hussein started this cruel war against Kuwait; tonight, the battle has been joined.

This military action, taken in accord with United Nations resolutions and with the consent of the United States Congress, follows months of constant and virtually endless diplomatic activity on the part of the United Nations, the United States and many, many other countries.

Arab leaders sought what became known as an Arab solution, only to conclude that Saddam Hussein was unwilling to leave Kuwait. Others traveled to Baghdad in a variety of efforts to restore peace and justice. Our Secretary of State, James Baker, held an historic meeting in Geneva, only to be totally rebuffed.

This past weekend, in a last-ditch effort, the Secretary General of the United Nations went to the Middle East with peace in his heart, his second such mission. And he came back from Baghdad with no progress at all in getting Saddam Hussein to withdraw from Kuwait.

Now, the 28 countries with forces in the Gulf area have exhausted all reasonable efforts to reach a peaceful resolution, and have no choice but to drive Saddam from Kuwait by force. We will not fail.

As I report to you, air attacks are under way against military targets in Iraq. We are determined to knock out Saddam Hussein's nuclear bomb potential. We will also destroy his chemical weapons facilities. Much of Saddam's artillery and tanks will be destroyed. Our operations are designed to best protect the lives of all the coalition forces by targeting Saddam's vast military arsenal.

Initial reports from General Schwarzkopf are that our operations are proceeding according to plan. Our objectives are clear: Saddam Hussein's forces will leave Kuwait. The legitimate government of Kuwait will be restored to its rightful place, and Kuwait will once again be free.

Iraq will eventually comply with all relevant United Nations resolutions, and then, when peace is restored, it is our hope that Iraq will live as a peaceful and cooperative member of the family of nations, thus enhancing the security and stability of the Gulf.

Some may ask, why act now? Why not wait? The answer is clear. The world could wait no longer. Sanctions, though having some effect, showed no signs of accomplishing their objective. Sanctions were tried for well over five months, and we and our allies concluded that sanctions alone would not force Saddam from Kuwait.

While the world waited, Saddam Hussein systematically raped, pillaged and plundered a tiny nation no threat to his own. He subjected the people of Kuwait to unspeakable atrocities, and among those maimed and murdered, innocent children.

While the world waited, Saddam sought to add to the chemical weapons arsenal he now possesses, an infinitely more dangerous weapon of mass destruction—a nuclear weapon. And while the world waited, while the world talked peace and withdrawal, Saddam Hussein dug in and moved massive forces into Kuwait.

While the world waited, while Saddam stalled, more damage was being done to the fragile economies of the Third World emerging democracies of Eastern Europe, to the entire world including to our own economy.

The United States, together with the United Nations, exhausted every means at our disposal to bring this crisis to a peaceful end. However, Saddam clearly felt that by stalling and threatening and defying the United Nations, he could weaken the forces arrayed against him.

While the world waited, Saddam Hussein met every overture of peace with open contempt. While the world prayed for peace, Saddam prepared for war.

I had hoped that when the United States Congress, in historic debate, took its resolute action, Saddam would realize he could not prevail, and would move out of Kuwait in accord with the United Nations resolutions. He did not do that. Instead, he remained intransigent, certain that time was on his side.

Saddam was warned over and over again to comply with the will of the United Nations, leave Kuwait or be driven out. Saddam has arrogantly rejected all warnings. Instead he tried to make this a dispute between Iraq and the United States of America.

Well, he failed. Tonight 28 nations from five continents, Europe and Asia, Africa and the Arab League have forces in the Gulf area standing shoulder to shoulder against Saddam Hussein. These countries had hoped the use of force could be avoided. Regrettably, we now believe that only force will make him leave.

Prior to ordering our forces into battle, I instructed our military commanders to take every necessary step to prevail as quickly as possible, and with the greatest degree of protection possible for American and Allied service men and women. I've told the American people before that this will not be another Vietnam, and I repeat this here tonight. Our troops will have the best possible support in the entire world, and they will not be asked to fight with one hand tied behind their back. I'm hopeful that this fighting will not go on for long and that casualties will be held to an absolute minimum.

This is an historic moment. We have in this past year made great progress in ending the long era of conflict and cold war. We have before us the opportunity to forge for ourselves and for future generations a new world order, a world where the rule of law, not the law of the jungle, governs the conduct of nations.

When we are successful, and we will be, we have a real chance at this new world order, an order in which a credible United Nations can use its peacekeeping role to fulfill the promise and vision of the U.N.'s founders. We have no argument with the people of Iraq. Indeed, for the innocents caught in this conflict, I pray for their safety.

Our goal is not the conquest of Iraq. It is the liberation of Kuwait. It is my hope that somehow the Iraqi people can, even now, convince their dictator that he must lay down his arms, leave Kuwait and let Iraq itself rejoin the family of peace-loving nations.

Thomas Paine wrote many years ago: "These are the times that try men's souls." Those well-known words are so very true today. But even as planes of the multi-national forces attack Iraq I prefer to think of peace, not war. I am convinced not only that we will prevail, but that out of the horror of combat will come the recognition that no nation can stand against a world united. No nation will be permitted to brutally assault its neighbor.

No President can easily commit our sons and daughters to war. They are the nation's *finest*. Ours is an all-volunteer force, magnificently trained, highly motivated. The troops know why they're there. And listen to what they say, because they've said it better than any President or Prime Minister ever could. Listen to Hollywood Huddleston, Marine lance corporal. He says: "Let's free these people so we can go home and be free again." And he's right. The terrible crimes and tortures committed by Saddam's henchmen against the innocent people of Kuwait are an affront to mankind and a challenge to the freedom of all.

Listen to one of our great officers out there, Marine Lieut. Gen. Walter Boomer. He said:

"There are things worth fighting for. A world in which brutality and lawlessness are allowed to go unchecked isn't the kind of world we're going to want to live in."

Listen to Master Sgt. J.P. Kendall of the 82d Airborne:

"We're here for more than just the price of a gallon of gas. What we're doing is going to chart the future of the world for the next hundred years. It's better to deal with this guy now than five years from now."

And finally, we should all sit up and listen to Jackie Jones, an Army lieutenant, when she says,

"If we let him get away with this, who knows what's going to be next."

I've called upon Hollywood and Walter and J.P. and Jackie and all their courageous comrades-in-arms to do what must be done. Tonight, America and the world are deeply grateful to them and to their families.

And let me say to everyone listening or watching tonight: When the troops we've sent in finish their work, I'm determined to bring them home as soon as possible. Tonight, as our forces fight, they and their families are in our prayers.

May God bless each and every one of them, and the coalition forces at our side in the Gulf, and may He continue to bless our nation, the United States of America.

—— Chapter Eleven ——

Get Personal

We have covered similes, analogies, and metaphors—three different but related rhetorical devices that speech writers often use to illustrate points by comparing one thing to another. We've discussed quotations—why they're effective, where to find them, and how to use them. The discussion of quotations is one of my favorite parts of this book. I love quotations. I enjoy browsing in a book of quotations, and I collect quotations. When I read or hear something I like, I jot it down and drop it in a file. If you write or deliver speeches, that's a good practice to adopt.

I also enjoy anecdotes, which to a speech writer are almost as useful as quotations. An anecdote is a short, factual, interesting, and often amusing narrative concerning a particular incident or person. The word *anecdote* comes from the Greek *anekdota*, which originally meant "unpublished." That's not necessarily the case today. Many anecdotes, especially about well-known people, are published and are readily available for use by speech writers.

An anecdote should be more than an odd biographical fact or a witty saying. An anecdote may be funny, but relating an anecdote is not to be equated with telling a joke. Most often, anecdotes reveal something about the subject—perhaps a particular character trait or a little-known fact. Humor is an often-desirable, but always secondary, purpose.

As a speaker or speech writer, you can use well-selected anecdotes for much the same reasons that you use quotations—to make a speech livelier, more interesting, and more credible. Like quotations, anecdotes can be found in books, magazines, newspapers, speech writers' newsletters, anthologies, and other sources. One of my favorite sources is *The Little, Brown Book of Anecdotes*, edited by Clifton Fadiman. No, the book is neither little nor brown. Little, Brown & Company is the name of the publisher.

Anecdotes in speeches fall broadly into two categories: those that come from the speaker's own life and experience and those that involve other people, who may or may not be known to the audience. In this book I have several times used personal anecdotes, drawn from my experiences as a speech writer, to illustrate points. I hope these illustrations have made the book more interesting, meaningful, and credible. Good speakers don't hesitate to use personal anecdotes to help them carry their messages.

What makes a suitable anecdote?

In deciding what makes a good anecdote for a speech, I apply five criteria:

1. It must be true, or at least perceived to be true.
2. It must give insight into the nature of the subject, the speaker, or the event.
3. It must be interesting or amusing.
4. It must be simple enough for the audience to grasp easily.
5. It must illustrate, support, or lead to a point that the speaker has made or wants to make.

One of my favorite examples of a personal anecdote has been used in more than one speech by a man I have mentioned previously in this book. His name is Jeff White. He's retired now, but I often helped him with his speeches when he was a highly respected corporate chief executive. He clearly enjoys telling the story of Willie White's mule. Although the story is a little longer than I would recommend for most speeches, it always holds the audience's attention. Here it is just as Mr. White told it in one of his speeches:

> Cap'n Willie White was one of the true characters of the little community of White's Neck, Virginia, where I came from. I don't know whether Cap'n Willie was a relative of mine or not: Just about everyone in White's Neck is named White, and most of those who are not are called "come-here people."
>
> Anyway, Willie White and his family are a vivid part of my own heritage. I can almost taste the biscuits his wife, Miss Mamie, used to make and hand out, dripping with butter, when we returned from a day of fishing. Cap'n Willie was one of those people who do a little bit of a lot of things and not much of anything. Mostly, he did what his father

and grandfather had done. He fished for crabs, and when
he wasn't tending his crab pots he did a little farming.

> *Some years ago I stopped by to see Cap'n Willie and*
> *found him plowing his corn patch with a decrepit old mule.*
> *He greeted me as if I had never been away, although I hadn't*
> *seen him in many years. And he called me "boy" as if I were*
> *still ten years old. I watched him for a while, sweating in*
> *the hot sun, walking behind that old mule. Finally, he*
> *stopped for a break and I asked him what he planned to do*
> *with all that corn he was going to raise. He answered that*
> *he would use the corn to feed the mule, and he mumbled a*
> *few choice words about how much corn the old mule could*
> *eat. I thought about that for a minute and asked him why*
> *he didn't get rid of the mule.*

> *Well, Cap'n Willie looked at me like I had asked just*
> *about the stupidest question in the world, and said, "Boy, if*
> *I got rid of my mule, how in hell could I work the corn."*

Good story, well told. It meets all five of my criteria for a good
anecdote. It is true. It reveals a lot about the teller—especially his
rural heritage. It's amusing; the punch line is classic. It's simple
enough for the audience to follow easily. And it makes the speaker's
point quite nicely. The speech was to a group of managers in the
speaker's own company. The point he wanted to make was that some
business segments and products are not profitable enough to justify
their existence and ought to be jettisoned. Like Cap'n Willie's mule,
they have no real reason to exist.

In a speech to the Economic Club of Detroit, John H. Johnson,
founder of *Negro Digest, Ebony,* and other magazines, used a personal anecdote, a very poignant one, to tell how he launched what
was to become a publishing and communications empire:

> *Everybody I talked to at every critical crossroads of my life*
> *told me no the first time. Even my wife told me no the first*
> *time. And my mother told me no the first time I asked her*
> *about the furniture. I said, "Mother, I need $500 to start this*
> *new magazine!" For the first time in all the years I'd known*
> *her, she balked. "Son," she said, "I just paid for this furni-*
> *ture, and I don't know anything about this new magazine!"*
> *And you must remember that we had managed to get off*
> *welfare and it had taken her a long time to pay for the furni-*
> *ture and she didn't intend to lose it. I pleaded with her, and*
> *she said, "I'll just have to consult the Lord about this." I*
> *called her in a couple of days, and she said she hadn't*

heard from the Lord. I said, "Maybe, I ought to come by and pray with you." So I went by for three or four afternoons and we prayed and cried together. Finally she said, "The Lord hasn't spoken, but I'm going to let you have it anyway."

Here's a personal anecdote about the speaker, from a speech I wrote for baseball great Hank Aaron to deliver to a group of student entrepreneurs:

I broke into pro baseball with the Indianapolis Clowns of the old Negro League. The day I went off to Indianapolis, my mother announced that if I wasn't hitting .300 at the end of the first month, I'd have to pack up and come home. Well, I did better than that. I was pretty proud, so I wrote my mother a letter and told her about it. She called me a few days later. But instead of telling me how great I was, which was what I wanted to hear, she said if I didn't raise my average to .400 I'd have to come on home. She still won't let me be satisfied.

The point Hank was making to the young students was that if you want to be successful in whatever you do, you can never afford to be satisfied with what you're doing at the moment.

On a similar subject, a speaker uses an anecdote about Thomas Edison to illustrate the fact that what is often called genius is merely perseverance:

Thomas Edison is said to have performed 50,000 experiments in his quest to develop the incandescent light bulb. At one point, a laboratory assistant grew so discouraged that he suggested the project be abandoned because they had worked so long and so hard without results. But Edison wasn't about to give up. He had set a goal for himself, and he was confident he would eventually reach it. His reply to the lab assistant went something like this: "Yes, it's true that we have worked long and hard and haven't found what we're looking for. But the results of our work have been excellent. We have a list of 50,000 things we know won't work."

The speaker makes his point:

Whether that story is literally true or not, it does shed some light on the nature of the genius who helped light up the world. The point is that genius or talent without persistence is of little value. Edison's assistant might have been a brilliant man. We'll never know. All we know is that he viewed 50,000 experiments as failure; Edison saw them as progress.

Here is an example from a speech by a mayor to the business community of his city:

I'm especially pleased that so many busy people have turned out at this most busy time of the year. I'm tempted to assume that the fine turnout is a tribute to me, or at least a testament to the good relations I have had with the business community over the years. On the other hand, I can't help thinking of a story attributed to Winston Churchill. After making a speech one day, the great man was asked by a member of the audience, "Doesn't it thrill you, Mr. Churchill, to know that when you make a speech, the hall is always packed?" To which Churchill replied: "It is quite flattering, Madam, but I always remember that if—instead of making a political speech—I were being hanged, the crowd would be twice as large."

Now, that's a sobering thought. But I'm not making a political speech, since I'm not, at the moment at least, running for anything.

That kind of anecdote is always good for a laugh. But, as I have said, humor is not a requirement for an anecdote. There is certainly nothing funny about John Johnson's praying with his mother over whether she should sell her furniture to enable her son to start a magazine.

To be (funny) or not to be

Humor does have a place in public speaking, but not everyone knows how or when to be funny.

A young minister of my acquaintance was invited to conduct a series of Bible study sessions at a men's prison. After his first visit, the warden invited him to have lunch with the prisoners. It was customary for lunch to be followed by a thirty-minute entertainment period. On this particular day, one of the prisoners rose and called out loudly, "Number 37." The room erupted in laughter.

Then another prisoner stood up and said, "Number 19," and again the prisoners laughed heartily.

This went on for several minutes. Finally, the puzzled minister asked the warden what was happening. "Well," the warden explained, "these men hear the same old jokes over and over, so they've compiled a list of their favorites. Instead of wasting time telling the jokes, they just give the numbers. Everyone thinks of the punch line and laughs."

So the next time the minister came to the prison, he opened his Bible study lecture by saying "Number 29." No one laughed. So he said "Number 12." Again, no one cracked a smile.

He tried several more. Same result. At the break he asked one of the prisoners why his "jokes" got no response. "Well, sir," the prisoner responded, "some people just don't know how to tell a joke."

That joke—and it *is* a joke, not an anecdote, because it is obviously not true—illustrates a couple of points about the use of humor in a speech.

The first point is, of course, the obvious one: Some people really *don't* know how to tell a joke.

The second is, if you're going to tell a joke, you don't need to announce it in advance. I didn't tell you that you were about to read a joke, and a speaker should not tell the audience they are about to hear one. I didn't feel I needed to say something like "I heard a joke the other day about a young minister" or "I'm reminded of a story about . . ." Surprise is an important element of humor. It probably dawned on you about halfway through my story that it was a joke. Surprise makes it more fun both for the teller and the listener.

The financier Warren Buffet, in a speech to the business school at Emory University, told a joke with a surprise ending to illustrate what he called the "copycat mechanism" that motivates some companies. Although Mr. Buffet did announce his coming joke, he still made good use of the element of surprise:

> To illustrate, let me tell you the story of the oil prospector who met St. Peter at the Pearly Gates. When told his occupation, St. Peter said, "Oh, I'm really sorry. You seem to meet all the tests to get into heaven; we're kind of lenient on oil prospectors. But we've got a terrible problem. See that pen over there? That's where we keep the oil prospectors, but it's all filled—we haven't got room for even one more."
>
> The oil prospector thought for a minute and said, "Would you mind if I just said four words to those folks?"
>
> "I can't see any harm in that," said St. Pete.
>
> So the old-timer cupped his hands and yelled out, "Oil

*discovered in Hell!" At that instant, the lock came off the
door of the pen and all the oil prospectors flew out, flapping
their wings as hard as they could for the lower regions.*

*"You know, that's a pretty good trick," St. Pete said.
"Move in. The place is yours. We've got plenty of room."*

*The old fellow scratched his head and said, "No, if you
don't mind, I think I'll go along with the rest of 'em. There
may be some truth to that rumor after all."*

The surprise in the joke came in what was in effect a second punch
line.

Humor is often best when and where it's least expected. Remember back in Chapter One when I was discussing the fear of public speaking and mentioned the fact that even Moses lacked confidence in his speaking ability? I reminded you that the Old Testament relates that when the Lord ordered Moses to lead the Children of Israel out of bondage in Egypt, Moses tried to beg off, saying, "Oh, my Lord, I am not eloquent, either heretofore or since thou hast last spoken to thy servant; but I am slow of speech and of tongue. Oh, my Lord, send, I pray, some other person."

And so the Lord sent Charlton Heston . . .

That line, "the Lord sent Charlton Heston" was intended to use the element of surprise. It came right in the middle of a serious discussion.

That is what's known as a "one-liner." A one-liner doesn't really have to have a point. To paraphrase an old poem, if ears were made for hearing, then humor is its excuse for being. A joke, on the other hand, should make a point or carry a message, as did my joke about the minister and the prison.

One of the funniest speeches I ever heard was a put-on from beginning to end. It started out sounding serious, but it was filled with meaningless phrases. After a few minutes the audience caught on and the laughter began. I regret that I don't have a copy to share with you. It was priceless.

Here is one that is equally priceless, another put-on, and a classic example of political satire. It was delivered to the Mississippi legislature sometime in 1952 by Judge Noah S. Sweat, Jr., when he was a state legislator. His contemporaries have called it "the most famous oration of the century." This clever speech, copyrighted in 1952 by Judge Sweat, received national attention and has been reprinted often, sometimes without credit:

*My friends, I had not intended to discuss this controversial
subject at this particular time. However, I want you to know*

that I do not shun controversy. On the contrary, I will take a stand on any issue at any time, regardless of how fraught with controversy it might be. You have asked me how I feel about whisky. All right, here is how I feel about whisky. If when you say whisky you mean the devil's brew, the poison scourge, the bloody monster that defiles innocence, dethrones reason, destroys the home, creates misery and poverty, yea literally takes the bread from the mouths of little children; if you mean the evil drink that topples the Christian man and woman from the pinnacle of righteous, gracious living into the bottomless pit of degradation and despair, and shame and helplessness and hopelessness, then certainly I am against it.

But . . .

If when you say whisky you mean the oil of conversation, the philosophic wine, the ale that is consumed when good fellows get together, that puts a song in their hearts and laughter on their lips, and the warm glow of contentment in their eyes; if you mean Christmas cheer; if you mean the stimulating drink that puts the spring into the old gentleman's step on a frosty, crispy morning; if you mean the drink that enables a man to magnify his joy and his happiness, and to forget, if only for a little while, life's great tragedies, and heartaches and sorrows; if you mean that drink, the sale of which pours into our treasuries untold millions of dollars, which are used to provide tender care for our little crippled children, our blind, our deaf, our dumb, our pitiful aged and infirm; to build highways and hospitals and schools, then certainly I am for it. This is my stand. I will not retreat from it. I will not compromise.

Why people laugh

Why do people laugh? What makes something funny? Why do equally intelligent people have such different senses of humor? Comedy writers, psychologists, and others have dissected humor and debated these questions. One thing we know is that people of different cultures have different ideas of what's funny. Americans may find the humor of Britons almost pointless, whereas Britons think American humor is unsubtle. An Englishman visiting an

American farm was told by the farmer, "We don't waste anything. We eat everything we can, and what we cannot eat, we can." All the Americans in the group laughed. When the Englishman returned home, he tried to repeat the play on words to a friend. It came out "We consume what we are able. What we cannot, we tin." Something, as the saying goes, was lost in translation.

I usually don't include jokes in speeches I write. I much prefer humorous sidelights, comments, and one-liners. In the first place, telling a joke well is not easy, and some speakers shouldn't even try. In the second place, using a joke to make a serious point can backfire. It can detract from the point it is supposed to make. Even so, if you, or the speaker you're writing for, are a skillful joke teller, and if you have one you're certain is appropriate, don't let my comments discourage you from putting it in.

As a public figure, Ronald Reagan was unsurpassed in his love for and ability to tell a joke. He had an exquisite sense of timing, owing, perhaps, to his training as an actor. His jokes usually made a good point, too. During the Cold War he often used jokes to compare the initiative-stifling economy of the Soviet Union with the free-enterprise economy of the United States. Here is a story he told during one of his speeches:

> *I am a collector of stories that I can establish are actually told by the people of the Soviet Union among themselves. And this one has to do with the fact that in the Soviet Union, if you want to buy an automobile, there is a ten-year wait. And you have to put the money down ten years before you get the car. So, there was a young fellow there that had finally made it, and he was going through all the bureaus and agencies that he had to go through, and signing all the papers, and finally got to the last agency where they put the stamp on it. And then he gave them his money, and they said, "Come back in ten years and get your car." And he said, "Morning or afternoon?" And the man that had put the stamp on says, "Well, wait a minute," he says, "we're talking about ten years from now. What difference does it make?" He said, "The plumber is coming in the morning."*

Reagan was also a master of self-deprecating humor. That's the art of poking fun at yourself, and it's a good way to put an audience at ease and, in Reagan's case, to disarm critics. He often joked about his age and that, no doubt, discouraged his enemies from bringing it up. In a speech to the Annual Dinner of the White House Correspondents Association, he said:

It's no secret that I wear a hearing aid. Well, just the other day, all of a sudden, it went haywire. We discovered the KGB had put a listening device in my listening device.

And at the annual Foundation Luncheon of the YMCA, he said:

Somebody did quite a research job, though, to find a picture of me in the Dixon YMCA band. This should lay to rest the rumor that photography had yet to be invented when I was that age.

Reagan also poked fun at his acting career, and that, too, probably was meant to preempt his critics. During a White House briefing for state and local officials, he said:

Well, at this point in my career, I'm used to a certain amount of skepticism. Back in 1966, when somebody told my old boss, Jack Warner, that I was running for governor of California, he thought for a minute and said, "No, Jimmy Stewart for governor, Reagan for best friend."

As president, Reagan had excellent speech writers, but I've always had the feeling that most of his humor came from his own fertile mind. He unquestionably has a marvelous sense of humor. He is always quick with a quip.

Humor with a purpose

Humor can be used as an icebreaker near the beginning of a speech to put both the speaker and the audience in a more relaxed frame of mind. It can be effective as a closer to ensure that the audience leaves on a happy note. It can be used throughout a speech to help the speaker make points and to make the points more memorable.

Using humor can help a speaker make a point on a sensitive subject. Texas Governor Ann Richards, keynoting the National Democratic Convention in 1988, used humor to get in a plug for women's rights:

But if you give us a chance, we can perform. After all, Ginger Rogers did everything Fred Astaire did. She just did it backwards and in high heels.

That was the same speech in which Mrs. Richards said of President Bush, "Poor George. He can't help it. He was born with a silver foot in his mouth." The remark was an oblique reference to the facts that Mr. Bush was born into a wealthy home and was sometimes distressingly bumbling in his discourse. The humor enabled her to say something that might have sounded petty if expressed in a humorless way.

You don't have to be a comedy writer to work humor into a speech, but you do need a good sense of what's funny. I feel that I have a good sense of humor, but I've never made a strong effort to write jokes or funny lines to include in speeches. Now and then a good line will pop into my head. When that happens, I use it. But I don't consciously try to make it happen. If you're inclined to try your hand at writing humor, there are books—and even computer software—available to help you get started. Comedy-writing courses are taught in some colleges.

I get most of my humor from other sources. Although you don't want to fall into the habit of using tired, old jokes, a bit of recycling can be useful. After all, experts tell us that all humor is created from a handful of formulas.

There are many sources of humor, both jokes and one-liners, that you can adapt for your particular purposes. Many speech writers subscribe to one or more newsletters devoted to humor. The jokes and lines found in these publications are likely to be fresher and based more on contemporary themes than those that come from anthologies. Even if a few members of the audience have heard the joke you tell, it almost certainly will be new to most of them. But what really makes a joke effective is not whether it's new, but how it's used in the context of the speech. A good line that crops up where humor is least expected can make a point stick in the minds of listeners even though the line is a bit gray-bearded. Many a hoary old line has been given a contemporary twist by a good humorist.

Humor in a speech does not have to be hilarious. A speaker, after all, is not a stand-up comic. Smiles and chuckles are better than belly laughs.

Some do's and don'ts

Here are some suggestions about the use of humor in speeches:

• *Never repeat a punch line.* The mark of a clumsy joke teller is repetition of the punch line. It's like saying, "I want to be sure you dumbbells got it, so I'm going to repeat it."

• *When you use a laugh line, don't pause and wait for the audience to start laughing.* That's begging. Instead, go right on. After the laughter starts—if it does—pause until it subsides.

• *Don't get flustered if your humor bombs.* Professional comics have their own ways to recover after a joke falls flat. Unless you're a professional, you're better off to go on and ignore the bomb.

• *Never ad lib a joke.* Don't tell one unless you have rehearsed it enough to have the pacing, timing, and punch line down pat. The success of a joke depends on timing, which is just as much a part of the telling as are the words. It's a good idea to try out your joke on two or three people who won't be in the audience.

• *Don't make your joke too complex. Or too long.* You want the audience to understand it easily, and you don't want them to doze off before you get to the punch line.

• *If you tell a joke, make sure it ties in with your topic.* Resist the temptation to tell a joke for the sake of the joke. If you're just bursting to tell a joke you've heard, but you can't find a way to tie it in to your subject, save it for the right occasion.

• *Humor can be slightly irreverent, but it should never be vicious.* Although the "silver foot" remark by Governor Richards about President Bush was both irreverent and biting, it could by no means be considered vicious. Will Rogers once said, "I ain't got it in for nobody. I don't like to make jokes that hurt anybody." Good rule to follow.

• *Never use ethnic humor.* There was a time when good-natured ethnic banter was acceptable. It still is to some people, but in these times of hypersensitivity, you're best advised to stay away from that kind of humor. Even in "roasts," which are supposed to be affairs in which anything goes, speakers have come to grief for using ethnic terms.

The same is true of humor based on religion, gender, physical disability, obesity, appearance, sexual orientation, and any number of other human characteristics. A joke about a blind person might be acceptable if the person telling it is blind. The same joke by a sighted person might be offensive.

• *Be careful about using profanity and off-color remarks.* Although mildly risqué remarks can spice up a speech for some audiences and some occasions, there's a line that a speaker should not cross. That's a line I can't draw for you. You have to know the audience, the occasion, and yourself. What's right for one audience may be totally out of place for another. What works for one occasion may not work for another. What one speaker can do well, another might botch. My advice is to avoid humor or language that is obscene, blatantly sexual, or scatological.

   • *Don't overdo it.* Unless you're a humorist, don't try to crack one joke after another. Keep the humor content of your speech in the right proportion to the serious content.

"Our Long National Nightmare"

On August 9, 1974, Gerald Ford was sworn in as President of the
United States, replacing President Richard Nixon, who had resigned
following the debacle known as Watergate. In assuming the presidency, Ford was acutely conscious of the fact that his was a difficult
task. His short speech at the swearing-in was a model of grace and
humility. A speech that contains but one memorable line might be
called a success. His had at least four: "I am acutely aware that you
have not elected me as your president by your ballots, and so I ask
you to confirm me as your president with your prayers," "If you have
not chosen me by secret ballot, neither have I gained office by any
secret promises," "This is an hour of history that troubles our minds
and hurts our hearts," and the best-known one, "Our long national
nightmare is over."

Here is the speech in its entirety:

The oath that I have taken is the same oath that was taken by George Washington and by every president under the Constitution. But I assume the presidency
under extraordinary circumstances never before experienced by Americans.
This is an hour of history that troubles our minds and hurts our hearts.

Therefore, I feel it is my first duty to make an unprecedented compact
with my countrymen. Not an inaugural address, not a fireside chat, not a campaign speech—just a little straight talk among friends. And I intend it to be
the first of many.

I am acutely aware that you have not elected me as your president by your
ballots, and so I ask you to confirm me as your president with your prayers.
And I hope that such prayers will also be the first of many.

If you have not chosen me by secret ballot, neither have I gained office by
any secret promises. I have not campaigned either for the presidency or the
vice-presidency. I have not subscribed to any partisan platform. I am indebted
to no man, and only to one woman—my dear wife—as I begin this very difficult
job.

I have not sought this enormous responsibility, but I will not shirk it.
Those who nominated and confirmed me as vice president were my friends and
are my friends. They were of both parties, elected by all the people and acting
under the Constitution in their name. It is only fitting then that I should
pledge to them and to you that I will be the president of all the people.

Thomas Jefferson said the people are the only sure reliance for the preservation of our liberty. And down the years, Abraham Lincoln renewed this
American article of faith asking, "Is there any better way or equal hope in the
world?"

I intend, on Monday next, to request of the speaker of the House of
Representatives and the president pro tempore of the Senate the privilege of

appearing before the Congress to share with my former colleagues and with you, the American people, my views on the priority business of the nation and to solicit your views and their views. And may I say to the Speaker and the others, if I could meet with you right after these remarks, I would appreciate it. Even though this is late in an election year, there is no way we can go forward except together and no way anybody can win except by serving the people's urgent needs. We cannot stand still or slip backwards. We must go forward now together.

To the peoples and the governments of all friendly nations, and I hope that could encompass the whole world, I pledge an uninterrupted and sincere search for peace. America will remain strong and united, but its strength will remain dedicated to the safety and sanity of the entire family of man, as well as to our own precious freedom.

I believe that truth is the glue that holds government together, not only our government but civilization itself. That bond, though strained, is unbroken at home and abroad.

In all my public and private acts as your president, I expect to follow my instincts of openness and candor with full confidence that honesty is always the best policy in the end.

My fellow Americans, our long national nightmare is over.

Our Constitution works; our great Republic is a government of laws and not of men. Here the people rule. But there is a higher power, by whatever name we honor him, who ordains not only righteousness but love, not only justice but mercy.

As we bind up the internal wounds of Watergate, more painful and more poisonous than those of foreign wars, let us restore the golden rule to our political process, and let brotherly love purge our hearts of suspicion and of hate.

In the beginning I asked you to pray for me. Before closing, I ask again your prayers, for Richard Nixon and for his family. May our former president, who brought peace to millions, find it for himself. May God bless and comfort his wonderful wife and daughters, whose love and loyalty will forever be a shining legacy to all who bear the lonely burdens of the White House.

I can only guess at those burdens, although I have witnessed at close hand the tragedies that befell three presidents and the lesser trials of others.

With all the strength and all the good sense I have gained from life, with all the confidence my family, my friends, and my dedicated staff impart to me, and with the good will of countless Americans I have encountered in recent visits to forty states, I now solemnly reaffirm my promise I made to you last December 6: to uphold the Constitution, to do what is right as God gives men to see the right, and to do the very best I can for America.

God helping me, I will not let you down.

Thank you.

—— Chapter Twelve ——

Statistics and Other Lies

We've considered at some length three devices that can liven up a speech and be used to make or reinforce serious points—quotations, anecdotes, and humor. Now let's look at a fourth one, one that might surprise you—statistics.

Of course, statistics can be made to prove almost anything. I heard about a statistician who always carries a bomb in his checked luggage when he travels on an airplane. He explains that the chance of a bomb being on a plane is one in a billion, but the chance of two bombs on the same plane is less than one in ten billion. So he feels ten times as safe when he brings a bomb.

When we think of statistics, we tend to think of a dry, tedious recitation of facts and figures. The use of statistics in a speech doesn't have to be that way. The key to using statistics to make or dramatize points, or to make a point more memorable, is to select a statistic that is dramatic, startling, or humorous. That's easy to say, but statistics being statistics, they aren't often dramatic, startling, or humorous. What you must do, then, is present them in a memorable way.

Make them memorable

Let's say you want to make the point that television is the most influential force in American life. You could say something like this: "A recent survey showed that the average American spends X number of hours watching television each week" or "X percentage of the American people rely on television for almost all their news and entertainment." Anything especially memorable in either statement? Well, no.

But how about this: "A recent survey found that 44 percent of the people didn't recognize George Bush when shown a picture of

173

him, but only 7 percent failed to recognize the smiling face and muscular body of Mister Clean. Maybe Mr. Clean ought to run for president. Or maybe President Bush ought to shave his head, grow muscles, and start doing TV commercials." Few in the audience will recall the percentages, but the vision of Mr. Bush with a shaven head is unforgettable.

Suppose you need to make the point that our public schools are not preparing students for intelligent citizenship. You could say, "49 percent of all high school students believe that the president can declare a law unconstitutional, and 50 percent of all high school seniors identify Israel as an Arab nation. Their elders, however, are no better: Half of all Americans believe that an accused person is guilty until proven innocent, and 42 percent can't name a nation that's near the Pacific Ocean." The percentages themselves are unimportant. The impressions are.

If junk-food consumption is your subject, you might mention the fact that Americans consume seventy-five acres of pizza every single day and that 7 percent of Americans eat at McDonald's every day.

If you're making the point that many retired people live in Miami, why not reinforce the point by saying that Miamians consume more prune juice than citizens of any other city in the United States? Or, even better, something like "Miami is the undisputed prune-juice capital of the U.S.A."

To dramatize the incredible cost of military hardware, you could tell the audience that if you had a block of silver that weighed the same as a B-1 bomber, you would still have only enough to pay for 6 percent of the bomber's cost.

And finally, if you're talking about the hazards of everyday life, your audience might be amazed to learn that one American a day drowns in the bathtub.

All of the statistics I've used are from the same source—an intriguing little volume called *The Harper Index Book*, published by *Harper's Magazine*. But there are many other sources of interesting statistics.

Make them understandable

Sometimes statistics just need to be compared with something that the audience can more easily relate to. For example, a billion is a number that is almost impossible for the typical person to comprehend. And a trillion—well, that really boggles the mind. So if you refer to a trillion dollars, you might as well be speaking a foreign language. Your audience just won't be able to grasp it.

A speech about the cost of the federal government's antipoverty efforts included this statement:

> *Since President Johnson launched his idealistic War on Poverty in 1965, this country has expended a whopping $5.4 trillion on programs for the poor. That's a lot of money.*

Ho hum. Zzzzzz. Everybody knows $5.4 trillion is a lot of money. So is $5.4 *billion*. And so, in fact, is $5.4 million.

With a little thought and research, the speech writer could have dramatized the point this way:

> *Since President Johnson launched his idealistic War on Poverty in 1965, this country has spent $5.4 trillion on programs for the poor. How much is $5.4 trillion? Well, if you had that amount today, you could buy every farm in the United States. You could also buy every factory and every office building. You could become a communications magnate that would make Ted Turner look like a piker. You could own every radio and TV station and every telephone company in the country. You could also buy every retail and every wholesale business, every hotel, every power company, every airline, every railroad, and every trucking company.*
>
> *And with the money left over after all those purchases, you could buy the nation's entire commercial maritime fleet.*

Makes you think, doesn't it?

If a trillion is an unimaginably large number, it follows that one-trillionth is an unimaginably small number. An oil-company executive, in a speech to the Society of Management Accountants, used a dramatic comparison to explain the meaning of "parts per trillion":

> *Advances in technology enable us to measure things that we could never measure before. Scientists, for example, are now able to speak in terms of parts per trillion. One trillionth is an awfully small number. One trillionth of the distance to the earth's moon is 1.5 hundredths of an inch. That's roughly like comparing the thickness of a human hair to the distance traveled one-way by the Apollo astronauts.*

Compare that use of statistics with this, from a speech to the Economic Club of Detroit by the head of a large insurance company. The speaker uses statistics to make a point about improper or unnecessary medical treatments:

> *Up to 50 percent of prescribed antibiotics are not indicated, resulting in a loss of a quarter- to a half-billion dollars annually. Of 1.6 billion prescriptions dispensed annually, up to 50 percent are taken incorrectly, resulting in a loss of $14 billion in health care. 40 percent of medications prescribed for the elderly may be "non-essential." 20 percent to 30 percent of all patients admitted to a hospital suffer an adverse patient occurrence. 44 percent of coronary artery bypasses may be unnecessary.*

In that brief passage, the speaker cited 6 percentages, along with some dollar figures. How many do you suppose his listeners were able to remember five minutes after hearing them?

There are occasions when using a lot of raw numbers may be necessary, but it is important to understand that the audience is not likely to remember them. If recalling the actual numbers is important, it's a mistake to use them as that speaker did. There are simply too many related numbers too close together. If the numbers, taken as a whole, leave the impression the speaker desires, then using the numbers can perhaps be justified.

Anecdotes can help

Still, there are other ways to accomplish the same purpose. One way is to use anecdotes. How much more interesting the insurance executive's speech would have been if the speaker had cited an actual example of a hospital patient who had suffered what he called an "adverse patient occurrence." I assume that is a bit of euphemistic jargon meaning that something bad happened to the patient in the hospital, and whatever it was wasn't related to what the patient was hospitalized for. After telling what happened to the patient, the speaker might have said something like this:

> *And that lady's experience wasn't at all unusual. It happens to between 20 and 30 percent of all hospital patients. Just think about that for a minute: If you go to the hospital, you have as much as a 30 percent chance of getting some-*

thing you didn't bargain for. Think how that affects medical costs—and insurance rates—in this country.

So, let me summarize my key points about statistics.

- Statistics don't have to be nothing but dull, dry figures. They can be interesting or even dramatic and can help make your points clear and memorable.
- You can sometimes express statistics in terms that your audience can relate to.
- Try to avoid using too many raw figures, especially very close together.
- Consider carefully whether using visuals would help make the material more understandable or more memorable. Before you make that decision, some points are worth examining.

Visuals? Maybe

If it is really important that the audience retain the actual figures, some type of visual aids—charts, graphs, slides, whatever—might be helpful. Whether visuals are appropriate depends on the audience, the occasion, and the kind of material to be presented. I have often written presentations to be delivered to financial analysts, who are accustomed to dealing with figures and are usually able to assimilate numbers delivered orally. Even so, visuals, if they're used well, make the speaker's task easier.

Some material just cannot be explained without illustrations. The adage that one picture is worth a thousand words does apply in some instances. If you are trying to tell an audience what a new building will look like, an architect's rendering of the building will get the job done better than any number of words.

Nevertheless, I am, as a rule, reluctant to use visuals in a speech. I think they detract from a speech more often than they add to it. The potential for boring the audience with visuals is far too great. Visuals dehumanize a speech. Who could feel warm and fuzzy about a slide or a flip chart?

I've known speakers who insisted on visuals, usually slides, for almost every speech. I suspect that in most instances, these speakers were looking for a crutch. Using slides would keep them from having to really say anything. Remember, most great speakers came along before the invention of the slide projector.

Use visuals effectively

Nevertheless, I've already conceded that for some audiences, on some occasions, and with some material, visuals may be useful or even necessary. Sales presentations, technical discussions, reports, presentations in which perfect understanding is required, and when a high degree of retention is desirable—these and others can benefit greatly from the proper use of visuals. I stress the word *proper* because there are right ways and wrong ways to use visuals. Here are some suggestions:

• *At the risk of being repetitious, my first suggestion is that you reject the idea of using visuals unless your material simply cannot be presented effectively without them.* Don't use visuals as a crutch or as an excuse for not preparing a solid, well written, thoughtful speech.

• *Don't let your visuals take over the speech.* Use them to support and reinforce, not to dominate, the message. Be selective. Use only the number necessary to do the job.

• *Never allow a visual to be seen until you're ready to discuss it, and don't leave one up after you've finished talking about it.* The last thing you want is to find yourself competing with your own material for the attention of the audience.

• *Avoid using handouts for people to look at as you speak.* Many in the audience will jump ahead and will miss what you say. Handouts are fine, but distribute them at the end of the speech.

• *Keep your visuals neat but uncomplicated.* Use plain, easily readable type and simple artwork. A visual that's too glitzy or clever will draw attention to it and from the speaker. A visual that's too complex cannot be easily understood. A good visual is usually self-explanatory.

• *Be sure that everyone in the audience can see the visuals clearly.* This is something to consider when you check out the venue in advance of the presentation.

• *Be careful how you stand in relation to your visual.* Don't block anyone's view.

• *Don't overuse a pointer.* A pointer is a useful device to guide the audience's attention. If you use one, point specifically to each item as you discuss it rather than simply using the pointer to make gestures. Put the pointer aside when you're not using it. Fiddling with the pointer, or with anything else for that matter, can distract the audience.

- *Stay in control.* Maintain good eye contact with the audience as you discuss the visuals. You want the audience to understand that the visuals are supporting what you say and not vice versa. The focus should always be on you.

- *If you use slides, have the room darkened only as much as necessary to make the pictures easily seen.* You do not want to be in the dark or keep your audience in the dark—literally or figuratively.

- *Avoid the verbal twitter that often accompanies the use of visuals.* Don't say things such as "The next slide will show that . . ." Just match your words to the slide and the audience will know what the slide shows.

- *If you use anything mechanical—projectors, slides, video monitors, whatever—remember Murphy's Law: Anything that can go wrong, will.* President Reagan once made a television appearance in which he was supposed to use a felt-tip marker. But the marker failed, and there were some awkward moments until a ghostly hand appeared in the picture with a new pen. The moral is, test everything. And it's not a bad idea to have a spare pen, as Mr. Reagan learned.

"THE DANGEROUS DECADE"

In the following speech, delivered on December 18, 1979, British Prime Minister Margaret Thatcher made effective use of anaphora, antithesis, and quotations:

As I speak today, 1979—and with it the 1970s—has less than two weeks to run. I myself will have some reason to remember both the year and the decade with affection. But in general few, I suspect, will regret the passing of either.

The last 10 years have not been a happy period for the Western democracies domestically or internationally. Self-questioning is essential to the health of any society. But we have perhaps carried it too far and carried to extremes, of course, it causes paralysis. The time has come when the West—above all Europe and the United States—must begin to substitute action for introspection.

We face a new decade—have called it "the dangerous decade"—in which the challenges to our security and to our way of life may if anything be more acute than in the 1970s. The response of Western nations and their leaders will need to be firm, calm and concerted. Neither weakness nor anger nor despair will serve us. The problems are daunting but there is in my view ample reason for optimism.

Few international problems today lend themselves to simple solutions. One reason is that few such problems can any longer be treated in isolation. Increasingly they interact, one between the other. Thanks to a still-accelerating technological revolution we become daily more aware that the earth and its resources are finite and in most respects shrinking.

The fact of global interdependence—I apologize for the jargon—is nothing new. Four hundred years ago South American gold and silver helped to cause inflation in Europe—an early example of the evils of excess money supply. Two hundred years ago men fought in India and along the Great Lakes here in America in order that, as Macaulay put it, the King of Prussia might rob a neighbor whom he had promised to defend.

But the popular perception of interdependence lagged far behind the fact. When I was in my teens a British Prime Minister could still refer to Czechoslovakia as "a far-away country" of whose quarrels the British people knew nothing; and an American President could still experience difficulty in persuading his people of the need to concern themselves with a European war.

Today it is painfully obvious that no man—and no nation—is an island. What President Cleveland once described as "'foreign broils" are brought into every home. The price of oil in Saudi Arabia and Nigeria, the size of the grain harvest in Kansas and the Ukraine—these are of immediate concern to people all over the world. The Middle East and the middle West have become neighbors and will remain so, uncomfortable though they may on occasion find it. The bell tolls for us all.

This has been tragically underlined in recent weeks. The world has watched with anger and dismay the events of Tehran. We have all felt involved with the fate of the hostages. Nothing can excuse the treatment they have received; for hundreds of years the principle of the immunity of the messenger and the diplomat has been respected. Now this principle, central to the civilized conduct of relations between states, is being systematically flouted.

We in Britain have respected and supported the calmness and resolution with which President Carter has handled an appalling situation. With our partners in Europe we have given full public and private support to his efforts to secure the unconditional release of the hostages. We will continue to support and to help in any way we can. Above all we have admired the forbearance with which the American people have responded to the indignities inflicted upon their fellow citizens. That restraint has undoubtedly been in the best interests of the captives.

The Iranian crisis epitomizes the problems which we face in trying to co-exist in a shrinking world where political, economic and social upheavals are endemic. Some would add religious upheavals to that list. But I do not believe we should judge Islam by events in Iran. Least of all should we judge it by the taking of hostages. There is a tide of self-confidence and self-awareness in the Muslim world which preceded the Iranian Revolution, and will outlast its present excesses. The West should recognize this with respect, not hostility. The Middle East is an area where we have much at stake. It is in our own interests, as well as in the interests of the people of that region, that they build on their own deep religious traditions. We do not wish to see them succumb to the fraudulent appeal of imported Marxism.

Because, to look beyond the Middle East, I am convinced that there is little force left in the original Marxist stimulus to revolution. Its impetus is petering out as the practical failure of the doctrine becomes daily more obvious. It has failed to take root in the advanced democracies. In those countries where it has taken root—countries backward or, by tradition, authoritarian—it has failed to provide sustained economic or social development. What is left is a technique of subversion and a collection of catch-phrases. The former, the technique of subversion, is still dangerous. Like terrorism it is a menace that needs to be fought wherever it occurs—and British Prime Ministers have had reason to speak with some passion about terrorism in recent years. As for the catch-phrases of Marxism, they still have a certain drawing power. But they have none in the countries which are ruled by the principles of Marx. Communist regimes can no longer conceal the gulf that separates their slogans from reality.

The immediate threat from the Soviet Union is military rather than ideological. The threat is not only to our security in Europe and North America but also, both directly and by proxy, in the third world. I have often spoken about the military challenge which the West faces today. I have sometimes been deliberately misunderstood, especially by my enemies who have labelled me the

"Iron Lady." They are quite right—I am. Let me, therefore, restate a few simple propositions.

The Soviet Union continues to proclaim the ideological struggle. It asserts that the demise of the Western political system is inevitable. It neglects the fact that few indeed who live in Western democracies show any sign of wanting to exchange their system for that operated by the Russians. In 1919, Lenin said:

"World imperialism cannot live side by side with a victorious Soviet revolution—the one or the other will be victorious in the end."

The Soviet government have not repudiated this threatening prediction. Indeed they broadcast their ambitions wholesale. They should not be surprised if we listen and take note.

Meanwhile they expand their armed forces on land, sea and air. They continually improve the quality of their armaments. They and their allies outnumber us in Europe. Their men, their ships, and their aircraft appear ever more regularly in parts of the world where they have never been seen before. Their Cuban and East German proxies likewise.

We can argue about Soviet motives. But the fact is that the Russians have the weapons and are getting more of them. It is simple prudence for the West to respond. We in Britain intend to do that to the best of our ability and at every level including the strategic. President Carter has shown that he intends to do likewise. And the Alliance last week decided to modernize its long-range theatre nuclear weapons. This in due course will help to balance the new and sophisticated weapons the Russians already have targeted on Europe. The strategic power of the U.S.A. in the Western Alliance remains paramount. But I would underline the contribution of the European members of NATO—a contribution which is never overlooked by the Russians.

Modern weapons are totally destructive and immensely expensive. It is in nobody's interest that they should be piled up indefinitely. It makes good sense for both sides to seek agreements on arms control which preserve the essential security of each. We in Britain have therefore supported the talks on Strategic Arms Limitation and on Mutual and Balanced Force Reductions. The British Government hopes that the SALT II agreement can be ratified.

I have been attacked by the Soviet Government for arguing that the West should put itself in a position to negotiate from strength. But in saying this, I have done no more than echo the constant ambition of the Soviet Government itself. I am not talking about negotiations from a position of superiority. What I am seeking is a negotiation in which we and they start from the position of balance, and if both sides can negotiate, genuinely, to maintain that balance at lower levels, I shall be well content. It is in that spirit that I approach the proposals which have recently been made by President Brezhnev and others.

The East/West conflict permeates most global issues. But other equally pressing problems have arisen. These affect above all the world economy and the relationship between the developed Western world and the newly emerging countries of Latin America, Africa and Asia.

No country can today escape economic involvement with the economies of others. In the U.K. external trade has always been of central importance to our economy. In the U.S.A. this has been less so. But recently you have become much more dependent on overseas countries. Ten years ago you imported 5 percent of your oil. Now it is 50 percent. But it is not just oil this has obvious consequences for your foreign policy. So, rich and poor, communist and non-communist, oil-producers and oil-consumers—our economic welfare is increasingly affected by the operation of the market. Increasingly affected by the growing demand of complex industries for scarce materials and by the pressure on the world's finite resources of fossil fuels.

All of this has coincided with a prolonged period of uneasiness in the world's economy. The immediate prospects are somber: Inflation will be difficult to eradicate; growth has fallen sharply from its earlier levels; there is a constant threat of disorder in the world oil market. News of recent price rises can only have added to the general uncertainty which is one of the most damaging consequences of the present oil situation. The task of economic management, both nationally and internationally, is becoming more and more difficult. The precarious balance of the world economy could at any time be shaken by political upheavals in one or more countries over which the rest of us might have very little influence.

In these circumstances, we all have a direct practical interest in the orderly settlement of political disputes.

These were some considerations which, in addition to the obvious ones, persuaded the new British Government of the need for a decisive effort to secure a settlement in Zimbabwe-Rhodesia. As you know, after months of strenuous negotiation, overall agreement was finally reached yesterday on the new Constitution, arrangements for free and fair elections, and a ceasefire. The agreement secured in London showed that even the most intractable problem will yield to the necessary combination of resolve and imagination. Concessions were made by all sides. Many difficult decisions were involved—not least for the British Government, which found itself acquiring a new colony, albeit for a short period. We are grateful for the forceful and timely support we received throughout the negotiations from the United States Government, and from President Carter personally, especially in the final stages.

We have no illusion about the practical problems of implementing this agreement on the ground, against a background of years of bitter conflict. But now is a time for reconciliation, and for restoring normal relations between all the states in the area. The Lancaster House agreement could prove a major step toward peaceful evolution and away from violent revolution in Southern Africa. We are encouraged to persevere with the Five Power initiative to achieve an all-party settlement in Namibia.

In this context I want to say a particular word about South Africa. There is now a real prospect that the conflicts on South Africa's borders, in Rhodesia and Namibia, will shortly be ended. This, combined with welcome initiatives in

South African domestic policies, offers a chance to defuse a regional crisis which was potentially of the utmost gravity, and to make progress toward an ending of the isolation of South Africa in world affairs.

We must not regard these problems as insoluble. The West has immense material and moral assets. To those assets must be added the clarity to see where our strengths should be used; the will and confidence to use them with precision; and the stamina to see things through.

Let us never forget that despite the difficulties to which I have referred, the Western democracies remain overwhelmingly strong in economic terms. We are, it is true, more vulnerable than before. Vulnerable because of our reliance on raw materials; vulnerable because of the specialization and complexity of our societies. It is vital, therefore, that we keep a steady nerve and that we concert our policies. We already agree on the basic requirements—on the need to defeat inflation; to avoid protectionism; to use our limited energy resources better. And as we deal with the problems our inherent vitality will reassert itself. There is, after all, no discernible challenge to the role of the Western democracies as the driving force of the world economy.

The political strength and stability of the West is equally striking. Preoccupied by passing political dramas, we often overlook the real sturdiness of our political institutions. They are not seriously challenged from within. They meet the aspirations of ordinary people. They attract the envy of those who do not have them. In the 35 years since the last war, they have shown themselves remarkably resistant to subversive influences.

Our democratic systems have made it possible to organize our relationships with one another on a healthy basis. The North Atlantic Alliance and the European Community are—and remain—free associations of free peoples. Policies are frankly debated. Of course the debates are often lively and occasionally heated. But those debates are a sign of strength just as the regimented agreements of the Communist alliances are a mark of weakness.

The argument now going on in the European Community is a case in point. The Community is used to debate, often difficult and prolonged. We are seeing at present something more serious than many of the disputes which have taken place in the past. But the interests that unite the members of the Community are stronger than those which divide them—particularly when viewed in the light of other international problems. I believe that these common interests will assert themselves. I am confident that an acceptable solution will be found and that the European Community will emerge fortified from the debate. And a strong Europe is the best partner for the United States. It is on the strength of that partnership that the strength of the free world depends.

The last asset I want to mention today is the West's relationship with the countries of the Third World. Neither recent events, nor past injustices, nor the outdated rhetoric of anti-colonialism can disguise the real convergence of interest between the Third World and the West.

It is we in the West who have the experience and contacts the Third World needs. We supply most of the markets for their goods and their raw materials. We supply most of the technology they require. We provide them with private investment as well as Government aid.

We do this not only for our own sake but also because we support the efforts of the countries of the Third World to develop their own economies.

I have only been able to touch on a few current international issues. There are many I have not mentioned. Nor would I wish anyone to think that I underestimate the difficulties, particularly on the domestic economic front, faced by Britain and our Western partners, including the United States. But these difficulties can and will be overcome provided we do not undervalue ourselves nor decry our strength. We shall need self-confidence to tackle the dangerous decade.

It is a time for action, action for the eighties:

—we must restore the dynamic to our economies

—we must modernize our defense

—we must continue to seek agreement with the East

—we must help the developing countries to help themselves

—we must conserve our resources of energy and especially fossil fuels

—we must achieve an understanding with the oil producers which benefits us all

—we must never fail to assert our faith in freedom and our belief in the institutions which sustain it.

The cynics among you will say that none of this is new. Quite right. It isn't. But there are no new magic formulae. We know what we have to do. Our problems will only yield to sustained effort. That is the challenge of political leadership.

Enduring success never comes easily to an individual or to a country. To quote Walt Whitman: "It takes struggles in life to make strength; it takes fight for principles to make fortitude; it takes crisis to give courage and singleness of purpose to reach an objective." Let us go down in history as the generation which not only understood what needed to be done but a generation which had the strength, the self-discipline and the resolve to see it through. That is our generation. That is our task for the '80s.

— CHAPTER THIRTEEN —

Closing the Speech

Someone has said that a speech is like quicksand: It's a lot easier to get into than out of. Actually, you can "get out of" a speech rather easily just by stopping when you've said everything you want to say. A simple and gracious "Thank you for allowing me to be a part of your program" will sometimes suffice.

But not usually. Most good speeches have strong closes. In the discussion of openings in Chapter Five, I mentioned the "speaker's grace period," that crucial period at the beginning of a speech when the speaker has the audience's full attention. The ending is a similarly crucial time, and the speaker who fails to make the most of it does not do justice to his efforts.

To craft a good closing requires some work. If you do not devote the necessary time and thought, you might miss a good chance to add additional impact to your message. Look at it this way: You have spent many hours researching your topic, developing a thesis, and writing the main body of the speech. Are you going to let all that hard work end with a whimper instead of a bang?

No? Okay, let's take a look, now, at some things to consider when you're writing a closing for your speech.

First, decide what you want your closing to accomplish. Of course, you want your audience to feel satisfied by the speech—that is, to feel they have gotten from it everything they expected. And you want them to leave with a favorable impression of the speaker and the organization he or she represents. Beyond these things, you might want members of the audience to do something, to believe something, or to feel a particular way about your subject. A strong closing can help make those things happen.

These things relate directly to the purpose of the speech, which we discussed in Chapter Three and in more detail in Chapter Four— that is, what you want the audience to do or think or feel as a result of what you say. Your closing should in some way reinforce that purpose—a sort of parting shot, if you will. The closing should also relate to the thesis of the speech, as defined and discussed in Chapter Three.

Types of closings

In listening to and reading many, many speeches, I have identified seven basic kinds of closings: summaries, wrap-ups, direct appeals, thesis closings, reference closings, inspirational closings, and humorous or anecdotal closings. In considering these types of closings, remember that closings, like openings, are rarely so neatly packaged. Most often, a good closing is a combination or two or more kinds and may have elements of several. My purpose in suggesting categories is to encourage you to think both logically and creatively about how best to close a speech and to fully appreciate the closing's potential for making the speech more effective.

In a *summary closing*, the speaker briefly summarizes the high points of the speech. A *wrap-up* is a closing in which the speaker closes the circle, so to speak, and brings everything together. In a *direct appeal*, the speaker does what sales trainers call "asking for the order." In other words, he asks audience members to take some specific action. The *thesis closing* is a restatement of the thesis, or main point, of the speech.

A *reference closing*, like a reference opening, is one that refers to the date, the location, an event, the weather, the speech subject, or almost anything that the speaker can tie to the subject. Examples of appropriate reference subjects were given in our discussion of reference openings in Chapter Six.

An *inspirational closing* is often a moving anecdote, a poem, or a quotation. In a *humorous* or *anecdotal closing*, the speaker tells a story or anecdote that makes a strong closing point.

Many of the rhetorical devices discussed in Chapter Nine, such as anaphora, triads, antithesis, and exaggeration, can be used effectively in closings.

Closings in action

Let's analyze some closings from actual speeches.

The conclusion of Lincoln's second inaugural address, March 4, 1865, provides a wonderful example of a direct appeal, or "asking for the order":

With malice toward none; with charity for all; with firmness in the right, as God gives us to see the right, let us strive on to finish the work we are in, to bind up the nation's wounds; to care for him who shall have borne the battle, and for his widow and his orphan, to do all which may achieve and cherish a just and lasting peace among ourselves, and with all nations.

Lincoln's appeal to the nation was clear and strong, a fitting way to conclude the speech.

Here is a closing, from a speech by an executive of Visa International, in which the speaker summarizes the main points of the speech:

In conclusion, let me emphasize that 1 see the potential role of the Federal Reserve in the securities markets as rather limited.

One, its primary objective should be to prevent the occurrence of disorderly markets, and not to maintain a certain level of the Dow Jones or the New York Stock Exchange Index.

Two, the Federal Reserve should act as guardian against the occurrence of systemic risks and not to prop up individual stocks. Thus, all intervention should be conducted in broadly based market composites and not in individual stocks.

The speaker makes three additional numbered points by way of summary, then brings them all together with this sentence:

Thus, I believe it is worthwhile to discuss the merits and problems associated with direct intervention by the Federal Reserve in the stock market aggregates.

To me, the sentence seems unnecessarily weak. I would much prefer a stronger wrap-up. In the final sentence, the speaker dusted off the business cliché, "If it ain't broke, don't fix it."

Here is a very good closing of a speech in which a business executive discusses the necessity of reducing the number of management levels in a corporation. The closing uses a couple of metaphors, two triads, and several strong, expressive verb forms:

This management system, designed to draw out the best in the 300,000 individuals who make up this company, is drawing it out. We're a long way from having those levers of responsibility in front of every workstation and desk in this company, but that is our ultimate objective. We know where competitiveness comes from. It comes from people—but only from people who are free to dream, free to risk, free to act.

Liberating those people, every one of them, is the great challenge we've been grappling with all over this company. And from what we've seen of the ocean of talent, initiative and creativity that is unleashed when we have the self-confidence to turn it loose, we are convinced your company is more than a match for anything the world can throw at us.

The two triads, one of which is anaphoric, are "free to dream, free to risk, free to act" and "talent, initiative and creativity." The two metaphors are "levers of responsibility" and "oceans of talent." The strong, expressive verb forms are "drawing out, liberating, grappling, unleashed, turn loose, and throw." The "oceans" metaphor seems slightly mixed by the use of the word "unleashed" (Can an ocean be unleashed?), but the overall effect of the closing is diminished only slightly thereby.

Here's an example of a closing that combines anaphora and a rhetorical question to create a stirring call to action:

Let's monitor performance, let's complain when promises are broken, let's use our electoral muscle to get the sort of government we deserve. Let's work to get more women elected to public office. Let's humanize government to make it not only accountable, but responsive, to the people who elected it. After all, who deserves it more than we?

Here is a good example of an inspirational closing. The title of the speech was "Vision of Detroit in 1987." The speaker combines a restatement of the thesis with an inspirational and seldom-heard quotation:

It's a vision we can make happen, starting with small steps, with individual efforts . . . you, me, large business, small business and government. This idea of individuals and families working together for the betterment of the community is hardly new. Indeed, it originated—not surprisingly—in ancient Athens, the birthplace of democracy. It's an idea we need to put into action in Detroit in the summer of 1988. I'd like to close with a quote from the oath of the Citizens of Athens that might well be the motto for the citizens of a greater Detroit:

"We will ever strive for the ideals and sacred things of the city, both alone and with many. We will increasingly seek to quicken the sense of public duty; we will revere and obey the city's laws; we will transmit this city not only not less, but greater, better, and more beautiful than it was transmitted to us."

Note the "we will" anaphora in the quotation from the Athens oath.

In the next example, a college professor speaking to a group of students uses three strong concluding paragraphs in which he combines metaphors, rhetorical questions, vigorous language, anaphora, antithesis, and direct appeals. In the first and last paragraphs, he refers obliquely to the title of the speech, which is "Stop the Waste," and pairs it with a contrasting phrase, "start the worth":

We cannot do everything at once, but we can do something at once. The point is, we can entrench these good habits if we start NOW. Start by stopping the waste and starting the worth! The easiest thing in the world is to think of college as a waste! What a cop out! What an excuse! In that way we can blame others for the shape we're in! When do we begin to take charge? When do we begin to take control? When do we begin to be master of our own life? To be of worth is to be valuable, to be precious, to be worthy. We need to start NOW to build good habits of oral communication, of written communication, and being enthusiastic.

Just remember: No horse gets anywhere till he is harnessed. No steam ever drives anything until it is confined. No Niagara is ever turned into light and power until it is tunneled. And no life ever grows great until it is focused, dedicated and disciplined. Stop the waste and start the worth!

President George Bush, speaking on "Aggression in the Gulf" to the General Assembly of the United Nations on October 1, 1990, closes with a wrap-up of the U.N. position on Iraq's invasion of Kuwait and includes an inspirational message of support for the U.N. Three strong anaphoric triads strengthen the two-paragraph conclusion. His badly mixed metaphor—"to swim, to march, to tackle"— does no serious violence to the generally strong closing, but something like "to swim upstream, to fight the undertow of negativ-

ism, to keep our focus on the distant shore of peace and stability"
would be better to continue the "swimming" metaphor:

> *The world must know and understand, from this hour, from
> this day, from this hall, we step forth with a new sense of
> purpose, a new sense of possibilities. We stand together,
> prepared to swim upstream, to march uphill, to tackle the
> tough challenges as they come, not only as the United Na-
> tions but as the nations of the world united.*
>
> *And so let it be said of this final decade of the 20th
> century, this was a time when humankind came into its
> own, when we emerged from the grit and smoke of the in-
> dustrial age to bring about a revolution of the spirit and
> mind, and began a journey to a new age and a new partner-
> ship of nations. The U.N. is now fulfilling its promise as
> the world's parliament of speech. And I congratulate you.
> I support you. And I wish you godspeed in the challenge
> ahead.*

The last example is from Governor Adlai Stevenson's gracious
concession of the presidential election to General Dwight Eisenhower, November 5, 1952. Governor Stevenson made several uses of
anaphora and one very good use of antithesis:

> *I have sent the following telegram to General Eisenhower at
> the Commodore Hotel in New York: "The people have made
> their choice and I congratulate you. That you may be the
> servant and guardian of peace and make the vale of trouble
> a door of hope is my earnest prayer. Best wishes. Adlai E.
> Stevenson."*
>
> *Someone asked me, as I came in, down on the street,
> how I felt, and I was reminded of a story that a fellow towns-
> man of ours used to tell—Abraham Lincoln. They asked
> him how he felt once after an unsuccessful election. He said
> he felt like a little boy who had stubbed his toe in the dark.
> He said that he was too old to cry, but it hurt too much to
> laugh.*

The late demagogic governor of Louisiana, Huey P. Long, once
used a simple way of signaling the audience that he was about to
wind up a thirty-minute speech: He said, "Now that I have but a
minute left . . ."

Recommended? Not.

"You Have Summoned Me to the Highest Mission. . . ."

Governor Adlai Stevenson never became president, perhaps because
history placed him head-to-head with the immensely popular war
hero Dwight D. Eisenhower. Stevenson was, however, an articulate
spokesman for the things in which he believed. The Democratic
party on July 26, 1952, nominated him for president, and his acceptance at the Democratic Convention reflects his essential decency
and intelligence. It contrasts dramatically with some of the political
oratory that seems to be the norm today. Notice particularly the closing, which includes a direct appeal beginning "Help me do the job
in the autumn of conflict and of campaign," plus an anaphoral triad,
a reference to the man he aspired to replace as president, and an
inspirational quotation:

I accept your nomination and your program.

I should have preferred to hear those words uttered by a stronger, a wiser,
a better man than myself. But after listening to the President's speech, I even
feel better about myself.

None of you, my friends, can wholly appreciate what is in my heart. I can
only hope that you understand my words. They will be few.

I have not sought the honor you have done me. I could not seek it because
I aspired to another office, which was the full measure of my ambition. And
one does not treat the highest office within the gift of the people of Illinois as
an alternative or as a consolation prize.

I would not seek your nomination for the presidency because the burdens
of that office stagger the imagination. Its potential for good or evil now and in
the years of our lives smothers exultation and converts vanity to prayer.

I have asked the merciful Father, the Father to us all, to let this cup pass
from me. But from such dread responsibility one does not shrink in fear, in
self-interest, or in false humility.

So, "If this cup may not pass from me, except I drink it, Thy will be
done."

That my heart has been troubled, that I have not sought this nomination,
that I could not seek it in good conscience, that I would not seek it in honest
self-appraisal, is not to say that I value it the less. Rather it is that I revere the
office of the presidency of the United States.

And now that you have made your decision I will fight to win that office
with all my heart and my soul. And with your help, I have no doubt that we
will win.

You have summoned me to the highest mission within the gift of any
people. I could not be more proud. Better men than I were at hand for this
mighty task, and I owe to you and to them every resource of mind and of
strength that I possess to make your deed today a good one for our country and

for our party. I am confident, too, that your selection of a candidate for vice president will strengthen me and our party immeasurably in the hard, the implacable work that lies ahead of all of us.

I know you join me in gratitude and in respect for the great Democrats and the leaders of our generation whose names you have considered here in this convention, whose vigor, whose character, and whose devotion to the Republic we love so well have won the respect of countless Americans and enriched our party.

I shall need them, we shall need them, because I have not changed in any respect since yesterday. Your nomination, awesome as I find it, has not enlarged my capacities. So I am profoundly grateful and emboldened by their comradeship and their fealty. And I have been deeply moved by their expressions of good will and of support. And I cannot, my friends, resist the urge to take the one opportunity that has been afforded me to pay my humble respects to a very great and good American whom I am proud to call my kinsman, Alben Barkley of Kentucky.

Let me say, too, that I have been heartened by the conduct of this convention. You have argued and disagreed because as Democrats you care and you care deeply. But you have disagreed and argued without calling each other liars and thieves, without despoiling our best traditions. You have not spoiled our best traditions in any naked struggles for power.

And you have written a platform that neither equivocates, contradicts, nor evades.

You have restated our party's record, its principles, and its purposes in language that none can mistake, and with a firm confidence in justice, freedom, and peace on earth that will raise the hearts and the hopes of mankind for that distant day when no one rattles a saber and no one drags a chain.

For all things I am grateful to you. But I feel no exultation, no sense of triumph. Our troubles are all ahead of us.

Some will call us appeasers; others will say that we are the war party.

Some will say we are reactionary.

Others will say that we stand for socialism.

There will be the inevitable cries of "throw the rascals out"; "it's time for a change"; and so on and so on.

We'll hear all those things and many more besides. But we will hear nothing that we have not heard before. I am not too much concerned with partisan denunciation, with epithets and abuse, because the working man, the farmer, the thoughtful businessman, all know that they are better off than ever before and they all know that the greatest danger to free enterprise in this country died with the great depression under the hammer blows of the Democratic party.

Nor am I afraid that the precious two-party system is in danger. Certainly the Republican party looked brutally alive a couple of weeks ago, and I mean both Republican parties! Nor am I afraid that the Democratic party is old and fat and indolent.

After one hundred and fifty years it has been old for a long time; and it will never be indolent as long as it looks forward and not back, as long as it commands the allegiance of the young and the hopeful who dream the dreams and see the visions of a better America and a better world.

You will hear many sincere and thoughtful people express concern about the continuation of one party in power for twenty years. I don't belittle this attitude. But change for the sake of change has no absolute merit in itself.

If our greatest hazard is preservation of the values of Western civilization, in our self-interest alone, if you please, is it the part of wisdom to change for the sake of change to a party with a split personality; to a leader whom we all respect, but who has been called upon to minister to a hopeless case of political schizophrenia?

If the fear is corruption in official position, do you believe with Charles Evans Hughes that guilt is personal and knows no party? Do you doubt the power of any political leader, if he has the will to do so, to set his own house in order without his neighbors having to burn it down?

What does concern me, in common with thinking partisans of both parties, is not just winning this election, but how it is won, how well we can take advantage of this great quadrennial opportunity to debate issues sensibly and soberly.

I hope and pray that we Democrats, win or lose, can campaign not as a crusade to exterminate the opposing party, as our opponents seem to prefer, but as a great opportunity to educate and elevate a people whose destiny is leadership, not alone of a rich and prosperous, contented country as in the past, but of a world in ferment.

And, my friends, even more important than winning the election is governing the nation. That is the test of a political party—the acid, final test. When the tumult and the shouting die, when the bands are gone and the lights are dimmed, there is the stark reality of responsibility in an hour of history haunted with those gaunt, grim specters of strife, dissension, and ruthless, inscrutable, and hostile power abroad.

The ordeal of the twentieth century, the bloodiest, most turbulent era of the Christian age, is far from over. Sacrifice, patience, understanding, and implacable purpose may be our lot for years to come.

Let's face it. Let's talk sense to the American people. Let's tell them the truth, that there are no gains without pains, that we are now on the eve of great decisions, not easy decisions, like resistance when you're attacked, but a long, patient, costly struggle which alone can assure triumph over the great enemies of man—war, poverty, and tyranny—and the assaults upon human dignity which are the most grievous consequences of each.

Let's tell them that the victory to be won in the twentieth century, this portal to the golden age, mocks the pretensions of individual acumen and ingenuity. For it is a citadel guarded by thick walls of ignorance and mistrust which do not fall before the trumpets' blast or the politicians' imprecation or even a general's baton. They are, my friends, walls that must be directly stormed by the hosts of courage, morality, and vision, standing shoulder to shoulder, unafraid of ugly truth, contemptuous of lies, half-truths, circuses, and demagoguery.

The people are wiser than the Republicans think. And the Democratic party is the people's party, not the labor party, not the farmers' party, not the employers' party. It is the party of no one because it is the party of everyone.

That, I think, is our ancient mission. Where we have deserted it we have failed. With your help there will be no desertion now. Better we lose the election than mislead the people; and better we lose than misgovern the people.

Help me do the job in the autumn of conflict and of campaign; help me to do the job in these years of darkness, of doubt, and of crisis which stretch beyond the horizon of tonight's happy vision, and we will justify our glorious past and the loyalty of silent millions who look to us for compassion, for understanding, and for honest purpose. Thus we will serve our great tradition greatly.

I ask of you all you have; I will give to you all I have, even as he who came here tonight and honored me, as he has honored you—the Democratic party—by a lifetime of service and bravery that will find him an imperishable page in the history of the Republic and of the Democratic party, President Harry S Truman.

And finally, my friends, in the staggering task that you have assigned me, I shall always try "to do justly, to love mercy, and walk humbly with my God."

—— CHAPTER FOURTEEN ——

"I have the honor to present . . ."

In the last several chapters, we've been exploring various aspects of the writing of a speech—from making an outline to using language well, to adding sparkle to the speech with appropriate quotations, anecdotes, statistics, and humor. Now I want to delve into a much neglected subject—the introduction of a speaker.

If you're a speech writer, you almost certainly will have many opportunities to write an introduction. If you're a speaker, or if you're active in an organization that regularly has guest speakers at its meetings, you will sooner or later be asked to introduce the speaker. How well you do so will affect the organization's impression of the speaker, the speaker's impression of the organization, and everyone's impression of you.

I think introductions are fun to do and fun to write. They give you an opportunity to be creative, and they challenge you to put a lot of meaning and a lot of information into a short time.

Most books on public speaking touch on introductions lightly if at all. Collections of speeches almost never include introductions. This may be understandable, you might say, because it is, after all, the speech, not the introduction, that's important.

But, wait a minute. An introduction *is* a speech. It may be short. It should be short; but it's still a speech. It should not be taken lightly. Many of the principles we've been discussing apply to introductions.

The sad story of Roger

Consider this scenario: Roger is a busy professional, and he's the program chairman for his service club. In that capacity, he has invited Mr. Maxwell Smythe, a British-born author of several books, including a Pulitzer Prize winner, to address the club. Because Mr. Smythe is much in demand as a speaker, Roger thinks it is a real coup to have him as a speaker. He has spread the word, and members of the club are anticipating a fine program. Attendance is certain to be near 100 percent, and the publicity chairman has invited the press. He thinks the local newspaper, at least one TV station, and a couple of radio stations will cover the speech.

So far, so good.

Roger doesn't know Mr. Smythe. He's even unsure how Mr. Smythe pronounces his name. Is the *y* in *Smythe* pronounced *eye* or as the *i* in the more familiar *Smith*?

Roger just happened to learn that the author would be in the city for a book signing. He contacted Smythe through his publisher and was pleasantly surprised when the author accepted the invitation. It would be Smythe's only appearance in the city, except for the book signing. No one else in the club knows Smythe either, so it will be up to Roger to make the introduction.

Now, less than a week before the scheduled speech, Roger begins to consider what he might say. *No problem,* he thinks. *I'll just get some information from the jacket of one of Smythe's books*, none of which, incidentally, Roger has gotten around to reading.

He goes to a bookstore to do his research. But he's disappointed to find that the book-jacket information is sketchy and doesn't include much information suitable for introducing a distinguished author. *No problem,* he thinks. *I'll get information from the publisher.* This time he strikes pay dirt. Someone in the publisher's PR department faxes Roger a bio sheet. Roger glances at the sheet, determines that it contains a lot of good information, and stuffs it into his coat pocket.

Fast forward now to the day of the speech. It's about three hours till show time. Roger has had a busy few days and he just hasn't had time to give much thought to the introduction. He has a couple of important appointments before it's time to leave for the meeting. *No problem,* he thinks, *the publisher's bio has everything I need. I can wing it.* He finds the sheet, still in the pocket of the coat he was wearing when he received it, and transfers it to the pocket of the suit he'll wear to the meeting.

Fast forward once again to the meeting and catch Roger's introduction:

> *In the interest of time, we have to go ahead with our program, so if you haven't finished your dinner, please continue.*

*Our speaker for this evening is Mr. Maxwell SmEYEthe
. . . er, Smith . . . Mr. Smythe was born in Watford, a suburb
of London, England, in 1933, the son of an engineer and a
school teacher. When Maxwell was only five years old, his
father accepted a job with an American firm, and the family
moved to Philadelphia, Pennsylvania. Maxwell attended
public schools in Philadelphia, excelling in both athletics
and academics and graduating a year ahead of his class.*

*At the age of 17 he enrolled in the University of Penn-
sylvania as a student majoring in electrical engineering.
After a year of engineering school, he abruptly changed his
major to English, disappointing his father, who had expected the son to follow in the father's footsteps. He announced that he intended to become a writer. After another
year, he dropped out of school and enlisted in the Army.
After basic training at Fort Benning, Georgia, he was promoted to private first class.*

*He was then sent to Korea, where he served with the
U.S. Eighth Army, winning the Bronze Star medal. He re-
turned from Korea in 1954 and was discharged from the
Army shortly afterward.*

*In 1955, while working as a salesman in Philadelphia,
he met Miss Peggy Manning, who was visiting Philadelphia
from Birmingham, Alabama. They were married on Christmas Day in 1955.*

*Maxwell held a succession of jobs for the next five
years, spending all his spare time writing. At the age of 27,
he published his first novel,* The Freshman, *a story about
college life. It was a critical success but brought little financial reward to the young novelist and his growing family,
which by then consisted of his wife, a baby daughter, and
twin boys, age four.*

*Since then he has published seven novels, all best sell-
ers, two volumes of poetry, and a biography of General William T. Sherman. His most recent novel,* Spring Forth in
Spring, *was awarded the Pulitzer Prize for literature last
year.*

*He and his wife make their home in Mountain Brook,
Alabama, a suburb of Birmingham.*

*It is a distinct honor to present our speaker for today,
Mr. Maxwell Smythe.*

Roger had simply read word for word from the sheet the publisher had furnished. That way, he reasoned, he could be certain it

was accurate. But, try to imagine how the audience—and the speaker—must have reacted to Roger's introduction.

Dull, dull, dull

The thing is, if I heard that introduction today it would not be the worst introduction I ever heard. What's wrong with it? It's dull, dull, dull. It has too many irrelevant details. It has no punch. It does not relate to the subject of Smythe's talk. In fact, it doesn't even mention the subject. It tells something of the accomplishments of Maxwell Smythe the famous author, but almost nothing of Max Smythe the person. It is, in short, a canned introduction. It *sounds* like a canned introduction.

Think about a couple of things: Here was a young man, evidently burning with the desire to be a writer. Why did he drop out of engineering and subsequently out of college? Why did he enroll in engineering school in the first place? He won a bronze star in Korea. How? What does he do when he's not writing? Curious minds want to know such things about their guest speaker.

Suppose that Roger had started his introduction something like this:

> *Max Smythe flunked college algebra twice when he was a freshman engineering student at the University of Pennsylvania more than 40 years ago.*
>
> *Today, he'll tell you that was the best thing he ever did. And there's good reason to agree, because if he had passed algebra, he might have become an engineer and the world would have been deprived of a body of literary works that includes a volume of poetry, a biography of General Sherman, and several excellent novels, five of which were bestsellers and one of which was a Pulitzer Prize winner.*
>
> *Max never wanted to be an engineer anyway. That was what his father wanted for him. And even today, the elder Smythe, who brought his family to the U.S. from England when Max was five years old, suspects his only son flunked algebra on purpose. He's probably right.*

How much more interesting that would be—in both tone and content—than the dry recitation of biographical information in the canned introduction.

Roger made several mistakes. First, he waited until just a few days before the speech to begin thinking about the introduction. With a little more time, he almost surely could have gotten some anecdotal information about Smythe. A phone call to the author's agent probably would have produced plenty of material. Besides, there's usually a lot of published material available on well-known people. Even with nothing except the publisher's bio sheet, he could have done a better job on the introduction. He could have tightened it up, organized it better, and omitted the least interesting details. He certainly could have skimmed through a couple of Smythe's books and constructed an introduction based on one of his stories or characters. He might have found something quotable from one of his poems.

In short, Roger failed to take the job seriously.

Smythe's mistake

Roger's mistakes were bad enough, but Smythe also made a mistake. His was failing to insist that his publisher have an imaginative, well-written introduction to go along with the bio sheet. Anyone who does a lot of public speaking, especially if public speaking is important to his livelihood, ought to have something prepared to send out to people who request it.

If you're writing a speech for a client, get in touch with the person who will introduce the speaker—that is, if your speaker doesn't object. Some speakers prefer to handle all contacts with the organization or the introducer. In companies that have public relations staffs, this is often a PR function. But as the speech writer, you have a vested interest in everything related to the speech you're writing. Make it your business to find out what the introducer needs and be sure that he gets it. You might even volunteer, tactfully of course, to write a suggested introduction. I stress *suggested* because the last thing you want is to give the impression that the introducer must use what you send. Nine times out of ten, the introducer will be grateful and will use your introduction word for word. That's what Roger did when he introduced Smythe. The difference is the introduction you provide will be well-crafted because you will have written it, whereas Smythe's was written by someone who didn't realize its importance.

Providing an introduction will do three things. First, it will ensure that your speaker receives an introduction that is worthy of the speaker and of the speech that the two of you have labored over. Second, it will ensure the accuracy of the information in the introduction. Third, it will almost certainly relieve the introducer of a burden.

The Rogers of the world are great in number. They need your help.

Purposes of the introduction

An introduction has three readily identifiable purposes: First, and perhaps most important, the introduction should tell *why* the speaker is there. It's well to remember that, with some exceptions, the introduction should introduce both the speaker and the speech. This does not mean that the introduction must mention the title of the speech, although it often does. It means that it should give a general idea of what the audience might expect to hear.

The second purpose of an introduction is to establish the speaker's qualifications and credentials. And here I want to stress the fact that qualifications and credentials are not necessarily the same thing. Let's take our friend Max Smythe. Although lacking a college degree, he might be better qualified than someone with, say, a doctorate in comparative literature. The person with the doctoral degree would have the credentials; the successful novelist, although a college dropout, would have the qualifications.

The extent to which qualifications and credentials are emphasized in an introduction depends upon how much the speech has already been publicized. If the organization has a bulletin, or the event a printed program, in which detailed information about the speaker is provided, the introduction should not repeat a lot of it. An anecdotal introduction is always better than a biographical introduction. Most introductions are a combination of the two.

The third purpose of the introduction is to pave the way for the speaker. It should act as a warm-up or an icebreaker. A bit of humor, an anecdote, or a pithy quotation may be appropriate.

Some do's and don'ts

Now, here are some do's and don'ts for you as an introducer or a writer of introductions:

• *Don't try to upstage the speaker.* Remember that the introduction is the appetizer, not the main course.

• *Don't make the introduction too long.* Two or three minutes ought to be long enough for most occasions. On the other hand, take whatever time is necessary to do a proper job. It's not so much the length that's important; it's the content.

• *Be sure you know how to pronounce the speaker's name .*If you're writing an introduction for someone else to deliver, and if the speaker has an unusual name, double-check the pronunciation and write it phonetically for the speaker's benefit.

• *Be sure your information is up-to-date.* If you get information from a book or a periodical, you need to make certain the sources are current.

• *Dare to be different.* There's an old axiom that says the speaker's name should not be mentioned until the very last thing. There's nothing really wrong with that, but in most cases the audience will already know who's speaking, so saving the name until the end doesn't do anything. If you're introducing someone whom most of the audience know well, try to find something different to say.

• *Please, please, don't say, "Our speaker is a person who needs no introduction."* If you do, your audience will be justified in wondering why you're bothering to give one. That's a cliché the world can do without.

• *If possible, wait until the audience has finished eating and the dishes have been cleared before you begin.* This is important for two reasons: First, your introduction will not get the attention it deserves if the people continue to concentrate on their food. Second, if you begin the introduction while the people are eating or the dishes are being cleared, you probably will not finish before the hubbub is over. The speaker will be forced to compete with waiters rattling dishes and refilling coffee cups. That is not a very good way to begin a speech.

How often I have heard a master of ceremonies at a meeting say something like, "For those of you who haven't finished eating, please continue and we'll move along with the program." How I long to hear one say, "If you haven't finished eating, speed up a bit because I don't intend to begin until everyone has finished."

That could be the best applause line of the evening.

• *Don't overdo it.* A flowery, too-detailed, or too-flattering introduction might be embarrassing to the speaker. I once heard a speaker say, after enduring an introduction filled with biographical minutiae, "Thank you, Charlie, for that very nice introduction. But I'm afraid you forgot to mention that I was an assistant patrol leader in my Boy Scout troop." The line got a chuckle, but what the speaker really wanted to say was, "Folks, it really wasn't necessary for Charlie to go into that much detail. He just got carried away."

Another good line to lighten the effect of a too-flattering introduction is "Thank you, Bob, for that generous introduction. May God forgive you for your excesses—and me for enjoying them so much." Still another: "That was a very fine introduction, but I want you to know that although I enjoyed it, I didn't inhale."

Some noteworthy intros

Because introductions are rarely published, it's not easy to find real introductions to use for illustrations. However, I have a few that you might find interesting. The first is an introduction of John H. Johnson, the founder of the publishing company that bears his name. This is the same speaker to whom I referred in the discussion of anecdotes in Chapter Eleven. He was speaking to the Economic Club of Detroit, January 30, 1989. The introducer is Gerald Greenwald, vice chairman of the Chrysler Corporation:

> *Our guest speaker today has a history every bit as dramatic as any Horatio Alger story.*
>
> *John Johnson was born in Arkansas, raised in Chicago, and spent his childhood years in poverty. When he was a senior in high school, his mother, a domestic, lost her job and the family went on welfare. Three months later, John got a great big job—$25 a month—as an office boy for the Supreme Life Insurance Company, which then was the largest black business in the North.*
>
> *There he got inspiration and he got an idea. He saw for the first time that blacks actually could be successful business people. And reading the papers for the company president and giving him a digest of the events in the black community persuaded John to start his own business—a monthly magazine condensing black-oriented articles that would be called* Negro Digest.
>
> *His friends thought he was crazy and cited the failure of a number of previously tried black-oriented magazines. John didn't listen. He persevered. He persuaded his mother— can you believe this?—he persuaded his mother to hock the family furniture for $500. He used the money to pay for direct mailings to potential subscribers, offering a charter subscription for $2.00. Three thousand people responded, and with the $6,000 he was now ready to publish the first issue of* Negro Digest.
>
> *He asked a leading Chicago distributor to handle newsstand distribution, but the company said no, saying the magazine had no chance of selling. Well, when there isn't natural demand, an entrepreneur like Johnny creates it. John got his friends to go around Chicago asking for the magazine. This convinced the distributor that there must be a demand out there.*

His success with Negro Digest *was an example of how one black man could succeed after witnessing the success of other blacks. This became John's publishing credo. He felt black Americans needed positive role models to help them fulfill their own potentials—stories about successful black men and women in commerce, in the arts, government and a host of other fields.*

This was a startling concept for the time; the idea came to John more than a decade before Martin Luther King carried a similar message.

Time and time again, John has defied conventional wisdom. The experts didn't think Ebony, *his second magazine, would last. When advertisers wouldn't buy space in it, he started a group of mail order companies and ran their ads in* Ebony. *The magazine survived* Life *and it survived* Look.

After Ebony *came other magazines; and then a nationally syndicated television show and three radio stations; the Supreme Life Insurance Company, of which he is now chairman; Supreme Beauty Products Company, a hair care company; and Fashion Fair Cosmetics, which was started when the large cosmetic companies refused to make shades dark enough for black women. And which today, I might add, is one of the top ten brands sold in department stores in the United States, the U.K. and France.*

Add all that together and you get the biggest black-owned company in the United States. John says his life is a story of turning disadvantages into advantages. It also happens to be the story of Chrysler in the '80s. Because we thought we had something in common, we reached out and asked John to join our Board of Directors four years ago. It's appropriate to note that John's appearance today comes a week after Chrysler and the NAACP agreed to discuss a fair share agreement to expand economic opportunities for minorities who are involved with our company.

John's topic today is "The Future of Minorities in America." Ladies and gentlemen, I'm proud to present an authentic American entrepreneur, John H. Johnson, publisher, chairman and chief executive officer of the Johnson Publishing Company.

Do you think the introduction is too long? What was your feeling as you read it? Did you think, "Get on with it, man, I want to hear Mr. Johnson, not you?"

Did the introduction make you eager to hear what Mr. Johnson had to say? Did the anecdotes make you feel warm toward the speaker?

Did the introduction include enough details about Mr. Johnson's business career, as opposed to anecdotes?

Do you feel it was overdone? That is, was it flattering or patronizing?

I think it was a pretty good introduction, but I believe it could have been shortened without doing violence to the content. The anecdote about Mrs. Johnson's selling the family furniture is wonderful, but Mr. Johnson, as you may recall from our previous discussion, used it in his speech. I wonder whether the fact that the introduction mentioned the story forced Mr. Johnson to modify his speech. Probably not. Most likely, Mr. Johnson's office furnished the information to Mr. Greenwald. Still, it would have been better if the introducer had not used the anecdote, since it was an important part of the speech.

Such are questions that you ought to answer about any introduction that you might write or deliver, and I suggest you read the Johnson introduction again and think about the questions as you read.

Mr. Johnson has a long and impressive list of accomplishments, and introducing someone like him is a real challenge. Mentioning all of the speaker's accomplishments, along with some basic biographical information, can make the introduction long and boring. At the same time, you want to do justice to the distinguished speaker. I was in a similar situation several years ago. An executive of the Philip Morris Company asked me to write an introduction of then Senator Mack Mattingly, who was to speak at a meeting of the company's management team at corporate headquarters in North Carolina. The executive had asked the senator's office for information for use in the introduction. Here is what he received and sent to me as my raw material from which to write the introduction:

Senator Mattingly is from St. Simons Island, Georgia. For twenty years, Mr. Mattingly worked for International Business Machines and for five years he owned his own small business. He graduated from Indiana University in 1957 with a degree in marketing. He served four years in the U.S. Air Force and was stationed at Hunter Air Field in Savannah.

He is married to the former Carolyn Longcamp and they have two daughters, both attending the University of Georgia. He is a member of the Christ Episcopal Church of St. Simons Island, the American Legion, and the Brunswick-Golden Isles Chamber of Commerce.

Mr. Mattingly is nationally known for his work involving economic and domestic policies. He has served on national economic tax policy committees. As the tax policy co-chairman, Mattingly co-authored the tax policy plank of the 1980 Republican Party Platform.

Since his election, Mr. Mattingly has been named to the powerful Senate Appropriations Committee, where he is chairman of the Legislative Branch Subcommittee. He was also named to the Governmental Affairs Committee and is chairman of the Congressional Operations and Oversight Subcommittee. He also serves on the Select Committee on Ethics and the Joint Economic Committee.

Some speakers would have used that information with few if any changes. But the executive hired me to write his introduction because he wanted something better. He asked me to come up with an introduction that would be unique. Here is what I wrote:

Along about midnight last November 4, most Georgians, except the most confirmed election-return addicts, were turning off their television sets and getting ready for bed. The most interesting race was no longer in doubt: According to media projections, Senator Herman Talmadge had been re-elected, thus continuing one of the nation's most enduring political dynasties, one that began in 1932 with the election of Senator Talmadge's father as governor of Georgia.

Few people had reason to doubt those projections. They might have been made by any reasonably astute eighth grader. But . . . astute eighth graders and sophisticated computer programs can be wrong. As the night wore on, Talmadge's lead began to dissipate and, by dawn's early light, Georgia had a new senator-elect. His name was Mack Mattingly. He is our speaker today.

Mack Mattingly may remain in the U.S. Senate for fifty years. He may become a great and powerful national figure. He may even be elected president. But . . . regardless of what he may or may not accomplish in the future, those of us who have followed Georgia politics closely will always remember him as the man who defied the odds and the experts to defeat a powerful, popular, and able senator.

Consider:

He defeated a Democrat in a state that, as an old saying goes, would "elect a yellow dog if it ran on the Democratic ticket." He is an outspoken Republican in a state that hasn't

been known to "cotton" to Republicans since Lincoln freed
the slaves. He is a businessman in a state where the farm
vote has often been the dominant force in statewide elections. And, most significantly, he is—or was—an amateur
in a game played by seasoned professionals.

Senator Mattingly comes from St. Simon's Island, one
of Georgia's fabled "Golden Isles" off the Southern coast.
Before entering the political arena, he was a small-business
man—a fact in which he takes considerable pride. Before
opening his own business, he worked for twenty years for
IBM. He was active for many years in Republican affairs
and, as co-chairman of the national tax policy committee,
he helped draft the tax policy plank of the 1980 Republican
platform. Senator Mattingly graduated in 1957 from Indiana University with a degree in marketing—and I might
point out that he has been known to do a little "marketing"
of President Reagan's economic philosophy. As a senator,
he's in a pretty good position to do so: He is a member of
the Joint Economic Committee, the Senate Appropriations
Committee, the Select Committee on Ethics, and the Governmental Affairs Committee. He is chairman of the Congressional Operations and Oversight Subcommittee.

It's particularly appropriate, I think, for us to have this
Georgia senator as our guest speaker. As you know, our
company has many interests in the state. We buy a lot of
Georgia-grown tobacco in Georgia markets. We have a large
sales force in the state; and, of course, there's the Miller
Brewery in the town of Albany—or, as they pronounce it
down there, ALL-BENNY.

Senator, we're honored by your presence. We look forward to your message.

Ladies and gentlemen, it's a pleasure for me to present
the junior senator from Georgia, the Honorable Mack Mattingly.

That introduction, I think, shows what can be done with a little
imagination and a little special knowledge. I was able to write a more
imaginative and interesting introduction because, as a Georgian, I
knew more about the Georgia political scene than did the North Carolina executive. That is probably the reason the executive gave me
the assignment rather than rely on one of his company's excellent
speech writers.

Now, I want to share two other imaginative approaches. In these,
I won't give you the full treatment, just the openings. The first is the

introduction of the chief executive officer of a large company. The CEO is the keynote speaker at a convention. He is being introduced by an employee of his own company:

> *Good evening, everyone.*
>
> *In thinking about what I might say to introduce our key-note speaker, it occurred to me that the most flattering intro-duction is the one that is often used for the President, which is, simply, "Ladies and gentlemen: the President of the United States." So I was tempted to introduce our speaker by saying, "Ladies and gentlemen: the president and chief executive officer of Wonder Widget, Inc."*
>
> *However . . .*
>
> *However, since we don't have the U.S. Marine Band to play "Hail to the Chief," I decided that I had better go a little further. I also considered the fact that this is my boss I'm talking about.*

After that beginning, the introducer goes into a fairly conventional introduction.

The next example is the beginning of an introduction of a speaker who had an exceptionally long list of accomplishments:

> *Good afternoon, everyone.*
>
> *Thomas Edison once said that if we did all the things we are capable of doing, we would literally astonish our-selves. Looking at the résumé of our speaker makes me won-der if I am about to introduce a very astonished fellow. I don't know what he's capable of doing, of course; I can only judge by what he has done—and what he continues to do. If I tried to mention all of his accomplishments and activi-ties, I'd be the speaker instead of the introducer. And you would miss out on a lot of wisdom and experience. I would, however, be derelict in my duty if I failed to mention a few highlights of his illustrious career.*

The opening was followed by some carefully selected highlights from the speaker's résumé.

I can summarize my advice about introductions very simply: Take them seriously.

"THE LUCKIEST MAN ON THE FACE OF THE EARTH"

Lou Gehrig bade farewell to baseball at Yankee Stadium on July 4, 1939. Suffering and dying from a crippling illness, Gehrig might have been expected to make and even been forgiven for making self-pitying remarks in his brief farewell address to his fans. He didn't. In fact, he hardly spoke of himself. He mentioned none of his many accomplishments. He spoke instead of others and what they had meant to him:

Fans, for the past two weeks you have been reading about a bad break I got. Yet today I consider myself the luckiest man on the face of the earth. I have been in ballparks for seventeen years and have never received anything but kindness and encouragement from you fans.

Look at these grand men. Which of you wouldn't consider it the highlight of his career just to associate with them for even one day?

Sure, I'm lucky. Who wouldn't consider it an honor to have known Jacob Ruppert; also the builder of baseball's greatest empire, Ed Barow; to have spent six years with that wonderful little fellow Miller Huggins; then to have spent the next nine years with that outstanding leader, that smart student of psychology, the best manager in baseball today, Joe McCarthy!

Sure, I'm lucky. When the New York Giants, a team you would give your right arm to beat, and vice versa, sends you a gift, that's something! When everybody down to the groundskeepers and those boys in white coats remember you with trophies, that's something.

When you have a wonderful mother-in-law who takes sides with you in squabbles against her own daughter, that's something. When you have a father and mother who work all their lives so that you can have an education and build your body, it's a blessing! When you have a wife who has been a tower of strength and shown more courage than you dreamed existed, that's the finest I know.

So I close in saying that I might have had a tough break; but I have an awful lot to live for.

—— Chapter Fifteen ——

More Than Words Can Say

Lou Gehrig was one of my heroes. Unfortunately, I never saw him play, although I have been lucky enough to see some of the latter-day baseball greats—Dimaggio, Aaron, Williams, and even Satchel Paige (in an exhibition game when Satch was past sixty-five).

Just about every field of endeavor has people we can hold out as heroes. In the entertainment field, one of my favorites is the old pro, the late Red Skelton. I miss him.

Some time ago, shortly after his death, I watched a television special featuring Red. He was at his lovable best when he acted out his skits without using words. His facial expressions, his gestures, and his body language were wonderful. He connected with me as surely as if he had been speaking directly to me. I had no doubt about the story he was communicating.

Before humans developed the ability to communicate with spoken language, there was body language. Animals use body language to supplement their oral communication. Your dog might bark to tell you he's happy to see you, but he also wags his tail and, unless you've trained him not to, jumps on you. He runs in circles, yapping happily. If an enemy approaches your dog, the friendly hound becomes a vicious mutt. Instead of yapping or barking, he snarls. Instead of wagging his tail, he raises his hackles and bares his teeth. Body language. It's the dog's main way to communicate. Other animals use it also. A horse paws the ground. A bull lowers his head. A cat rubs against your leg. A rattlesnake shakes its tail to warn you to get out of its way.

Speakers use it, too

As a speaker, you use body language for better or worse. You might not think of it that way, but that's what it is. Researchers have estimated that a person is capable of twenty thousand distinct gestures, each of which has its own meaning. This vocabulary, if we can be justified in calling it that, dwarfs the working vocabulary of the typical English-speaking person.

According to *American Speaker*, a program for speakers and speech writers, research by a leading communications expert has shown that the visual impact of a speech accounts for an astounding 55 percent of the audience's impressions. This compares with 38 percent for vocal impressions—the speaker's tone of voice, range, enunciation, and so forth—and only 7 percent for verbal impressions. So, are we forced to conclude that what a speaker says is less important than how he says it or how he looks while saying it?

Not at all. The point is that verbal, vocal, and visual impressions combine to create an effective, memorable speech. The vocal and visual elements of the speech affect how the verbal message is received. If the vocal and visual elements are favorable to the speaker, the message has a better chance of being well received and fulfilling its purpose. Words convey information; nonverbal communications add meaning to the information. Sometimes, body language can tell us more than words alone can say.

The key to a good speech is for the verbal and nonverbal language to say the same thing. The old cliché from a long-forgotten western movie, "Smile when you say that, Podnuh," gives us the incongruous picture of angry words emanating from a smiling face.

When you listen to someone on the radio, you have no visual element to consider, unless you happen to know what the speaker looks like. Even then, the image you have is static. However, you'll likely form some sort of image as you listen, based on the vocal elements I've mentioned. Your impressions of the speaker affect the way you receive the messages of the program. That's because the speaker's voice, perhaps as much as his or her actual words, are part of the message.

If the speaker sounds sincere, confident, relaxed, and knowledgeable, we tend to believe what he says. If he mispronounces words, if he sounds phony, if his voice is thin and high-pitched, if he talks too fast or too slowly, or if he speaks indistinctly, the words are sure to be less credible.

If nonverbal aspects of a speech account for 55 percent of the audience's impression, as the research cited above indicates, then the importance of nonverbal communication cannot be overstated.

Let's go back to what is commonly called "body language," which is defined as gestures, mannerisms, and movements. Communications experts have written books about body language. Most body language is unconscious, which is to say that it's something we do without thinking. Psychologists tell us that just by the way we sit or stand or use our hands, we may unknowingly convey aggression, openness, hostility, defensiveness, sincerity, fear, or other attitudes and emotions. For example, standing with your arms folded across your chest is said to be a defensive posture.

The study of body language is called kinesics. It is not, by any means, an exact science. A certain body movement may mean one thing in one culture and quite another thing in another culture. There's also evidence that body language varies with the spoken language. Thus, German body language might be different from English body language.

I don't pretend to be an expert in kinesics. I can, however, offer some practical suggestions about how to make body language work in your favor and how to avoid certain habits that may detract from your public-speaking persona.

Getting to know you

It's important to know yourself. Strangely enough, most of us don't know ourselves very well. A person may have a nervous habit that is apparent only to a spouse, a friend, or someone else who knows the person well. The pressure of standing before an audience may cause the person to exaggerate the habit. That's why a video camera is a useful device for speakers' training. If you could see a video of yourself delivering a speech, or practicing a speech, you could probably detect many problems that would be fairly easy to correct. This is absolutely the best way to evaluate what you say, how you say it, and how you look while you're saying it.

If seeing yourself on video is impossible, ask your spouse or a friend whether you have any distracting mannerisms. After you have made a speech, ask someone in the audience to evaluate your body language, gestures, and appearance. Be sure you make it clear that you're not asking for a general opinion of your speech. Approving remarks such as "I liked your speech" are of little value. You need specific comments. Constructive criticism is hard to come by. Most people, especially friends and colleagues, don't like to criticize. If someone tells you your speech was "good" or "great," don't take the comment too seriously. If the person says you mumbled, slouched, mispronounced words, or whatever, believe it.

Posture is an important part of body language. The best posture for a speaker is to stand up straight, arms at his side, legs slightly apart, weight balanced equally on both feet. You want to feel and look relaxed, but not to the point of slouching or leaning on the lectern, which will make you look tired or bored.

One of the problems most of us have when we speak is what to do with our hands. With some speakers, the hands seem to have a will of their own. They do all sorts of things the speaker doesn't want them to do and may not even know they do. They need to be brought under control.

Don't stand with your hands clasped in front of you or your arms crossed over your chest. In body language, these positions are said to mean, "Keep your distance." Don't fidget with anything such as keys, a pointer, or a pencil as you speak.

The best place for your hands is at your side except when you're using them to make an appropriate gesture, to refer to a visual, or to manipulate your speech notes. Having made that observation, however, I will say that keeping your arms rigidly down all the time might make you seem too stiff. You can relieve this stiffness by putting one hand in your pocket briefly now and then or by allowing one hand to rest gently on the lectern. For men at least, putting one hand in the trousers pocket is a natural act that creates a feeling of informality. Do not jam both hands in the pockets and leave them there. And don't hold the lectern in a double-handed death grip. That makes you look nervous, and it will make you feel nervous.

Don't use too many gestures. Gestures are to speaking what punctuation marks are to writing. Used sparingly, they add clarity and emphasis to the message; overused, they can be distracting to the audience. Imagine reading a sentence that had a comma or an explanation point after every word or two. And, imagine! listening, to a speech, in which the speaker punctuated! every! phrase by pounding! his fist, on the table! Nerve-wracking, wouldn't you say?

A certain management guru and author of several fine books on management did a series of commentaries on a televised business program. This man punctuated almost every word with a karate chop of his right hand. It was so distracting that I could barely concentrate on what he was saying. I thought it remarkable that the show's director evidently didn't point this out. I have a feeling that the speaker was so concerned about being seen as just a talking head that he used the constant gesturing as a way to enliven his commentaries. Whatever his reason, it didn't work. Better a talking head than a chopping hand.

Be careful about the kind of gesture you make. For example, don't point your finger at anyone in the audience. To some people, pointing is a threatening or intimidating gesture. If you have reason to single out an individual, as you might during a question-and-answer period, try to do it in a way in which you don't have to point.

For example, you can use words and eye contact. Say, "Yes, the lady in the blue dress has a question," and look directly at the woman so as to exclude others.

My best advice is to keep body movement of any kind at a minimum. Use only gestures and movement that serve some purpose. Above all, make your gesture appropriate to the context, or, in the parlance of the theater, "suit the action to the words."

We might make the same observation about facial expressions. I know a man who owns a heating and air-conditioning business. He does his own television commercials, and when he speaks of the glories of having your heating system checked at the beginning of each season, he seems always to wear a frown. He can't help it; it's the way his facial muscles work. He would look equally foolish with a perpetual grin. In neither case would his facial expression make me want to use his company's service. I suppose he ought to stick to radio.

When you speak, your facial expressions are nonverbal communications as surely as are gestures. They can convey a full range of emotions that the audience will associate with the message. Unfortunately, the association the audience makes may be invalid because the speaker's emotions, and thus his facial expressions, may be affected by tension or even fear. Most of the time, you're unaware of your facial expression of the moment. Relaxing your tensions and overcoming your fear can help ensure that your expressions will be in keeping with the messages you wish to convey.

Try to look relaxed and pleasant most of the time. An occasional smile can't hurt anything.

The eyes have it

Eye contact is certainly a part of body language and is included in every book and every course on public speaking. It's extremely important to maintain good eye contact with the audience, but it is necessary to understand exactly what it means. The phrase "eye contact with the audience" is often used, but it seems to me to be a contradiction, for it is not possible to maintain eye contact with more than one person at a time. The idea is to go from person to person in the audience and make eye contact with each one for a second or so. The contact should not be too fleeting or it will seem furtive. But looking directly into the eyes of a person for too long may make the person uncomfortable.

Jeff Cook, in his book *The Elements of Speechwriting and Public Speaking,* offers a sort of formula for using eye contact effectively.

He advises looking at one person while you express one idea. The sequence, he says, goes something like this:

- Look at your notes.
- Absorb one idea.
- Make eye contact with one person.
- Express the idea.
- Then go on to another idea and another person.

I had never heard that system before, but it seems to make good sense. If it works for you, fine. Whatever method you use, there are four things to keep in mind:

1. *In maintaining eye contact with members of the audience, don't allow yourself to become distracted by something that's going on.* If, for example, a member of the audience has dropped a pencil and is trying to retrieve it, look somewhere else in the room for your eye contact.
2. *Never try to look out into space over the heads of the audience.* That is not making contact.
3. *Hold eye contact with the same person long enough to have a meaningful connection, even if you don't accept Jeff Scott's one-person-per-thought formula.* Moving from person to person too fast will give you a herky-jerky appearance.
4. *If a short pause is indicated at the end of the thought, hold the eye contact through the pause.*

Pauses that refresh

A pause is a form of body language. Pauses can be used for dramatic effect, for emphasis, and as transitions. In the discussion of transitions in Chapter Nine, I made the point that a long pause in a speech could have the same effect as a subhead or a typographical bullet in writing. A very slight pause usually comes at the end of a paragraph, a long one at the end of a topic.

A pause also gives a speaker a chance to breathe deeply and may help him relax and pace the speech well. You might find it helpful, as I do, to write the word *pause* at appropriate spots in your speech text to remind the speaker when to pause. This could be especially helpful if the speaker has a tendency to talk too fast.

If at first you have the feeling you're exaggerating your pauses, they're probably just right. What might seem like a long pause to you probably will not seem so long to your audience. The next time you listen to a really good speaker, especially one such as an actor or a TV commentator who is well-trained, listen for the pauses. Be conscious of when they appear, what purposes they serve, and how long they are.

Other than body language, the two forms of nonverbal communication are the way you look and the way you sound.

The way you look

Your appearance can have a powerful effect on your audience. Politicians, perhaps more than anyone else, are very much aware of this. How many times have you seen a candidate appear on television in shirt sleeves, often with his collar unbuttoned and his tie loosened? President Jimmy Carter liked to wear a sweater when he spoke to the nation from the oval office. Ronald Reagan loved to be seen wearing boots, jeans, and a western-style hat. These modes of appearance are all calculated to give audiences certain impressions. If they seem too contrived they can backfire. Remember Michael Dukakis in the tanker's helmet?

I thought George Bush looked out of character in shirt sleeves. To me, he seems like a coat-and-tie man. Every time Jimmy Carter showed up on TV trying to look like my next-door neighbor, he surrendered some of the aura that surrounds a president. Reagan, on the other hand, always looked natural in his western hat, but I suppose that's because I had seen him in so many western movies.

How should you dress for a speech? It depends mainly on the occasion, but partly on your own style. I once attended a Rotary Club meeting in a rural county. The speaker was the county agricultural agent, and he wore a business suit. You could almost smell the moth balls. The guy seldom wore anything other than jeans and a sport shirt. In his business suit, he looked as out of place as Bill Clinton at a Moral Majority convention.

If you're speaking at, say, a convention in a resort, and just about everyone in the audience is dressed for the golf course, you'll be more comfortable in slacks and a golf shirt than a business suit.

But that's an exception. Most of the time, you ought to dress as if you were going to an important appointment. For a man, this means a business suit and a conservative tie, or perhaps a navy blazer with gray slacks. For a woman, it means a tailored dress or suit accented by tasteful jewelry.

Dress comfortably. Don't wear something that doesn't fit quite right. If you have a favorite garment and it's appropriate for the occasion, by all means choose that over something that you might not like quite as much. Maybe the audience won't know the difference, but you will. If you feel that you look your best, you will be more confident, and confidence will make you look and feel better when you speak.

I've done some college teaching, and I always wore a coat and tie to class. No matter that most of my students looked as if they had bought their clothes at a yard sale. Some professors came to class looking about the same as their students. I could be wrong, but I always thought they gave up some of the respect that their position demanded when they tried to look like one of the gang.

The way you sound

If looking your best is important, sounding your best may be even more so. Most of us can never hope to have a voice as rich as that of James Earl Jones, Julie Andrews, or Richard Burton. But most of us can improve our voice and thus our speaking image. Those professionals underwent many years of training to develop their voices to the point that they could project from a stage to a large audience. Every speaker, however, should be aware of how much a good voice, properly used, can add to the effectiveness of a speech.

Audiences draw conclusions from the speaker's voice. A person with a soft voice may be assumed to be timid; a high-pitched voice may mark the speaker as effeminate; a strong, deep voice is associated with masculinity or authority. These impressions aren't necessarily accurate. In the movie *The Untouchables*, the little guy playing the FBI accountant had a high-pitched, almost whiny voice. But when the chips were down, when the law officers came up against Al Capone's mobsters, the accountant was a tiger. His courage almost put even Eliot Ness to shame. Accurate or not, the impressions an audience gains from a speaker's voice are significant.

In the introduction to her short, but useful, book *Speak to Win*, Dr. Georgiana Peacher said:

> *Your speaking voice is a powerful instrument of human relations. It is often the first yardstick by which other people measure your attractiveness—and even your ability.*
>
> *Like a violin, your voice can be resonant and melodious, or it can sound weak or discordant and harsh. It can help you win the respect of your colleagues and subordinates, or it can be a factor holding you back from positions of authority. Furthermore, you yourself are influenced by*

*the sound of your own voice, and your confidence in your-
self will be enhanced if it is firm, clear, and musical.*

When I think of speech training, I recall the wonderful scene in
the old flick *Singin' in the Rain.* A speech coach had been employed
to help a beautiful but inarticulate movie star convert from silent
films to the new talkies. The coach was having her endlessly repeat
phrases such as "How Now, Brown Cow," and "Moses supposes."

And don't forget Professor 'Enry 'Iggins laboring to rid Eliza
Doolittle of her Cockney accent.

Serious voice training can indeed be a long and laborious process. Dr. Peacher prescribes a regimen that should continue for, in
her words, "at least six months or until your voice is completely re-
educated and you are spontaneously using it in a correct and relaxed
manner under all conditions."

But don't let that discourage you. Nothing quite so tedious is
necessary for most people who just want to improve their voice for
public speaking. You can get good results by following a few simple
principles.

Don't try to make your voice do something it was never meant
to do. There's a popular notion that a low-pitched voice is always
more pleasant. If you think a lower pitch is necessarily better, try
telling that to fans of Luciano Pavarotti, tenor, or Beverly Sills, so-
prano. Your optimum pitch is the pitch that enables you to speak
naturally and clearly with a minimum of strain.

I once knew a young man whose ambition was to be a radio
announcer. He had a pleasant voice, but he was never satisfied with
it. He wanted a deeper voice, so he was constantly straining to lower
the pitch. He succeeded only in sounding strained because he was
strained. I always suspected that the straining did more harm than
good to his larynx.

A good voice is largely a function of proper breathing. You can
improve your voice by improving your breathing. Practice breathing
deeply through your mouth, using your abdominal muscles to draw
air into your lungs. Exhale slowly, without forcing the air out. This
will help relax your vocal cords. Do this exercise five to ten minutes
at a time, a couple of times a day. You can do it standing erect, sitting
at your desk, or lying on your back. Try it in bed at night. It might
even help you fall asleep.

Good posture and proper breathing go together, and both contribute to voice quality. Get into a good-posture habit, not just when
you're making a speech. Good posture helps reduce nervous tension,
which can make your voice sound reedy or nasal. When you speak,
you should have the feeling that the words are coming from deep

inside rather than from the throat. This will add to the richness and timbre of the sound.

And, by all means, take care of your voice. Cigarette smoking, shouting or screaming, and excessive throat clearing can damage your vocal cords.

No matter how good your voice is, you must use it correctly. Reading aloud, especially poetry, is a good way to train yourself to enunciate clearly. Recording and playing back what you have read can help you eliminate bad habits of which you may not even be aware. Most of us have bad speech habits, and when we become aware of them, we can and should correct them.

Some people have the habit of allowing the voice to rise at the end of almost every clause or sentence, making everything seem like a question. For example:

> *Yesterday my wife and I went to the MOVIES* [?]. *We saw* Dances with WOLVES [?]

Ending a statement with rising inflection gives a sort of tentative quality to what is said, as if the speaker is unsure of himself. It robs the statement of authority. To the audience, it can be distracting at best, irritating at worst. For some reason, the habit seems to go naturally with the disgusting expression "you know." It's remarkable how often I hear "you know" following a rising inflection:

> *Yesterday my wife and I went to the MOVIES* [?], *you know. We saw* Dances with WOLVES [?], *you know. My wife thought Kevin Costner was WONDERFUL* [?], *you know.*

With very few exceptions, a speaker's inflection at the end of a statement should be *down*. That's the point of natural emphasis.

And speaking of "you know," that and similar expressions that clutter the discourse of many otherwise articulate people have no place in a speech. They are the verbal equivalent of clearing your throat. The process of preparing a written text for a speech should help you eliminate such expressions.

Pronounce it right

My final comments on nonverbal communication relate to the pronunciation of words. Yes, I know, pronunciation is a verbal act. But to me it falls into the nonverbal category because it has nothing to do with meaning. If I say "potAto" and you say "potAHto," we send the same information even though we might be sending a slightly different message. At least it tells something about the speaker. But what? Well, for one thing, it tells me that you're not from my part of the country.

Suppose you hear a speaker say "nuc-yu-lur" instead of "nuclear" or "ath-uh-lete" instead of "athlete." Again, the information we receive from "nuc-yu-lur" and "ath-uh-lete" is the same as from "nuclear" and "athlete," but we get the message that the person who says "nuc-yu-lur" and "ath-a-lete" is, to say the least, just a bit careless of pronunciation. Could that mean the person is also careless with facts?

Some words, especially proper names, are pronounced differently in different regions of the country. In Atlanta, Ponce de Leon, a well-known street, is pronounced to rhyme with "nonce," "the," and "neon." In other parts of the country, the name might be pronounced "PonSAY day LeOWN." In both New Hampshire and North Carolina, there is a city named Concord. In New Hampshire, it's "CONKurd," but in North Carolina it's "CONcord." Houston (HOUSEton) County, Georgia, is spelled the same as Houston (HY-USton), Texas.

I would be the last to suggest that you eliminate regional pronunciations from your speech, but blatant mispronunciations such as the all-too-common "nucyular" have nothing to do with regionalism and everything to do with indifference to our language.

If there are words that you habitually mispronounce, and you know you're doing it, make a list and practice the correct pronunciation. If you're not sure how a word is pronounced, check your dictionary.

To delve a bit more deeply into the subject of pronunciation, invest in a copy of Charles Harrington Elster's *Big Book of Beastly Mispronunciations.* This is an authoritative guide to pronouncing many often-mispronounced words.

In summary, don't take the nonverbal elements of speech making lightly. After all, they account for 55 percent of the impressions you will leave with your audience.

"Gaining Strength and Respect in the World"

The following speech was delivered by Ambassador Jeane J. Kirkpatrick, United States Permanent Representative to the United Nations, at the Reagan Administration Executive Forum on January 20, 1984. Note how effectively Mrs. Kirkpatrick used anaphora with several successive repetitions of "I didn't know" and "I knew":

We have all, I suspect, learned a good deal in the past three years. I personally have learned so many things I never suspected were true about government and politics—that I feel like sending recall notices to my former students.

What I didn't know about the United Nations three years ago would fill a book I don't intend to write.

I didn't know that the Soviet Foreign Minister would attack us for interfering in the internal affairs of Afghanistan.

I didn't know that the Foreign Minister of the Ethiopian government—accused by Amnesty International of burning high school students in oil—would attack us for gross abuses of human rights.

I didn't know that the Poles who had just suppressed Solidarity would accuse us of totalitarianism.

I didn't even know that we would not be able to get subjects like the Libyan invasion of Chad or the repression of the Baha'i in Iran onto the agenda of the General Assembly while "they" could keep Israel's "crimes" perpetually before that body.

The fact is, when I went to the United Nations three years ago, I didn't know much about that institution in which, as Sam Levenson said, whole peoples are sentenced to death by elocution.

A few things, however, I did know.

I knew that the elections of 1980 marked the end of our national identity crisis—that the period of great national self-doubt and self-denigration had given way to a returning confidence in the legitimacy and success of our society, our institutions and ourselves.

I knew, too, that this returning confidence in the basic decency of Americans and in the relevance of our experience to the contemporary world coincided with a time of unprecedented expansionism by the Soviet Union.

I knew they had never been stronger, and that we had never been as weak by comparison; and that this "new correlation of forces," as they like to call it, constituted a dangerous threat to liberal, democratic, Western societies and to the independence and sovereignty of smaller, non-Western societies as well.

Like a clear majority of other Americans, we all knew that the defeatism, delusions, and self-doubts that had displaced our traditional American optimism during the Carter years were not, as they liked to suggest, "a sign of growing American maturity in a complex world."

It was a symptom of despair.

Political scientists sometimes like to argue that it is impossible to tell what an election means—especially when they don't like the election's outcome.

But it was not, really, very difficult to understand the meaning of the 1980 elections:

The election of Ronald Reagan was a victory for those who rejected the idea of inevitable American decline.

The inauguration of Ronald Reagan—endowed with unique significance by the simultaneous release of our hostages, which closed the most humiliating episode in our national history—signaled a new beginning for America; a new beginning based on restoration of a strong economy and a strong defense, based above all on a vigorous commitment to freedom in domestic and foreign affairs.

Our nation's subsequent recovery in domestic and foreign affairs has been sustained by the consensus that brought the Reagan/Bush team to office and has in turn sustained growing national health and returning capacity to believe in ourselves, our worth and our future. That recovery has progressed so that today, the "sick society" syndrome of the Vietnam era is finally behind us. The self-doubt, pessimism and associated paralysis of those dismal times have been replaced by a new optimism.

A great many recent polling data, relevant to broad, basic and significant orientations, make this clear. Some 66 percent of all voters today approve the American quality of life. Some 62 percent believe this nation's best times are still ahead of us. There is also increased clarity and agreement about our principal adversary. Some 61 percent of Americans believe communism is the worst form of government, up from 54 percent only five years earlier. Today only 9 percent of Americans, the lowest point since 1956, have a favorable opinion of the Soviet Union. This negative opinion is associated with the widespread belief (by 81 percent of Americans) that the Soviets and Cubans are encouraging turmoil and terrorism around the world and, more specifically, a substantial majority of both Democrats and Republicans think those same Soviets and Cubans promoted trouble and turmoil in Grenada and in Central America. Some 75 percent of all Americans believe the U.S. Government should counteract these activities.

Over 60 percent of Democrats as well as Republicans and independents see the Soviet Union as an immediate danger to the United States. Over half of all three groups—Republicans, Democrats and independents—agree that President Reagan's policy of firmness will prove effective in preventing greater problems. 93 percent of Americans believe it would be better to fight if necessary than to accept Russian domination, though most of us believe that firm leadership will make it unnecessary. On a range of foreign policy questions, from the general to the particular, from Lebanon to Grenada, there are some differences between rank-and-file Republicans, Democrats and independents, but these differences are small as compared to the broad consensus about basic matters. Moreover, for the first time since 1964 the confidence of the public in the good sense and good faith of those who govern them is again on the rise.

Strangely enough, the broad consensus about ourselves, the goals of our foreign policy, the nature of our adversaries, and what we should do in various situations is not reflected—certainly not fully reflected—in the positions taken by leading contenders for the Democratic nomination today, any more than it is reflected in many partisan discussions of foreign policy or in many votes in the Congress.

The shared understandings and consensus broad enough to support a bipartisan foreign policy exist; but, much too often, public discussion of foreign affairs is still dominated by the harsh, bitter, polemical spirit that so deeply scarred the American conduct of foreign affairs in the period since debate on the Vietnam War turned mean and pushed our disagreements over the limit of civil debate to the edges of violence and beyond. Remember the nasty riots that were called "disturbances"? —The Viet Cong flags? The most violent manifestations of that era are mercifully past, but the bitterness of many of those divisions remains and distorts, I believe, national discussion of how to implement, through our foreign policy, the effective protection of democratic values and of the West.

Neither public opinion polls nor election outcomes have so far lured a good many of our opposition leaders back from the attractions of adversary elitism, from what Mark Shields has called "reflexive anti-Americanism." Democratic Congressmen and candidates doubtless know that great majorities of Americans support strong defense and a prudently assertive foreign policy, but many continue to embrace elitist liberal points of view. As Mark Shields, a Democratic commentator, put it in a most recent issue of "Public Opinion" magazine, "Democrats insist they favor some weapons system or another, but it's never the one which is before the Congress in any given year. . . . Of course, say the Democrats, there is some place in the world where we should tell the Soviets, 'Enough'; but it is never the place where we are currently embroiled."

So far they just have not caught on to the fact that the American people are no longer ready to give everybody except the government the benefit of the doubt. Too many liberals remain bogged down in what they apparently consider the "good old days" of the anti-war movement and the counterculture.

Most of us have moved on. Most Americans decline to be "willing victims," and are no longer ready to assist in the legitimization of our defeat and disappearance.

When I arrived at the United Nations, someone asked what would be the difference between this new administration's policies and the previous one's.

I said, "We have taken off our 'kick me' sign."

He said, "Does that mean that if you're kicked, you'll kick back?"

"Not necessarily," I responded, "but it does mean that if we're kicked, at least we won't apologize."

In his book on How Democracies End, the distinguished French commentator, Jean-François Revel, observed that in the West people are embarrassed to call the struggle between democracy and totalitarianism by its own name; that they prefer instead to speak of the "competition between East and West" or the "struggle between the superpowers," as if the "superpowers" were politically, morally equivalent.

The people know better.

In New York, at the UN, some people tried to suggest that the liberation of Grenada was the moral equivalent of the invasion of Afghanistan. We asked them: Where were the grateful Afghans lining the streets of Kabul shouting, "God Bless Andropov?"

The Grenadians know the difference. So do the American people.

We know the difference, too, between a foreign policy that is based on appeasement and recklessness and a foreign policy that is steady and strong.

We know that in the past three years President Reagan has given us a strong, steady policy that has paved the way for a renaissance of freedom in the United States and in the world.

And let us be clear: In giving this nation strong, steady leadership, Reagan has been Reagan.

I feel certain you are as grateful as I that the President has given us an opportunity to participate in this extraordinary reconstruction.

Thank you.

—— Chapter Sixteen ——

The Final Stages

You have now been through the process of researching, outlining, and writing a speech. Your speech has been written. You have an opening that will get the speech off to an exciting start, a closing that will send the audience on their way feeling that they've heard from a speaker who's a cross between Reagan and Cicero, and a middle that's packed with useful information, colorful metaphors, beautiful analogies, revealing anecdotes, and a few touches of humor. Now all you have to do is show up, make your speech, and enjoy the accolades.

Well, no. There are still a few things left to do:

1. You need to give your speech a thorough editing.
2. You have to prepare your speech for delivery. That is, put it in the form that you will carry with you when you step up to the lectern.
3. You must practice so that you know your speech thoroughly.

These three imperatives are the subjects of our discussion in this chapter. This discussion is written as if you are both writer and speaker, but the principles are applicable if you're the speaker or the writer.

Editors-R-Everybody

If you're a speech writer working in a corporate or government environment, you'll have plenty of "editors"—probably more than you want or need. Everyone, it seems, is a frustrated writer and cannot resist the impulse to edit someone else's hard work.

Peggy Noonan, the talented writer who crafted some of President Reagan's best speeches, relates some of her White House experiences in her book, *What I Saw at the Revolution*. In the book she tells of writing a speech for the president to deliver to students in Shanghai. In her first draft of the speech, she included this paragraph:

> *My young friends, history is a river that takes us as it will. But we have the power to navigate, to choose direction, and make our passage together. The wind is up, the tide is high, and the opportunity for a long and fruitful journey awaits us. Generations hence will honor us for having begun the voyage . . .*

Ms. Noonan relates that a State Department functionary, in reviewing the draft, had numerous changes, including elimination of the metaphor of history as a river. His reason was that the metaphor was "politically unhelpful" because, in his words, "the 'history is a river' claim is more in line with standard Marxian theory regarding historical determination than it is with the idea that man can affect his fate."

"A speech," Ms. Noonan writes, "is a fondue pot, and everyone has a fork. And I mean everyone."

I have been fortunate in that for most of the speeches I have written, the process involved working directly with the speaker. That, however, has not invariably been the case. I recall being asked to write a speech for a corporate CEO to deliver to his company sales force. When I arrived at what I expected to be the initial interview with the speaker, I was astonished to find that the CEO wasn't there. Instead, I faced seven executives, each expecting to have "input" into my "output."

I wrote the speech without having interviewed the speaker. When the draft came back to me, it had detailed comments and heavy editing from all seven executives. Most of the comments were worthless, and some were in direct conflict with others. I accepted the ones that were useful, discarded the others, and found a way to get my draft to the CEO without sending it through the vice-presidential gauntlet again. If I had been forced to consider all the "input," I might have been unable to "outget" the speech in time for the meeting. That kind of editing you don't need.

Let it rest

Once you have completed your speech draft, put it aside for a few days if time permits. Forget about it. Let it rest. It's amazing how often some of the phrases that you thought were so clever, the jokes that were so funny, and the statistics that were so compelling will change while the speech is reposing in your desk drawer. Actually, the speech will never leave your subconscious mind. Your mind will continue to work on it, and when you get back to it, ready to do your editing, you'll be able to look at it more objectively.

It's also a good idea to get another objective opinion. Ask the help of someone who doesn't have a vested interest in the speech. Even if you get such help, the responsibility for producing a well-edited speech is yours. Editing your own work requires an extraordinary amount of self-discipline.

During editing, you should begin to "hear" your speech, at least in your imagination, as it will be heard by members of the audience. That's an almost magical time when the speech becomes real.

Editing your speech

To do a really thorough job of editing, you need to consider five broad areas. They are content, organization, style, language, and grammar.

Edit for content

In editing your speech for content, question everything. Check every statement, every statistic, every quotation for accuracy. Examine every metaphor, analogy, quotation, statistic, and illustration for suitability. Ask yourself: Will this metaphor invoke the right picture in the minds of the audience? Will that analogy really help to enlighten? Will this anecdote reveal anything of importance about the subject or speaker?

Be especially critical of your humorous touches. It's so easy to offend someone without meaning to. If you have any doubt about a joke or a comment, leave it out. If you feel you just can't do without it, at least test it on two or three people to see how they react.

Most important, look at the overall content of the speech and ask yourself once more whether it fulfills the basic purpose of the speech as stated in your prewriting phase. Ask yourself also whether it meets the expectations of the sponsoring organization. Is it the right length? Is it suitable for the audience and the occasion?

Edit for organization

Next: Edit your speech for organization. Now is the time to be certain the speech is coherent, that it hangs together, that it is a unified presentation rather than just a collection of ideas and information. Be certain that all the points and subpoints are arranged in logical sequence, with each one building on the previous one. Remember the discussion of transitions? When you go from one thought to another, is the transition smooth?

Edit for style

Editing for style will probably produce the most changes. Style, the way I am defining it, involves how word combinations, sentences, and paragraphs are put together to create the meanings and impressions you want to convey with your speech.

Sentence length and structure are a part of style. Short sentences are usually easier to read and are often more direct and more dramatic. If you have many long sentences, break them up into shorter ones. Sentences that follow the normal word order—subject, verb, object—are generally preferable to sentences in which the order of these elements is different. A lot of sentences with dependent clauses may be needlessly complex. Prepositional phrases strung together can damage the rhythm of a sentence.

Simplicity has a certain eloquence all its own. Never underestimate the power and grace of a simple, declarative sentence.

Watch out for unintentional rhyme, alliteration, or unusual combinations of words that the speaker might stumble on. Most people have phrases that give them trouble. For example, I have always had a problem saying "raw oysters." For some reason, when I try to say "raw oysters," it often comes out "roy osters." Be aware that word combinations that are perfectly acceptable in print might cause problems in speech.

Edit for language

When you edit your speech for language, remember the discussion of language in Chapters Seven and Eight. Here, I review briefly some of the things you need to be concerned about. These are in no particular order:

• *Overuse of jargon.* Jargon, you recall, is language peculiar to a particular profession. If you know the audience will be composed of people who are not members of your profession, go easy on the jargon. It can be both tiresome and confusing to people who don't use it or hear it regularly.

• *Use of too many long words.* Short, gutsy words usually are more powerful and more memorable.

• *Infrequent use of contractions and personal pronouns.* In editing a speech for language, as in editing for style, consider whether the language preserves natural speech patterns and rhythms. To make your speech more conversational, use personal pronouns and contractions liberally. It is possible, I suppose, to overdo both, but you're more likely to err on the side of underuse of these very human words. If you find you've used these devices infrequently, increase their use.

• *Use of too many generalities rather than concrete words.* If you want to be understood specifically, you must speak in specific, concrete language.

• *Overuse of the passive voice.* A succession of passive sentences can weaken a speech and make the speaker sound wimpish. The active voice is usually more vigorous and interesting.

• *Use of clichés.* We can't avoid clichés altogether, but a few go a long way. As someone has said, we ought to avoid clichés like the plague.

• *Too many "concept words."* A good speech paints pictures in the listener's mind. Bold, colorful, descriptive words and strong verbs are much better for that than the kind of words I have called "concept words."

• *Misuse of words.* Chapter Eight provides a short list of commonly misused words. These are words you should be alert for in editing your speech, but the list is by no means complete. Every speech writer ought to own a comprehensive usage manual. The usage manual I recommend is listed in Appendix B.

• *Undesirable tone.* Avoid the use of language that indicates the "child" or "parent" rather than the "adult" is the dominant personality of the speaker at the moment.

• *Use of profanity and obscenity, especially sexual or scatological terms.* To be safe, avoid this kind of language entirely. An occasional *damn* or *hell* is probably acceptable for most audiences. So is tasteful and purposeful use of slang.

Edit for grammar

The fifth and final editing area I want to mention is grammar. I say *mention* rather than *discuss* because I could not do justice to the subject in this book. There are other books and other ways better suited for brushing up on grammar. The main point I want to make is this: Although perfect grammar does not produce a perfect speech, too many instances of bad grammar can damage an otherwise good speech. Moreover, bad grammar leaves the audience with a bad impression of the speaker and thus might diminish the credibility of the message.

On the other hand, strict adherence to what some people believe are "rules" can make a speaker sound stilted. For years students have had to contend with prohibitions against certain constructions, but many of these prohibitions have little validity in writing and none in speaking. For example, most teachers frown on sentence fragments, and it's true that good writers keep the use of sentence fragments to a minimum. But sentence fragments can be dramatic in a speech. Very dramatic. Better than long, rambling sentences. Much better.

And you need not feel self-conscious about beginning a sentence with *and* or *but* when it seems right. And end a sentence with a preposition if that seems like the best word to end it with, as I have done throughout this book to give the text a conversational tone. Split infinitives? No problem. The world's best writers split infinitives and have been doing it for centuries.

As you edit your speech, try to determine whether you have gone overboard in attempting to comply with some of these so-called rules. If so, consider recasting your sentences to make them more closely follow natural speech patterns and rhythms.

High-tech help

If you write on a word processor, I suggest you run your speech through a grammar checker if your program includes one. I'm not suggesting you rely too heavily on a grammar checker. It can be helpful, but it is by no means infallible. A grammar checker does not take the place of a good grammar handbook. You'll find my recommendation for a handbook in Appendix B.

Word processors have made editing and revising far easier than they once were. If you don't like a paragraph where it is, move it to another location and try it there. Although I wrote speeches and other materials for many years on an old Royal standard typewriter, I wonder now how I produced as much as I did without the help of my computer.

On the other hand, if Abe Lincoln had had a laptop on that train trip to Gettysburg, his famous address might have been three times as long and one-third as effective.

My final thought on editing is this: Editing cannot turn a bad speech into a good one, but editing can turn a good speech into a better one. To help you in editing your speeches, I have developed a checklist based on this discussion. It appears in Appendix A.

Preparing for delivery

Once you have edited your speech and are satisfied with the content, organization, style, language, and grammar, it's time to prepare the speech for delivery. Remember, now, that I'm referring to a speech that has been written out word for word.

Many important speeches are read, as I have pointed out, and if precision is essential for, let's say, legal or political reasons, reading may be necessary. In no case, however, is it wise to memorize a complete speech. Let me modify that. If you happen to be a trained actor accustomed to memorizing lines for plays, then it might be okay to memorize a speech. For most of us, though, memorizing is a very bad idea.

Although I have strongly advocated written speeches, nowhere have I said that just because a speech is written, it *must* be read or delivered word for word. I have said that a speech *can* be read effectively. It's simply a matter of knowing how to read aloud skillfully, so that the audience forgets, or doesn't care, that the speech is being read. If the content is interesting and the speech is delivered with the right pacing and emphasis, the audience will not care. On the other hand, if the speaker keeps his head down constantly, speaks in a monotone, and frequently stumbles, the audience is not likely to react favorably.

Bear in mind that when you see Peter Jennings, Dan Rather, or Diane Sawyer speaking earnestly from the tube on the evening news, you're seeing someone who most likely is reading. These people are professionals who know how to read aloud and hold the attention of their audiences. They can do it so skillfully that you're unaware they're reading.

Reading aloud is difficult for most of us because we're accustomed to reading silently and our eyes and minds tend to race ahead. It is, however, a skill that can be developed. The best way to develop the skill is to practice. Read something, anything, into a tape recorder. As you listen to the recording, pay attention to how you emphasize words, how fast you read, and so on. If you are not satisfied, record the same material again and again if necessary. You will improve each time.

To deliver a speech by reading with proper pacing and emphasis, you must know the speech well. Knowing it allows you to read without keeping your eyes glued to the text and thus will enable you to keep good eye contact with the audience. It will also ensure that you don't run into words or combinations of words that might cause you to stumble.

To prepare your speech for delivery by reading, have the speech produced in large type. Don't use italics or any other fancy or unusual typeface. A typeface with serifs is more readable than sansserif type. This is the kind of type you find in the body of most newspapers and magazines. The lines should be double-spaced.

Forget about conventional punctuation. Devise your own system. For example, you might elect to use a virgule, or what is known as a slash mark, to indicate the end of a sentence. Use a series of dots for a slight pause. For a longer pause, for example, between thoughts or discussion points, skip an extra space between lines. Use underlining, boldface, or all caps for words you want to emphasize.

If there are words, especially names, that may be difficult to pronounce, write them out phonetically to remind yourself of the proper pronunciation. I prefer to have numbers written out exactly as you say them rather than in figures. For example, instead of "$1,237,521,000" write "one billion, two hundred thirty-seven million, five hundred and twenty-one thousand dollars."

Make the lines of type shorter than you would for other manuscripts. Try not to break up phrases. For example, if your speech contained the phrase "at the end of each line," you would want to have the entire phrase on the same line rather than having "at the" on one line and "end of each line" on the next.

Never hyphenate a word at the end of a line, and never end a page in the middle of a sentence or even a paragraph. Try to keep each page a complete unit. By that I mean if you begin a unit of information or thought on one page, end it on the same page. This will prevent you from pausing where no pause is needed.

If you feel the need to give yourself instructions, write them in pencil at the appropriate point. A speech I once wrote called for the speaker, a banker, to emphasize a point by holding up a credit card. I suggested she make a note in the margin of the text to remind her to do it. She declined, saying she would have no problem remembering. Later, she confessed that she forgot. It wasn't a big thing, of course, but it would have added a little bit of interest to the speech.

Some speakers like to have their speeches typed on index cards—either 3×5 or 5×8. I prefer to have a speech typed on standard $8^{1}/_{2} \times 11$ paper, using only the upper half or less of each page. This means you have fewer words to cope with on each sheet. Your eyes can take in a limited amount of copy at once. Everything beyond that amount is competition. With fewer words on the page, you're less likely to lose your place in the text and better able to get back on track after some minor distraction.

It's true that with fewer words to the page, you'll have more pages to handle and you'll have to manipulate them more often. Believe it or not, this can work to your advantage. The slight pause that occurs when you go from one page to another can improve your pacing. It will give the audience a bit more time to absorb your messages.

Using full-size sheets of paper only half full of copy is better than using half sheets for a very good reason: When the full-size sheets are lying flat on the lectern, as they should be when you're speaking, you do not have to bend your neck as much to look down at the upper half of each page as you do to see the lower half. This makes it easier to keep in contact with the audience and makes your reading less obvious. If you use half pages, the pages are likely to slide down to the bottom of the lectern.

The important thing is to have the speech manuscript as unobtrusive as possible. Do not staple the sheets together. The best system for going smoothly from page to page is to have the sheets—or cards, if that is your preference—lying flat slightly to the right side of the lectern. As you finish each page, let your left hand gently slide it to the left. Be sure to number the sheets. In case they somehow get jumbled, you can get them back in order easily if they're numbered.

Besides reading, there are two other ways to deliver a speech. One is to deliver it without the benefit of text or notes. The other is to deliver it using an outline or notes prepared from your written manuscript.

None but the brave—or foolish

The ability to deliver a speech without the use of notes or a manuscript is a talent few people have. For most, attempting to do so is foolhardy for several reasons. First, you run considerable risk of omitting something that you intended to say, no matter how good your memory is or how well you know your speech. I've been conducting seminars on business writing for many years. I know the material well, but I always use notes in a thirty-minute introduction to the seminar. Once, conducting a seminar at an advertising agency in New York, I found myself without my notes. They were in my checked luggage somewhere in the airline's never-never land. I had to wing it—no pun intended. It was not a disaster, but I did forget a few things that I would have said if I had had my notes.

Without notes, it's difficult to get a quotation exact no matter how well you know it. Figures also are easily forgotten. If you have notes or a text, you can use statistics and quotations more confidently.

A second problem is the difficulty of keeping track of your time. Without something to guide you, you could get carried away and talk too long. You might spend too much time on one point and not leave enough time for others. Or you might run out of gas, finish too soon, and leave a gap in the program.

Thirdly, when you speak without notes, you are more likely to slip into bad habits and speech patterns, such as overuse of the vacuous expression "you know."

Speaking from notes or an outline

Speaking from notes or an outline made from the written text might be the best way to deliver a good speech. At least, it's a good middle ground between reading and speaking without notes.

I want to stress that speaking from notes or an outline does not mean that you don't need to write the speech word for word and edit it thoroughly. The reasons for writing the speech are valid no matter how you deliver it. For starters, you can use the written text as the basis for the outline from which you will speak. Do not make the mistake of assuming that this is the same as the outline you make before you begin to write a speech.

To prepare to speak from an outline, go through the text and reduce it to a few main points. Underline words or phrases that will serve to remind you of the points when you speak. Then transfer the key words and phrases to 3×5 index cards. You don't have to write the exact words, just whatever you feel you need to jog your memory. Use one card for each thought or information unit. Assigning numbers and letters to your points will help keep your thoughts organized.

To illustrate how this works, consider the following passage from a speech titled "Time Management and Effective Delegation":

> *Stepping back away from business to look at a bigger picture for a moment, the most obvious limitation on our ability to control our time is the need to sleep. Thomas Edison was famous not only for his ability to organize research and create inventions, but also for his ability to go without sleep. Many of his colleagues attributed his success to the fact that he could work for days without ever taking a break—he seemed to be in complete control of his time. When his body*

said, "Take some time off," it appeared that he could ignore it.

He delighted in the image that grew up around him as a tireless worker, but he admitted in his old age that he needed as much sleep as anyone else—he simply mastered the trick of sleeping for a few minutes at a time, sitting at his desk or workbench.

Edison appeared to be in control, but he was only managing his time. He happened to be very good at it, and the results of his remarkable life are proof that he was a very good manager of every minute he had.

If I were reducing that speech to notes or an outline, here is what I would write on the index card for the passage you've just read:

a. Need to sleep—our limitation
b. Edison—famous for ability to go without sleep
c. Colleagues attributed his success to this
d. Could ignore signals from his body
e. Delighted in the image
f. Mastered trick of sleeping few minutes at a time
g. Results of life proved he was good time manager

What I did was take a passage of almost two hundred words and reduce it to seven points totaling fewer than fifty words. If you follow this procedure, the key words and phrases on the cards should bring the points immediately to mind as you refer to them in the speech—*if you know the speech well.*

When you deliver your speech, you might not use the exact words of written text, but the points should bring to mind much of the original phraseology—*if you know the speech well.* To fix the phrases in your mind, use the full written text, not just your notes, when you rehearse the speech.

Your key words should be written large enough to be easily read. And, of course, the cards should be numbered in case they get jumbled. For a twenty- to thirty-minute speech, you might have as many as twenty-five cards. Use them as you would use the cards or sheets in a speech that you read—as unobtrusively as possible, of course.

If you use quotations and want to use them exactly as written, copy each one in full on a separate card to be inserted in the right place among your note cards. As I mentioned in Chapter Ten on the use of quotes, a good device for getting into and out of a quotation is to pick up a card and let it be obvious to the audience that you're reading. You will be saying, in effect, that this quotation is so important that you want to make certain to get it exactly right. When you put the card down, that effectively closes the quote.

If you do a good job of making your outline, you're not likely to leave out anything important. That is, once again, assuming you know your material thoroughly.

How to practice effectively

The key to delivering a good speech—whether you read it, speak from notes, or speak extemporaneously—is to know the speech very well. If you're reading, knowing the material will make the speech go smoother and with less chance of stumbling over words and phrases. If you're speaking from notes or an outline, the good words and phrases you labored over during the writing of the speech will come to you more readily. Practice may not make perfect, but it can keep a speaker from making a damned fool of himself.

After you have completed the speech and edited it thoroughly, read it over silently several times. Then read it aloud several more times, paying special attention to timing, pacing, pauses, tone, and emphasis. If you have someone you can trust to be an honest critic, read it to that person a couple of times and ask for sincere criticism.

When you're satisfied that you're delivering the speech with the right pacing, emphasis, and so forth, read it into a tape recorder. Then listen, and if you don't like the way it sounds, do it again. You can use the tape in a technique called visualization.

Trainers in various fields—especially sports—recommend visualization. The principle is sound, and it can help you make a better speech. Listen to your tape recording at least once a day until the day of the speech. If you commute to your job, listen as you drive or ride the train. Just before going to sleep is an excellent time to listen. But whenever you listen, listen actively. Visualize yourself on the podium. Visualize the eye contact, the gestures, the body language. Envision yourself enjoying the applause after the speech. The handshakes. The congratulations. The promotion you'll get when your boss finds out how talented you are.

This technique works. It helps the speech become well-fixed in your mind, and it gives you the confidence you need to face your audience. Try it; you'll like it.

"EULOGY FOR RICHARD M. NIXON"

Although Richard Nixon resigned the presidency in disgrace, his accomplishments while he was in office and his conduct after he left office earned him the respect of many national leaders. This respect is reflected in the following eulogy delivered by Senator Robert Dole on April 27, 1994. Notice the effective repetition of the phrase "how American" at the close of four successive paragraphs:

I believe that the second half of the twentieth century will be known as the "Age of Nixon." Why was he the most durable public figure of our time? Not because he gave the most eloquent speeches, but because he provided the most effective leadership.

Not because he won every battle, but because he always embodied the deepest feelings of the people he led.

One of his biographers said that Richard Nixon was "one of us." And so he was.

He was the boy who heard train whistles in the night and dreamed of all the distant places that lay at the end of the track. How American.

He was the grocer's son who got ahead by working harder and longer than everyone else. How American.

He was the student who met expenses by doing research at the law library for 35 cents an hour, while sharing a rundown farmhouse without water or electricity. How American.

He was the husband and father who said that the best memorial to his wife was her children. How American.

To tens of millions of his countrymen, Richard Nixon was an American hero—a hero who shared and honored their belief in working hard, worshipping God, loving their families, and saluting the flag.

He called them the "silent majority." Like him, they valued accomplishment more than ideology.

They wanted their government to do the decent thing, but not to bankrupt them in the process.

They wanted its protection in a dangerous world. But they also wanted creative statesmanship in achieving a genuine peace with honor.

These were the people from whom he had come, and who have come to Yorba Linda these past few days by the tens of thousands—no longer silent in their grief.

The American people love a fighter, and in Dick Nixon they found a gallant one. In her marvelous biography of her mother, Julie recalls an occasion where Pat Nixon expressed amazement at her husband's ability to persevere in the face of criticism. To which the President replied, "I just get up every morning to confound my enemies."

It was what Richard Nixon did after he got up every morning that not just confounded his enemies, but turned them into admirers.

It is true that no one knew the world better than Richard Nixon. As a result, the man who was born in a house his father built would go on to become this century's greatest architect of peace.

But we should also not underestimate President Nixon's domestic achievements.

For it was Richard Nixon who ended the draft, strengthened environmental and nutritional programs, and committed the government to a war on cancer. He leapfrogged the conventional wisdom to propose revolutionary solutions to health care and welfare reform—anticipating by a full generation the debates now raging on Capitol Hill.

I remember the last time I saw him—at a luncheon held in the Capitol honoring the 25th anniversary of his first inaugural.

Without a note, President Nixon stood and delivered a compelling speech, capturing the global scene as only he could, and sharing his vision of America's future.

When it was over, he was surrounded by Democrats and Republicans alike, each wanting just one more word of Nixonian counsel, one more insight into world affairs.

Afterward, the President rested in my office before leaving the Capitol. Only he got very little rest. For the office was filled with young Hill staffers, members of the Capitol Police, and many others . . . all hoping to shake his hand, get an autograph, or simply convey their special feelings for a man who was truly "one of us."

Today, our grief is shared by millions of people the world over. But it is also mingled with intense pride in a great patriot who never gave up and who never gave in.

To know the secret of Richard Nixon's relationship with the American people, you need only listen to his own words.

"You must never be satisfied with success," he told us, "and you should never be discouraged by failure. Failure can be sad. But the greatest sadness is not to try and fail, but to fail to try . . . in the end, what matters is that you have always lived life to the hilt."

Strong. Brave. Unafraid of controversy. Unyielding in his convictions. Living every day of his life to the hilt. The largest figure of our time, whose influence will be timeless. That was Richard Nixon. How American.

May God bless Richard Nixon. May God bless the United States of America.

—— Chapter Seventeen ——

And So to Speak

"The human brain is a wonderful organ," said the entertainer George Jessel. "It starts to work as soon as you are born and doesn't stop until you get up to deliver a public speech."

If your brain seems to slip out of gear at the very thought of making a speech, it might be of some comfort to know that you're not alone. Unreasonable fear of public speaking is much more common than you might expect, and anyone who has never experienced it can't possibly understand how it feels.

You may recall from Chapter One that *The Book of Lists* ranks fear of public speaking number one among the fourteen things Americans fear most, along with the fear of high places, the fear of sickness and death, and the fear of insects. It's far, far ahead of even sickness and death.

If you have that all-consuming fear, you must learn to overcome it before you can begin to develop your speaking techniques or even to accept your first significant speaking engagement. This might sound like a chicken-and-egg proposition: You can't make speeches until you overcome your fear, and you can't overcome your fear without making speeches. Let me share with you my own experience.

A personal experience

Many, many years ago, as a young man recently discharged from the army and more recently married, I accepted a job as editor of a small-town weekly newspaper. It was inevitable that I would be asked to make a talk. My first invitation to speak came from a women's club. It was a small group that met in a private home. That was fortunate, because I was able to speak sitting down. I don't think I could have stood, I was so frightened. There was I, a college-educated former army officer, quaking in fear of a small group of very nice ladies who were eager to learn a little bit about the exceedingly complex job of editing a country newspaper.

It seems silly now . . . absurd, actually; but at the time it was serious. It was so serious that I took out a bank loan to finance the modest cost of taking the Dale Carnegie Course in a neighboring town. The course didn't make me a good public speaker, but it did help me overcome my unreasonable fear.

You can overcome

If you have the problem, you can overcome it, probably not all at once, but gradually. Here's how: Begin to accept, or even seek out, minor opportunities to talk on your feet. Anything that will get you out of your seat and on your feet can be nothing but beneficial. Volunteer to read a devotional in your church or synagogue, make announcements at club meetings, accept club offices or committee chairmanships. Join a discussion group or a book club. You might even call a radio talk show and express your views on a subject you feel strongly about. Don't laugh. Many callers to radio talk shows begin by saying how nervous they are to be on the air.

It's also a good idea to sign up for a course in public speaking. You'll probably be surprised to find many of your classmates have the same fears that you have. Workshops and seminars on public speaking are offered periodically in major cities. If you live near a college, check its schedule of evening courses. Many schools offer courses. Professional and trade associations such as the American Management Association offer public-speaking seminars. If there's a Toastmasters Club in your area, that's also a good bet. That organization has a good program of self-improvement.

These activities, and probably others you can think of, will help you gradually shed the inhibitions that keep you from even trying to speak in public. Remember, we're talking about overcoming your fear, not turning you into a polished public speaker. Fear of speaking is largely fear of failure. Success in small things will give you confidence that you can succeed in larger ones. When the fear is gone, you'll be left with normal, healthy nervousness.

Healthy nervousness?

Yes, healthy. It's natural to be nervous before you speak. Seasoned actors suffer from stage fright now and then and may even forget their lines. TV anchors feel nervous before they go on the air. And even the best speakers have moments in which they wish they were anywhere doing anything.

The difference between nervousness and fear is that fear is debilitating, but nervousness is controllable. It's also useful. It keeps you from being overconfident.

If nervousness seems to be a problem, it's a far less serious one than overconfidence. Dr. Kenneth McFarland, who was once voted Number One Public Speaker in America by the U.S. Chamber of Commerce, relates this anecdote in his book, *Eloquence in Public Speaking*:

> *I was recently scheduled to be the third and final speaker for the morning session of a national convention. When I reached the lobby of the convention hall someone yelled, "Hi, Ken!" It was the second speaker of the morning. He was having a short beer at the concession stand. I asked if he had already been "up to bat." He said "No, I don't start for ten minutes yet." In the conversation it developed he had not yet been in the main auditorium, he had not seen a program, he had not talked with the chairman, he had not heard the previous speaker, he did not know whether there was a convention "theme." He was calmly drinking his beer and awaiting his turn.*

Now that was a self-confident speaker. Or, in my opinion, an *over*confident speaker. I like what author Jeff Scott Cook has to say on the subject:

> *Many people are afraid of giving speeches. And many who aren't probably should be. For every introvert fighting back terror to recall his meticulously prepared speech, two extroverts go boldly where no thought has gone before.*

Yes, self-confidence is wonderful; overconfidence can be destructive. Overconfidence is when you're certain the bull market will last another five years; self-confidence comes from having done all you can to make sound investment decisions. Overconfidence is when you think you know exactly what the professor will ask on the final exam; self-confidence comes from having studied everything she might ask. Overconfidence is when you use a 5-iron for a 185-yard shot because you once hit a 5-iron that far; self-confidence comes from having practiced with a 5-iron so that you know how far you can hit it.

And *over*confidence is when you *assume* everything will go right for your speech. *Self*-confidence comes from having made sure by thorough preparation and careful attention to details.

When you're scheduled to speak, don't be as nonchalant as Ken McFarland's fellow speaker. Be on the site well in advance. Allow yourself time to check out every variable. Once again, remember Murphy's Law, which says that if anything *can* go wrong, it *will*.

Leave nothing to chance

If you're using audiovisuals, make certain all equipment is working properly. If the program chair did her job, this will all have been taken care of. Don't bet your reputation on it.

Test the microphone. Have someone stand in the back of the room while you say a few sentences. The sound level should be adjusted so that you can talk into the mike in your normal voice and make yourself understood. Incidentally, you may find that you don't even need the mike. If you can do without it, don't use it.

Be sure you know how to adjust the mike so you will be able to move it to the right position for you after the previous speaker has used it. The idea is to make the adjustment before you start to speak. Avoid the awkwardness of having to say, "Can everyone hear me okay?" or something like that.

Ask the program chairman, the host, or master of ceremonies if there have been any changes since your most recent contact. What is your position on the program? Who will precede and follow you? Who will be at the head table?

When you're comfortable that everything checks out okay, you'll be more confident when you mount the podium. If you still have the jitters, here are some suggestions:

• *While you're awaiting your turn at the lectern and when you rise to speak, think about the audience.* They're a great group of people waiting eagerly to hear what you have to say. If you're concentrating on the audience, you can't be thinking of how you look, whether you'll goof up, whether you'll make a good impression.

• *If you're troubled by dry mouth, try sucking on a piece of hard candy while you're waiting to speak.* This will stimulate the saliva glands in your mouth.

• *Try not to clear your throat while you're speaking.* Instead, pause and take a swallow of water. Excessive throat clearing can make the problem worse.

• *Practice deep, rhythmic breathing to help relax the body and the vocal cords.* When you take a deep breath and let it out slowly, you can feel the tension drain away.

• *Eat lightly before a speaking engagement.* Although you don't want to be weak from hunger, a heavy meal can make you mentally and physically sluggish. When your stomach is full of food, blood is diverted from your brain to your digestive system.

• *Go easy on the cocktails.* Alcohol doesn't make you more articulate, it just makes you think you are. There's quite a difference. While one drink, or possibly two, might help you relax, more than that could spell disaster.

All these things can help, but the very best cure for nervousness is preparation. If you have prepared your speech properly and have followed my suggestions for practicing, you will know your material thoroughly and you'll have the confidence you need to make a good speech. And, as you continue to accept speaking invitations, you will improve, especially if you go back to this book again and again to review the fundamentals.

And now for a few questions

After making an important discovery, a scientist was so much in demand as a speaker at scientific gatherings that he hired a chauffeur to drive him to his speaking venues. Over a period of months, he and the chauffeur became close friends. On one occasion, the scientist complained that he was tired and needed to rest.

"Professor," the chauffeur said, "I've heard your speech so many times that I could deliver it myself." Well, one thing led to another, and the professor decided to give it a whirl. They stopped at a gasoline station and changed clothes. The chauffeur put on the professor's business suit and the professor donned the chauffeur's uniform.

The chauffeur did indeed deliver the speech flawlessly. Everything went fine until the question-and-answer (Q&A) period. A member of the audience asked a very difficult question. Unable to answer and uncertain what to do, the chauffeur looked at the scientist, who was sitting in the front row. All he got from his friend and employer was a smile.

Then, in a flash of brilliance, the chauffeur said to the questioner, "That, sir, is quite simple. In fact, I really believe my driver could answer it." Whereupon he gestured to the scientist, who stood and responded to the question. That's what is known as savoir faire.

As a speaker, you will often be asked to allow time for questions. If you do plan to have a Q&A period, consider announcing it in advance so your audience won't be tempted to interrupt your speech to ask questions. Or, you might prefer to have the master of ceremonies announce the Q&A period. After you have made your eloquent closing, as discussed in a previous chapter, you sit down and the master of ceremonies stands up and says something like, "Our speaker has graciously agreed to remain for a few questions."

A potentially embarrassing situation is to offer to answer questions and not get any. This usually means that no one wants to go first. You can sometimes stimulate questions by asking one yourself and answering it.

A Q&A period can be difficult, especially if you're not prepared for questions. If your answers are fuzzy or indefinite, you and your speech can lose credibility. To prepare for a Q&A session, jot down potential questions and give some thought to how to answer them. If you have a friend or colleague to review your speech, ask him or her to think of possible questions.

No matter how well you prepare, there's always the chance that someone will ask an unanticipated question that you don't quite know how to answer. If that happens, don't try to bluff your way through it. It will probably be obvious to the audience that you're on shaky ground. Simply say something like "I don't know the answer to that, but if you'll give me your address after the meeting, I'll find the answer and drop you a line." Reasonable people will respect you for admitting that you don't know everything.

Keep your answers short and to the point. I've known speakers to take so long to answer a question that it was almost as if they were making another speech.

Never engage in a debate with a questioner. If a questioner persists, say something like "You make an interesting point. I'd like to discuss it with you if we had a little more time." Then go on to the next question.

When you have answered a question and the person seems not to understand, try to express your answer differently. One time. Just don't go on and on rephrasing the answer. You may never satisfy the questioner, and you'll surely bore the rest of the audience.

Not every situation is suitable for questions, but when questions are appropriate, the speaker can use the Q&A period to add to the benefits that he or his organization expects to receive from the speech.

Business benefits

If you're involved in business or a profession, or if you represent some organization or cause that values public support or acceptance (And what business or organization doesn't?), you should be aware that public speaking can be a powerful marketing and public relations tool. I have touched on this before, and now I want to discuss it in detail and give you some suggestions about how you can make the most of the marketing and PR opportunities public speaking offers.

Some companies and some individuals aggressively seek speaking invitations with such opportunities in mind. There is nothing crass about this. Look at it this way: Most organizations are on the lookout for guest speakers for their meetings. If you fill a spot, you do the organization a favor. When you make an interesting, informative, and entertaining talk, you do the audience a favor. If your own organization benefits in some way, then everybody wins. Of course, speeches that are blatantly commercial are usually frowned upon. But a speech doesn't have to be blatantly commercial to benefit a company or even a commercial product. Bear in mind also that if a group invites you to speak, they expect you to speak on your specialty, whatever that might be.

Many companies encourage their executives to make speeches. Some even provide speech training conducted either in-house or by outside experts retained by the company. A few operate speakers' bureaus and will furnish an appropriate speaker to almost any group or organization that requests one.

Operating a speakers' bureau and supplying speakers more or less indiscriminately can be expensive for a company and time-consuming for busy executives involved. Many companies that offer speakers prefer to seek speaking engagements before certain target audiences in order to concentrate on particular demographic groups or geographical areas. They're usually interested in audiences that include people who are considered to be opinion leaders. The criteria for selecting these targets are as varied as the interests of the organization that furnishes the speaker.

For example, if your company operates manufacturing plants in several cities and plant-community relations are important, you will certainly want to have speakers appear on the program of service clubs in plant cities. If your company makes a product or provides a service primarily for older people, you should seek speaking invitations from senior citizens' clubs. And so on.

Opportunities abound

Service clubs such as Rotary, Lions, Kiwanis, and Jaycees are almost always eager for good programs. And usually they are excellent audiences. If you expect to have, or want to have, no more than one speaking invitation in a town, try to target the best. Among service clubs, Rotary tends to have many community leaders among its membership. But the Lions and Kiwanis Clubs follow closely. Jaycees is a younger and often more activist organization whose members are often looked upon as future community leaders.

School groups such as PTAs and business organizations such as chambers of commerce are also good possibilities. Business organizations have a high percentage of community leaders among their memberships.

For service clubs, a telephone call to the state headquarters of an organization will usually produce the name of the local club president and program chairman. A letter or phone call to one of them will often result in a speaking invitation. Of course, if the program can be arranged by a local representative of the company, so much the better.

The right messages

Careful consideration should be given to the messages the company wishes to incorporate into speeches. Again, I stress that this does not mean blatantly commercial messages. As an illustration, suppose you work for a chemical company and are filling a speaking invitation in a plant city. An interesting subject might be called something like "The Chemistry Set in Your Kitchen," a discussion of the safe handling of chemicals commonly found in homes. Your speech might include a description of the chemical industry's concerted effort to put public health and safety first on its agenda. The implicit message would be, of course, that your company, as a member of a responsible industry, is acting responsibly in the community.

Some companies have one or more prepared speeches for their speakers to use in the program. I don't recommend this. I feel each speaker should develop his or her own speech and find the right ways to incorporate the company's messages. If a stock speech is used, the speaker ought to tailor it for the occasion, the city, or the organization.

Leveraging the speech

When you make a speech to an audience of, say, fifty people, what you see is what you get. It's sensible, then, to look for ways to extend the benefits of the speech beyond this narrow group of people. I call this leveraging the speech—increasing its value exponentially.

Publicity is the best way to leverage a speech. Several steps should be taken to help ensure that the speech is well-publicized:

It's important to send to the program chairman, or whoever extended the invitation, a short news release along with a biographical sketch and a photo of the speaker. This should be done well in advance. The program chairman can use the material in the club bulletin or the printed program and send it to the local news media. Or, if you prefer, the company's PR department can distribute the news release.

Depending on the occasion, the speaker, and the subject, the speech could have significant news value. It's a good idea to take a couple of extra copies of your speech to the meeting just in case any news media representatives show up. Reporters appreciate having a printed copy because it frees them from the necessity of taking notes. Moreover, it helps ensure that you will be quoted accurately. When I handled press relations for corporate annual meetings, I always gave copies of the chairman's speech to business writers who attended. Reporters seemed to appreciate this courtesy.

The copies you hand out should be conventionally punctuated and typed, not arranged for use at the lectern according to our discussion in Chapter Sixteen.

If you have reason to believe that the speech will interest people in a broader area, distributing a news release based on the speech to appropriate media is a good idea. Your distribution list should include trade publications in the industry of which the speaker is a part. In many companies, preparing these news releases is done routinely by the public relations department.

The speech in print

Another effective way to leverage a speech is to have it printed for distribution to groups such as shareholders, employees, opinion leaders, and government officials. This, of course, is appropriate only for major speeches. And let me stress that speeches used in this way must not be obviously commercial or self-serving.

There's no special format for printed speeches, but I prefer a folder that fits in a standard business envelope. As I write this, I have before me a printed copy of a speech by William S. Anderson, who at that time was chairman of the NCR Corporation. The title of Mr. Anderson's address was "The Technology Race: How America Could Lose," a subject that ought to interest a great many people. It was the kind of speech that tends to be widely quoted and reprinted, often in *Congressional Record.*

On the first page of the folder is a small photo of Mr. Anderson and a single-paragraph description of the speech. Inside is a series of quotations from the text, "bulleted" and set in larger type than that of the body copy. The quotations serve somewhat the same purpose as an executive summary of a long report. They enable a busy person to get the essence of what Mr. Anderson said without reading the full text. They are also calculated to make someone want to read the speech. The speech itself is attractively presented, with the first line of each paragraph in boldface type. Altogether an effective presentation of a worthwhile speech.

The title of Mr. Anderson's speech, although not especially clever, was attention-compelling and descriptive of the content.

For a reprinted speech, a good title is essential.

What's in a name? Plenty

Every speech ought to have a title. If the organization sponsoring the speech prints a program or a bulletin, the speech title may give the audience its first impression of the speaker. If you read that someone was going to speak on "The Technology Race: How America Could Lose It," you likely would think, *This is going to be a speech about the future of my country. I had better listen.*

The title of a speech can be used in the introduction of the speaker and in the speaker's opening.

The question about titles boils down to this: How descriptive should the title be? Should it really tell what the speech is going to be about, or should it serve mainly to pique the interest of the audience? A good case can be made for either approach. Certainly, there's merit in the idea of letting your potential audience know what to expect. Still, life is a lot more fun when there's a little mystery along the way.

Several years ago, I wrote a speech that I titled "Automation and the Insurance Industry." It was about how telecommunications and computers have revolutionized the insurance underwriting process. The title was bland but fairly descriptive: Most in the audience would know what to expect if they read it. Thinking about it now, I wish I'd titled it "We Got Algorithms: Who Could Ask for Anything More?" George Gershwin would approve. I think the audience would have also.

Another speech in my file is titled "Privacy in the Information Age." The speech refers to the fact that George Orwell, in his novel *1984*, envisioned a society in which citizens would be completely controlled by sophisticated technology in the hands of an oppressive, omnipotent government. The speech made the point that 1984 came and went without Orwell's prediction having come true. A more intriguing title for that speech might be "Orwell Got It Wrong" or "*1984*? It Hasn't Happened . . . Yet."

Speech writers and speakers rarely spend a lot of time or energy in creating good titles for the speeches they work so hard on. I confess that I've written my share of bland, unimaginative titles. But now and then, when I have put my mind to it, I've been able to come up with something different. In most cases, it was worth the extra effort.

It really doesn't matter how far out you get with the title, as long as the speech makes the meaning of the title clear and ties it securely to the subject. This can be done gradually so that the audience begins to make the connection in the first few pages. If the connection is too subtle or too tenuous, you need to let the audience in on it fairly early. Keeping the audience in suspense too long may be cruel and unusual punishment. I once worked with a speaker who wanted to title his speech "Opening the Organizational Bow Tie," a reference to a favorite analogy. I considered the analogy a bit vague, but I followed his wishes and built a speech around it. In my draft, I explained the analogy early. In his revision, he delayed the explanation until page thirteen of the twenty-one-page script. I thought it was wrong to keep the audience guessing that long.

Title sources

Where do good title ideas come from? Often you can get inspiration from the body of the speech itself. The "We Got Algorithms" title mentioned above was inspired by a statement in the speech that without computerization, labor costs of underwriting would "drive today's premium algorithms off the chart."

The Bible, Shakespeare, mythology, and other literature are rich sources of title ideas.

So are quotations, classical and modern. Some of the rhetorical devices discussed at length in previous chapters—alliteration, anaphora, triads, exaggeration, and so on—can be adapted as speech titles. Sports terminology can be effective, if the audience is likely to know the term you select.

Here are some effective speech titles. Some of them are my own; most are from speeches I have heard or read:

• *"Death and Taxes: Was Ben Franklin Right?"* This was a reference to Franklin's aphorism that nothing is certain but death and taxes. The central theme was that planning can help minimize estate taxes.

• *"Minerva's Owl: Building a Corporate Value System"* This title, the speaker explained, refers to a saying that "Minerva's owl takes flight in the gathering darkness." Minerva is the goddess of wisdom. The owl symbolizes wisdom.

• *"Two Faces of Progress"* This speech opened with a reference to the Roman god Janus, for which January is named. Janus had two faces looking in opposite directions. The idea was that progress involves looking both backward and forward.

• *"On the Wings of a Butterfly"* An allusion to the so-called butterfly effect, the theory that the motion of a butterfly's wings in an Amazon forest can affect events around the world.

• *"Skating Where the Puck Is"* A reference to a statement attributed to the hockey player Wayne Gretzky. When someone asked Gretzky how he managed to score so many goals, he answered, "I always skate where the puck is going to be, not where it's been."

• *"How to Succeed in Business by Really Trying"* This was the title of a speech to student entrepreneurs, stressing the importance of hard work. The title played on the name of the Broadway show *How to Succeed in Business Without Really Trying.*

• *"The Media and the Terrorist: A Dance of Death"* A communications specialist made this speech to a group of airline security people. The title dramatized the role of news coverage in terrorism.

• *"A Loaf of Bread"* This speech was delivered at a Boy Scout dinner. The title referred to a poignant anecdote about wasted life.

• *"Playing Poker With American Industry"* This speech compared poker—a game of guesses, chance, and bluffs—with chess—a game of long-term strategy. It suggested that the United States, in dealing with other countries, plays poker with American industry.

• *"Technology and the Three Rs"* An automotive executive, speaking at a convention of elementary school principals, was making the point that even in this high-tech era, we neglect the three Rs—reading, writing, and arithmetic—at some peril.

• *"We're Good, but Not That* Good" This was a speech by a CEO to employees of his company. The point was that although the company was doing well, it was not the time to become complacent.

• *"Zipping, Zapping, and Other Lethal Weapons"* I love this one. The speech was delivered by an ad agency executive at an industry convention. The thesis, from which the title was derived, was that with cable TV and VCRs, broadcast networks and local TV stations are gradually losing control of consumers' viewing decisions. The "zipping and zapping" refers to zipping from station to station and zapping out commercials on recorded programs.

*   *   *

We are now at the end of our discussion of how to write and deliver a speech. I hope that if this book has done nothing else, it has convinced you that you have it within yourself to make a great speech—or, if not a great one, at least a damn good one.

All that remains to say is "Good luck."

"A New Birth of Freedom"

No discussion of speaking and speech writing would be complete without President Abraham Lincoln's Gettysburg Address. The occasion of this speech, you'll recall, was the dedication of the national cemetery at Gettysburg, Pennsylvania, on November 19, 1863. Lincoln reputedly wrote the speech on the back of an envelope while traveling by train from Washington to Gettysburg. Whether this is true is open to question, but there is no question that the speech is a marvel of simplicity and brevity and a wonderful example of the art of the great speech. It is a fitting way to conclude this book. As you read Lincoln's immortal words, note the brilliant use of triads, anaphora, and antithesis:

Four score and seven years ago, our fathers brought forth on this continent a new nation, conceived in liberty, and dedicated to the proposition that all men are created equal.

Now we are engaged in a great civil war, testing whether that nation, or any nation so conceived and so dedicated, can long endure. We are met on a great battle-field of that war. We have come to dedicate a portion of that field as a final resting place for those who here gave their lives that that nation might live. It is altogether fitting and proper that we should do this.

But in a larger sense we can not dedicate, we can not consecrate, we can not hallow this ground. The brave men, living and dead, who struggled here, have consecrated it far above our poor power to add or detract. The world will little note, nor long remember, what we say here, but it can never forget what they did here. It is for us, the living, rather to be dedicated here to the unfinished work which they who fought here have thus far so nobly advanced. It is rather for us to be here dedicated to the great task remaining before us that from these honored dead we take increased devotion to that cause for which they gave the last full measure of devotion; that we here highly resolve that these dead shall not have died in vain, that this nation, under God, shall have a new birth of freedom; and that government of the people, by the people, for the people, shall not perish from the earth.

—— Appendix A ——

An Editing Checklist for Speech Writers

Editing for content

☐ Is the speech accurate in all respects—facts, figures, names, etc.?

☐ Are your quotations, metaphors, analogies, etc., suitable? Do they add clarity and enlightenment?

☐ Is your humor suitable for the audience and the occasion? Is there anything that might offend?

☐ Does the overall content support and advance the stated purpose of the speech?

☐ Does the thesis come through clearly?

☐ Does the speech meet the expectations of the sponsoring organization?

Editing for organization

☐ Is the speech organized logically, with points and subpoints?

☐ Have you used "thought modules" to build the speech?

☐ Is the speech a unified presentation rather than just a collection of ideas and information?

☐ Are transitions strategically placed to help move the speech along from one point to another?

Editing for style

☐ Does the speech contain unintentional alliterations or word combinations that might be awkward for the speaker?

☐ Are any of the sentences too long or too complex?

☐ Do most sentences follow the normal (subject-verb-object) word order?

☐ Are there sentences with a succession of prepositional phrases?

Editing for language

☐ Does the speech make frequent use of short, "gutsy" words—vivid nouns and strong verbs—as opposed to long, lifeless "concept" words?

☐ Does the speech contain many generalities where specific, concrete language would communicate better?

☐ Does the speech rely too heavily on clichés and jargon?

☐ Have you used contractions and personal pronouns freely?

☐ Does the language create the impression you want to convey?

Editing for grammar and usage

☐ Have you followed the generally accepted norms or grammar without being overly pedantic and without sacrificing colorful expressions or colloquialisms that may be appropriate?

☐ Does the speech make excessive use of the passive voice?

☐ Are all words used correctly?

— Appendix B —

Resources for Speakers and Speech Writers

Publications and services

The Executive Speaker Company (Box 292437, Dayton OH 45429) offers a variety of publications and services to help you be a better speaker or speech writer. They are:

• *The Executive Speaker*, a twelve-page monthly newsletter that serves as a clearinghouse and digest for recent speeches by executives. Each issue features examples of the best openings and closings from speeches, along with a line or two of analysis that points out what made the opening or closing work. Other regular features include "In Between" (examples of the use of speech-writing techniques drawn from the bodies of recent speeches), and "Quotable" (a collection of quotations from recent speeches that epitomize the speech or offer a valuable insight on an issue of current interest). A subscription to *The Executive Speaker* ($132 per year) includes several supplementary indexes. Each index includes bibliographical listings of the latest one hundred speeches that have been added to The Executive Speaker Library of more than six thousand speeches. The speeches are indexed on more than four thousand topics, as well as by speaker and company, and subscribers can order the full texts of any of the speeches listed in the index for $.35 per page ($.40 for nonsubscribers).

• "The Executive Speaker Compendium" combines the last five years of *The Executive Speaker* newsletter into a single reference volume, which contains more than three hundred of the best openings, more than three hundred point makers, more than two hundred closings and summaries, and more than three hundred quotations. The 400-page compendium is $279.

• "Speech Search," a service that provides a bibliographical listing of speeches in the library on any of more than four thousand key words. For example, you can order a list of all the speeches in the file that have anything to do with entrepreneurship, leadership, mergers and acquisitions, technology, competition, the global economy, philanthropy, volunteer activities, public relations, and thousands of other topics. The fee is $25 for the basic search and $.35 per page.

• *Executive Speeches*, a bimonthly journal featuring the full text of ten to twelve of the best recent speeches by executives. Periodically, special issues of *Executive Speeches* are dedicated to a single topic. Past issues have focused on ethics, restructuring, education, customer service, motivation, and productivity. There are also periodic special collections of commencement speeches and other special-occasion speeches. Subscription: $60 per year.

• *The Quote . . . Unquote Newsletter*, a quarterly eight-page publication dealing with the origin and use of quotations, proverbs, and popular phraseology. It includes observations and insights of British author and BBC radio personality Nigel Rees as well as questions and answers submitted by subscribers on the authorship and history of phrases and quotations. Subscription: $40 per year.

Other publications and services

• *Speechwriter's Newsletter*, a monthly publication of Lawrence Ragan Communications, 316 N. Michigan Ave., Suite 300, Chicago, IL 60601, 800-878-5331, includes tips for speech writers, brief articles of interest to speech writers, anecdotes, quotes, analyses of current speeches, industry news.

• *The American Speaker*, 1101 30th St., NW, Washington, DC 20007. This publication provides a wealth of useful information in a thoroughly indexed binder, with monthly updates.

Anecdotes and quotations

• *The Home Book of Quotations*, compiled by Burton Stevenson, Greenwich House, 1984; distributed by Crown Publishers, Inc., New York.

• *The Oxford Dictionary of Modern Quotations*, compiled by Tony Augarde, Oxford University Press, 1991.

• *1,911 Best Things Anybody Ever Said*, compiled by Robert Byrne, Fawcett Columbine, 1988.

• *The Little, Brown Book of Anecdotes*, edited by Clifton Fadiman, published by Little, Brown & Company, 1985. This collection of fascinating yarns about people from Aaron to Ziegfield makes good reading even if you never use one of them.

• *Golden Treasury of the Familiar*, edited by Ralph L. Woods, Avenel Books, 1980, includes 952 pages and more than a thousand entries including all those "evergreen" things you've always known but can never remember where they came from or exactly how they go. Indexed by titles, familiar lines, and authors.

• *And I Quote*, by Ashton Applewhite, William R. Evans III, and Andrew Frothingham, described as "the definitive collection of quotes, sayings, and jokes for the contemporary speechmaker." Published by St. Martin's Press, 1992.

• *The Ultimate Book of Business Quotations*, by Stuart Crainer, AMACOM, 1998, is "an unconventional compendium of quips, quotes, and sayings."

Speech anthologies

• *Lend Me Your Ears: Great Speeches in History*, revised and expanded edition, 1997, a collection of some two hundred speeches, compiled and introduced by William Safire. Published by W. W. Norton, New York. Safire's analyses and insightful commentary make this book well worth a place in any speaker's or speech writer's library. Includes a remarkable variety of speech types—inspirational, farewell, commencement, sermons, lectures, political.

• *The Business Speaker's Almanac*, edited by Jack Griffin and Alice Marks, published by Prentice Hall, 1994. Includes forty-four of the best speeches of the year by business executives. Chapter topics include management, research and development, education and business in the world market, competing today and tomorrow, women in business, minority viewpoints, and trends and predictions. Also includes a section on openers, quotations, anecdotes, and closings. Indexed by speaker, topic, audience, and occasion.

Computer resources

• "World's Greatest Speeches," CD-ROM (Windows), a collection of four hundred of the world's best known speeches, plus more than one hundred bios of speakers. Produced by Softbit, Inc., 1 Whitewater, Irvine, CA 92715.

• "The New American Library of Quotes" (Windows), a collection of more than ten thousand quotations. Great Bear Software, 1100 Moraga Way, Moraga, CA 94556.

• "Idea Fisher," an idea-generating program to simulate brainstorming, produced by Idea Fisher Systems, Inc., 2222 Martin St., #110, Irvine, CA 92715. Windows Version 6.0. Several add-ons, including a speech-writing module, are available.

• "IdeaBank"®, 11 Joan Drive, Chappaqua, NY 10514 (e-mail: francis@ideabank.com), an on-line base of quotations, anecdotes, humor, and calendar-related historical and biographical information, accessible by personal computer through the Internet and through a private long-distance line. The material is updated almost daily. For additional information and a free trial period, visit Idea-Bank's Web site (www.idea-bank.com).

• "Well . . . There You Go Again! The Humor That Shaped America." CD-ROM, with more than eight hours of audio clips of quips, jokes, and anecdotes told by Ronald Reagan during his first administration. Also includes the full text of fifty of The Great Communicator's major speeches. $49.95. For information call 800-278-3245.

Audio and video

• "Great Speeches of the 20th Century," a boxed set of four audiotapes of segments of speeches (actual voices) of well-known public figures of the 20th Century. Produced by Rhino Records, Inc., 2225 Colorado Ave., Santa Monica, CA 90404-3555.

• "Historic Presidential Speeches, 1908–1993," a boxed set of tapes with actual voices, also from Rhino Records.

• "Great American Speeches," a two-volume videotape set, more than four hours of speeches by such notables as Theodore Roosevelt, Huey Long, Gen. George Patton, Gen. Douglas MacArthur, Malcolm X, the Rev. Jesse Jackson, Dr. Martin Luther King, Jr., Barry Goldwater, Ronald Reagan, and Mario Cuomo. Narrated by Jody Powell. Pieri & Spring Productions, 800-441-1399.

• Fans of Ronald Reagan should know of a two-cassette audio album of The Gipper's favorite quips, jokes, and anecdotes—two and one half hours—told by Reagan himself. Compiled by N. R. Mitgang and Malcolm Kushner and available from Durkin Hayes Publishing,

2221 Niagara Falls Blvd., Niagara Falls, NY 14304; 716-731-9177. Also in bookstores at $16.99.

• *The Write Way*, by Richard Dowis and Richard Lederer, a complete course in writing, grammar, and usage on 13 audio cassettes. Available from Verbal Advantage, 1150 Calle Cadillera, San Clemente, CA 92673; call 800-765-5522 for prices.

Useful books

• *The Big Book of Beastly Mispronunciations*, by Charles Harrington Elster, Houghton Mifflin, 1998. This book is just what its subtitle suggests—"The Complete Opinionated Guide for the Careful Speaker." An excellent resource for speakers who want to "say it right."

• *The Handbook of Good English*, by Edward D. Johnson, Facts On File, 1991. This is one of the best grammar handbooks ever. Its explanations are clear and its arrangement makes it easy to use.

• *The Write Way: The SPELL Guide to Real-Life Writing*, by Richard Lederer and Richard Dowis, Pocket Books, 1995. This is a good, all-around guide to better writing. It was published under the auspices of The Society for the Preservation of English Language and Literature (SPELL), P.O. Box 118, Waleska, GA 30183. Available in bookstores.

• *A Dictionary of Modern American Usage*, by Bryan A. Garner, Oxford University Press, 1998. Possibly the most comprehensive usage manual available. A must for the speech writer who wants to "write it right" all the time.

Index

rhythm, 119, 229
Richards, Ann, humor used by,
    167–168
Rogers, Will, on jokes, 169
Roosevelt, Franklin Delano
    declaration of war speech of,
        10–11, 61, 62
    inaugural address of, 146
    and simplicity of language, 90
    triads used by, 117
Rotary Clubs, 246
rule of three, 116–119
Rusk, Dean, 150–151

Safire, William, and use of allitera-
    tion, 122
scatological language, 170
school groups, 246
Schwarzkopf, Norman, on leader-
    ship, 145
Scott, Sir Walter, triads used by,
    117
self-confidence, 4, 6, 241–242
self-deprecating humor, 68
    Ronald Reagan's use of, 166–167
    in reference opening, 75–76
seminars, public speaking, 240
sentence fragments, 229–230
sentence(s)
    editing, for style, 228
    emphasis in, 117
    triads composed of, 119
service clubs, 246
Sessions, William, personal refer-
    ences used by, 92
"sewerage/sewage," 109
sexual language, 170
Shakespeare, William, 123, 146,
    249
"shall," 109
Shaw, George Bernard, 150
similes, 124–125
simplicity
    of language, 69, 88–91
    of sentences, 228
sincerity, 21
Singin' in the Rain, 218
Skelton, Red, 210

slang, 229
slides, 179
Smith, Al, 120
Society for the Preservation of En-
    glish Language and Literature
    (SPELL), 89
Socrates, 123
Sorensen, Ted, on John F. Kenne-
    dy's speeches, 31
Speak to Win (Georgiana Peacher),
    217–218
specific language, 93–94
speech patterns, 229
speech training, 218
SPELL (Society for the Preserva-
    tion of English Language and
    Literature), 89
split infinitives, 230
stage fright, 53–54
statistics, 173–177
    memorable presentations of,
        173–174
    sources of, 174
    use of anecdotes with, 176–177
    use of comparisons with,
        174–176
Stevenson, Adlai
    concession speech of, 191
    nomination acceptance speech
        of, 192–195
style, editing for, 228, 253–254
summary closings, 187
suspense
    in openings, 66
    and titles, 249
Sweat, Noah S., Jr., Mississippi leg-
    islature speech of, 164–165

"tandem," 109
techniques, rhetorical, see rhetori-
    cal devices.
TelePrompTers, 33
Tennyson, Alfred Lord, 123
thanks in openings, 60–61
"that," 109
Thatcher, Margaret, speech by,
    180–185
thesis closings, 187